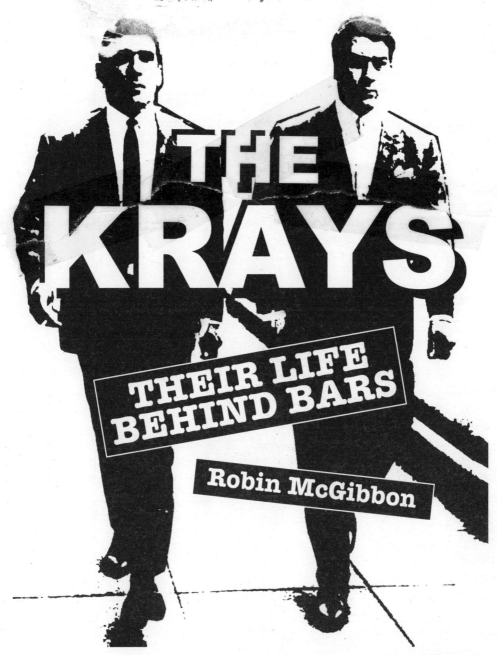

THE KRAYS

THEIR LIFE BEHIND BARS

Robin McGibbon

GREAT NORTHE

Great Northern Books
PO Box 213, Ilkley, LS29 9WS
www.greatnorthernbooks.co.uk

ISBN: 978-1905080-88-5

Design and layout: David Burrill

Printed and bound in the UK by CPI Mackays, Chatham ME5 8TD

CIP Data
A catalogue for this book is available from the British Library

To my wife, Sue

A deeply caring human being,
and an inspiration, not only to
me, but to everyone she meets.

About the Author

Robin McGibbon is a former national newspaper sub-editor and publisher, who ghost-wrote Barbara Windsor's best-selling autobiography, *All of Me*, and *Me and My Brothers*, for the Kray twins' elder brother, Charlie.

He has written and co-written nine other books, including biographies on Paul Gascoigne and Mick Hucknall, and a TV tie-in on Battersea Dogs' Home for BBC Books. He is currently working on a crime/sex novel, based on his Fleet Street experiences.

Acknowledgements

Originally, this book was going to be just the stories behind some of my letters and phone calls to and from the Kray twins. I have to thank several people for helping to make it more than that.

Flanagan insisted on coming first, and so she should: but for her, I'd never have met the twins. I'm grateful to Flan for taking me to Parkhurst, in 1985, and for being a reliable, helpful and amusing friend for nearly 40 years.

Special thanks to Reg's pal, Steve Tully, now living peacefully by the sea, Charlie's loyal mate, John Corbett, and Steve Wraith, who runs a company organising sporting dinners. All helped willingly whenever asked.

I'm indebted to Anne Marie Doyle, Jane Jarrett, Jane Bull and Bernice Farrell, at Southborough Library, for whom nothing is ever a problem, to Terry O'Neill for his generosity, reporter Shan Lancaster for her tireless searching, Matthew Butson, at Getty Images, for never being too busy, Peter Maguire, for the cuttings, Alastair Stewart and Jamie Shepherd at ITN, for detecting that date, the ever cheerful David Mears for oiling the mechanics of the operation, and IT wizard Graham Johnson for his Trojan efforts at the moment of crisis.

Thanks also to Hilary Ritchie and Jo Timson, at Addenbrooke's Hospital, Aaron Dean, of Gorringe's auctioneers, Richard Clemence, of Lanmere London, Jill Litchfield, at the Multiple Schlerosis Society, Tom Petrie, Les Martin, Kate Kray and 'Arry-boy' Nye. And, especially, to Jacquie and Stuart McLean and Peter and Mac Tompsett for their most welcome umbrellas.

I must also thank Bradley Allardyce for an enlightening visit, Mike Harris for enthusiastic input, Simon Melia for the "film treatment," Jack Leigh, who didn't want to help, but did, and the indefatigable Richard Barber for that photo of the Krays' wartime home. And to Wilf Pine and his charming wife, Ros, for making Sue and I most welcome at their home at such a stressful time.

Finally, I must give extra special thanks to the irrepressible, ever reliable, Dave Courtney for his invaluable help, generously and entertainingly given. Good luck in Hollywood, poppet.

Foreword

WHEN people I didn't know well heard I was visiting the Kray twins - Reg in prison, Ronnie in Broadmoor – they invariably asked if I was frightened. One, shocked to hear that I'd had the nerve to shout and swear at Reg, even asked if I had a death wish. The answer to both questions is No. I'm not particularly brave or stupid, or both, but when Ronnie and Reg agreed to see me, in 1985, they had been locked up for seventeen years, and as far as I was aware, posed no threat to anyone, except, perhaps fellow prisoners, and staff looking after them. More important, the Krays had always been careful to nurture their image by using the media and, as a well-connected national newspaper journalist, I'd been recommended as someone who could be useful to them; an invited guest, if you like, who might be able to make them money and generate favourable publicity.

Ah, but what if I upset them, or didn't deliver my promises? Didn't the once-feared vicious killers still have friends on the outside who could sort me out? The answer to that, as far as I was concerned, was No. The terrifying control the twins had had in the sixties was largely gone, and the only real power they wielded now was in prison. True, they might still have one or two "heavies" on the outside, but nothing would have happened to me: although I wasn't introduced to Ronnie and Reg by older brother Charlie, they were aware I knew him well, having published his autobiography, *Me and My Brothers*, after his release from prison, in 1975. And while that didn't make me part of the family, it did put me among the inner circle of their regular visitors and, as such, not someone they would hurt.

So, no, throughout the ten years I was in touch with the twins, I was never frightened. Not once. Not even after Reg and I had had one of our fiercest rows. Or when I'd had the cheek to ask Ronnie about his fondness for young boys.

As for Charlie, I can't imagine that anyone was ever frightened of him. As everyone who knew him would testify, he abhorred violence: he was a quiet, well-mannered gentleman, with old fashioned values, who'd rather throw a party than a punch. It was just his bad luck that he was linked in the public mind with two notorious gangsters with whom he had nothing in common except his surname.

Obviously, it was not possible to include *all* the twins' letters, or cover everything they told me - face to face, and on the phone. But there is enough to provide an insight into how their minds worked, after so many years' incarceration. The book differed from its original concept because friends of all three brothers became friends of mine, and wanted to share their experiences. To me, much of what they revealed – published here for the first time - was deeply shocking, and I have to admit that, had I known at the time, I would have behaved differently, not only to the twins, but Charlie, too.

Robin McGibbon, March 2011

Chapter One

I'D NEVER have met the Krays had it not been for sex.

If I hadn't been told a sex magazine was making thousands of pounds every month, I wouldn't have launched one myself and met a glamorous, bubbly, blonde model who had been Violet Kray's personal hairdresser, and knew her three sons. It was the early seventies and I'd left my job as a sub-editor on the *Daily Sketch* to become a director within the Mecca entertainment empire. I'd been persuaded to join the company by its managing director, Eric Morley, who saw huge potential in an idea I'd been developing for three years with two friends, also journalists. However, the scheme, promoting restaurants and clubs to overseas visitors, had not taken off, and we knew our days were numbered. While waiting for the axe to fall, we started ploughing our energies into a new venture – an innovative guide to London, and it was while correcting the page proofs one September evening, in 1971, that our printer, a genial gentleman named Bob Stevens, asked what would prove to be a fortuitous question – and change our lives.

"You're very proud of your new idea," he said. "How much do you expect to make from it?"

One of my partners, who dealt with the financial side of the venture, told him our anticipated first year's profit.

"I thought as much," Bob said, with a knowing smile. "I'm printing a magazine that's earning more than that every *month*."

We knew the magazine he was talking about: a small-format publication, called *Search*, that dealt, mainly pictorially, with rubber and sado-masochistic fetishes. We suspected it was selling well because we'd seen the owner arrive on Press day, expensively dressed, and dripping with trendy designer jewellery, at the wheel of a gold Mercedes sports car. But we were so focussed on our own publication we hadn't given his much thought. We did now, though.

"So what *is Search* making?"

"More than five grand," Bob said.

"A month!"

"Every month," he said. "And circulation is growing."

Bearing in mind that, at Mecca, my two partners and I were on sixty quid a week, before tax, and grateful for Capri 2000 company cars, we were mightily impressed.

"So, what are you suggesting, Bob?" I said. "That we start a rival magazine?"

"Not a rival," he said. "*Search* has cornered the kinky market. I'm thinking of a straight sex magazine. There isn't one."

Almost together, the three of us said: "But we know nothing about the sex industry."

"You're all journalists," Bob said. "Surely you can write about anything, if it pays."

There was some truth in that. When one of my partners and I had launched a free newspaper, near our homes, in Kent, we'd had to dream up "think pieces" to fill spaces round the ads. And, as a newspaper sub-editor, I'd written scores of captions for photographs, based on nothing but my imagination. But a sex magazine?

The potential income was enticing, of course. In 1971, one could buy a house for less than what *Search* was making in two months. But there was more to consider than the money – or, indeed, whether we were equipped to produce a marketable sex publication. The legal implications, for a start. At the time, laws governing obscenity in print were hazy, following a landmark ruling that DH Lawrence's sexually-explicit novel, Lady Chatterley's Lover, was not obscene, due to its literary merit. But police were still under pressure to prosecute purveyors of so-called "dirty books." Did we, as three law-abiding citizens, want to risk being charged with publishing obscene material – and suffer the shame and embarrassment that would cause? The legal risks aside, did any of us actually want to be associated with the sex industry? Were we prepared for our friends and business contacts to know how we earned our living?

In the end, we were hurried into making our minds up by a most disappointed Eric Morley, who gave us the heave-ho in September. We walked out of our Shaftesbury Avenue offices, facing a gloomy future, with no salary, no car – and the limited potential of the guide to London our only financial hope.

Deciding we should, at least, explore the sex market, we agreed to invest some time and effort, finding out whether we had it in us to write titillating copy. If we couldn't, we'd split up and go our separate ways. If we felt we *could*, then we'd look into ways to finance the magazine. We spent a week pounding out our sexual fantasies on typewriters in our respective homes, then reconvened to read each other's efforts. What happened next, and over the next ten years, is probably another book, but, basically, we voted unanimously to give the magazine a go – and, three months later, *Experience* was born. Although we'd written all the stories, we gave the A5 publication a promotional edge by selling it as "*a sex magazine for men written by women*" – and for that we needed photos of sexy girls to go with our erotic stories. Which is how I came to meet the bubbly blonde model with shapely legs, in a Soho snooker club, late one February morning, in 1972.

We were producing the first colour issue and, to maximise the effect, were using Maureen Flanagan - or simply Flanagan, as she insisted on being called – to pose provocatively among the coloured balls. Watching her stretch her naked body over the green baize was enough to put any snooker player off his stroke – but the skinny young guy practising, at near running pace, on a nearby table, wasn't the least bit interested. I knew little about the game, but I recognised him as Alex Higgins, who had won the world snooker championship the previous night. The opportunistic journalist in me sensed a scoop and, after watching him clear a 147 break in no more than 15 minutes, I asked Alex if he'd mind having a photograph taken, potting a ball round the naked Flanagan.

In those days, I was breezing through life, never expecting a negative reaction to my ideas, so I wasn't surprised when Alex said he'd be delighted; after all, he was only weeks away from his 23rd birthday and heady with the ultimate snooker success. However, as I was setting up the picture, one of Alex's pals asked what publication Flanagan was working for. When I told him, he advised Alex that, perhaps, he ought to phone his manager, in the north of England, to tell him what he was doing. And when the hugely amiable and co-operative world champ agreed, our goose, as they say, was cooked. The manager didn't think a photograph of his newly-crowned star and a naked blonde was a good idea at all – so the speedy Irishman who'd stormed to the world title like a hurricane, hurried back to his practice and "Flan" continued baring all, leaving my partners and I reflecting on what might have been. Given the topicality of Alex's triumph, a Sunday paper would certainly have gone for the picture – and with my Fleet Street connections I'd probably have got a mention for *Experience*, which would have been priceless promotion for a fledging publication fighting to spread its wings.

As it turned out, the magazine didn't need any publicity. The idea of a team of sexy young women writing explicitly about their bedroom experiences and fantasies caught the imagination of a certain section of the public and, although circulation was restricted to street bookstalls and sex shops, sales swiftly soared to 50,000 copies a month. Within a year, we had made enough money to launch a legitimate book-publishing company, specialising in celebrity autobiographies, TV tie-ins - and fiction, if it was a particularly original idea. I called it Everest Books and, leaving my two partners to nurture the sex side of our business, I spent the next year building it up. And that's why, in the autumn of 1975, I came to meet Charlie Kray.

He had been released from Maidstone Prison in January that year, after serving six years eight months of a ten-year sentence for supposedly getting rid of the body of Jack "The Hat" McVitie, a heavy-drinking, drug-taking South London hoodlum, murdered by Reg Kray in 1967. Charlie was eager to earn a few quid by writing his autobiography and had walked into Everest's offices, a few hundred yards south of the Thames, in Blackfriars Road, to try to persuade us to publish it.

To be perfectly truthful, as Charlie would say, I wasn't sure the book was right for Everest. Although I must have edited reporters' copy about the Krays – even written some of the headlines – their name and notoriety, surprisingly, meant little to me. Certainly my publishing pulse didn't race with excitement as it had the previous year when I'd signed Malcolm Allison, the football manager, and BBC disc jockey Pete Murray for their autobiographies. In fact, if it hadn't been for one of my staff – a young former newspaper reporter named Ken Follett – I might not have even have agreed to meet Charlie.

Ken was a hugely likeable young Welshman, and I'd given him a job after meeting him at the launch of our first book, a novel written by one of his colleagues on the London *Evening News*. He told me he was writing a novel himself and asked if I'd like to read what he had written. I said I would, and, two days later, the first seventy pages of a London-based crime thriller, *The Big Needle*, arrived, with an accompanying letter, telling me, with an arrogance that I would learn was Ken's stock in trade, that his wife, "who is nothing if not forward thinking, would like Michael Caine to play the lead in the film."

I enjoyed the story and Ken's racy style so much I missed my train home to Maidstone that evening and, a few months later, agreed to publish the novel. I saw more in Ken than an author, however. He was young, vibrant and ambitious and I felt he could be a useful asset to a young, vibrant and ambitious company. When he told me he wanted to quit journalism and get into publishing, I took him on as an editor. University educated, with a fast wit and even faster brain, Ken quickly became someone I admired and trusted, so when he walked into my office to ask if he could bring Charlie Kray in to meet me, I agreed.

I had no idea what Charlie would look, or sound, like, but if I expected a burly, cocky hoodlum, with a broken nose and uncouth manners to match a foul mouth, I would have been mistaken. The man who offered me his hand that morning was the most charming, softly-spoken and well-mannered gentleman one could wish to meet. He was good-looking, too, tall and slim, and elegantly dressed in a brown suit, highly-polished brown shoes and crisply-ironed white shirt, with cufflinks, and neatly-knotted tie. He asked, ever so politely, in a warm London accent, with a well-modulated, gentle tone, if I minded him smoking, then proceeded, in the friendly, self-effacing manner I would come to know so well, to charm me.

Was it any wonder that, an hour later, I was sold on the idea of publishing Charlie's memoirs? Ken's instinct was right: the man, and the story he wanted to tell, was irresistible. I agreed for Ken to draw up a contract, giving Charlie and his ghostwriter, Jonathan Sykes, a £2,000 advance, payable in three stages: on signature of the contract, delivery of an acceptable manuscript and publication, the following year. At the time, I had no qualms about the deal. As the new kid on the publishing block, it was important for Everest to acquire titles that would attract publicity and get our name in the trade magazines, and Charlie certainly helped here: although it blighted his life, he was immensely proud of the Kray name, and it certainly boosted the company's profile, and mine.

However, in view of what I learned a few years later, I do feel I was gullible and naïve for not being circumspect about what Charlie planned to write. Such was my general confidence and optimism, I didn't think for a moment to ask him what Everest was going to get for its investment. Neither did Ken. We simply let Charlie and his ghostwriter get on with it. We should have insisted on an honest, revelatory book, worthy of newspaper serialisation, not a bland, boring whitewash. But *Me and My Brothers*, in 1976, *was* bland, boring, and while not a whitewash - Charlie did not paint the twins, Ronnie and Reggie, who were both serving life sentences for murder, as charity-minded angels - it did lack the honesty his story warranted. The reason was, of course, that neither of them, had admitted having anything to do with the killing of Jack McVitie, which, infuriatingly for Charlie, made it impossible for him to reveal how and why he was jailed for a crime that he knew - and the police must strongly have suspected - that he did not commit.

If only those sceptics who believed the Krays were business geniuses who'd salted away fortunes before their arrests could have been in my office in the months leading up to the publication of *Me and My Brothers*! Charlie would pop in to see me, ask, very charmingly and courteously, if I had a few minutes, then plead with me for a further advance. When I said No, he'd offer me a percentage of his share of the film of the twins' lives, in return for cash now. I didn't ask any details, because I knew the film world was awash with good stories that never made the screen, riveting scripts that were gathering dust. In any event, if there was genuine interest in a movie, I felt Charlie would have mentioned it at the outset, to encourage me to increase his advance.

Years later, however, I learned that a Kray film was, at least, being talked about at that time. It came about through Wilf Pine, former manager of the Black Sabbath rock band, who had been introduced to Charlie by Laurie O'Leary, a childhood friend of the twins, shortly after his release. Broke and unemployable, Charlie was thrilled when Wilf offered to loan him his five-bedroomed house on the Kent coast, near Herne Bay, and happily moved in that summer with a woman he had fallen in love with before his arrest in 1968. Diana Buffini, an attractive, hard-working woman in her thirties, was married with a son, Dean, and a daughter, Claudine, but had left the marital home in Leicester to be with Charlie after he contacted her on his release. Charlie hated his prison pallor so much he spent half an hour every day under Wilf's sunbed and, throughout that first summer of his freedom, would lay in the garden or on the beach, deepening the tan that would be his trademark. He loved being brown so much that Wilf would joke: "If you put Charlie by a 500 watt bulb long enough, he'd try to tan up!"

Even though they had been incarcerated for seven years, the twins were desperate to have a film made about their lives. And when Wilf mentioned that he knew Joe Pagano, of New York's Genovese Mafia family, Charlie seized on it. "Joe must have contacts in the movie business, Wilf. Would you ask him if he can do anything to make a film happen?"

Wilf agreed and, that September, flew to New York to meet Pagano, taking with him several copies of *The Profession of Violence*, a biography of the twins that had been published three years after their convictions. After reading the book, Pagano told Wilf: "I can't believe how nutty those guys are. But it's a hell of a story. I'll see what I can do."

Unfortunately for all three Kray brothers, nothing came of it. But at least Charlie was not totally bullshitting when he was trying to squeeze money out of me in 1975. As I would discover over the next twenty years or so, he was always scratching around for money and would think nothing of bending the truth to get some.

Since that entertaining snooker photo session, I'd kept in touch with the bubbly blonde, by inviting her and her shapely pals to Everest book launches. So, when I decided to launch a series of books – with a feminine spin – to compete with a rival publisher's "Confessions" of a cheeky lad-about-town, Flanagan was the first person I thought of. When I said I needed a glamour girl to put her name to *"Intimate Secrets of an Escort Girl, Actress, Model, etc."* – amusing, sexy escapades, written by a professional writer – she jumped at it, insisting only that the cover photographs were taken by her favourite photographer Ben Jones, who I'd worked with on the *Daily Sketch*.

Sadly, neither *Intimate Secrets*, nor a long list of celebrity-based books, could save Everest – or me, come to that – from crippling financial problems, caused by my decision to publish the memoirs of an egomaniacal, vitriolic and incomprehensibly unreasonable human being named Dorothy Squires. In the 1940s and early 1950s, she was Britain's most popular and highly-paid vocalist, but her star had faded and she blamed everyone but herself for that. I soon discovered that she wanted to use her memoirs to wreak literary vengeance on all those she believed had wronged her – and to hell with the fears my lawyers expressed over the libellous claims she made. The book was never published and one of my other authors said that, because I'd refused to give in to her demands, I'd taken over from her former husband, the actor Roger Moore, as her *bête noire*. As a result, she forced me into not one, but four, hugely expensive High Court actions. The stress took me to the brink of a nervous breakdown and though I won all four cases and was awarded substantial damages – which Dorothy never paid! - Everest was losing money, and the negative publicity drove the proverbial nail into the company's coffin. In the early eighties, it went into voluntary liquidation.

With the bottom having fallen out of the sex market, I was thankful to be offered a job as a news sub-editor on the *Daily Express*. Now married for the second time – to a former advertising executive, named Sue – but still financially committed to four children from my previous marriage, a regular income was a godsend. And it didn't bother me one jot that I was back doing what I'd done fifteen or so years before. Indeed, after what I'd been through, I was positively thrilled to be among bright, witty colleagues – and well-paid for a four-day week. Then, in the spring of 1985, Flanagan called with a proposition. And my life as one of the Kray brothers' most trusted friends was about to begin.

Chapter Two

FLAN wanted me to write her autobiography, covering not only her friendship with the Kray family, but her life as a top model, one of *The Sun's* early Page Three Girls, and her work on TV in the Monty Python, Benny Hill and Dave Allen shows. She'd led a colourful life and I was tempted because Flan would have been a joy to work with and had the personality to promote the book well. But the thought of ghost-writing a book was daunting: how would I be able to interview Flan, transcribe tape recordings and write the manuscript, while holding down an often high-pressure job on a national newspaper?

In the end, I told Flan I wouldn't ghost her life story, but I had a friend who'd be ideal. His name was Peter Batt and he was a legend in the national newspaper industry. Although an alcoholic, who had been sacked from almost every paper he'd worked on, he possessed an extraordinary and enviable writing talent. He was born in Stepney, no more than two miles from Vallance Road, at around the same time as the twins, and had just been employed by the BBC to create characters and write scripts for its new series, *EastEnders*. Who better to write the life story of one of the Kray family's closest friends?

Well, we all make mistakes, and I made one, thinking that Flan and Peter would adore each other. Within half an hour of meeting at my home in Beckenham, it was clear they couldn't stand each other. Beneath the happy-go-lucky giggle and apparent self-confidence, Flan is deeply insecure and craves love, admiration and respect. Peter, on the other hand, can seem arrogant and boorish. I believed Peter would slip into the ghost-writer role easily, listen to what Flan had to say, then write it in her style, using his flair to make her story flow, but it was quickly apparent that he'd want to write her story *his* way, not hers. That, clearly would never work and the frosty meeting ended with me driving Peter to the nearest station to catch a train home to Wimbledon, while Flan stayed chatting to Sue. When I got back, I apologised for Peter's behaviour, promised to find another ghost-writer, and then the conversation turned, not unnaturally, to the Krays, particularly Charlie, whom all three of us liked. I was curious to know if he shared any similarities with the twins. Certainly it didn't appear so from the book *Everest* published.

"None at all," said Flan. "Mind you, there's not much similarity between Ronnie and Reggie now."

"Really?" I said.

Flan nodded. "You'd be amazed how different they are."

"In what way?"

"The way they behave on visits for a start," Flan said. "Reg is very intense and businesslike and always arrives with a pile of papers, listing all the things he wants done. Ronnie is more laid back. He'll stroll into the visiting hall slowly and settle down for a leisurely chat. Reggie is always on edge. Ronnie calm."

As I pondered this, Flan said: "You wouldn't think they were brothers, let alone twins."

"That's fascinating, Flan," I said.

"Yeah, it is" she said. "Particularly when you visit one, then go to see the other a couple of days later, as I do."

"How often do you visit?" I asked.

"Since Violet passed away, I've gone to Parkhurst every month for three years. I was visiting her in hospital and she held my hand and made me promise that I'd visit Reg after she was gone. I was surprised because I knew Ronnie was her favourite son, but she wanted Reg to have a female visitor, and there'd be no one but me who'd be prepared to trek to the Isle of Wight. She wasn't worried about Ronnie, she said, because, being in Broadmoor, he would have loads of visitors, male and female. I go to see him every six weeks or so. As you know Charlie so well, you should meet them, Rob. Do you want to go with me one day?"

I wasn't sure what to say to that. As I didn't start work at the *Express* until late afternoon, I did do occasional freelance work – interviews with TV stars mainly – but the thought of trying to get in to see the Kray twins had not occurred to me. Now, however, it was appealing. At the very least, I might be able to sell a first-person piece on how the once-identical Terrible Twins had changed during their seventeen years in captivity.

"It would be an experience for you, Rob," said Flan. "Have a think about it."

"I don't have to, Flan," I said. "I'm not going to look a gift horse in the mouth. I'd love to meet them with you."

"Leave it to me," she said. "I'll speak to Reg first. See if he'll fix VOs for us."

"VOs?"

"Visiting orders. He's on maximum security. Visitors need a VO to get in the prison. And Reg has to authorise it. Have you never visited anyone in prison before? No?" Flan gave her throaty laugh. "What a place to go for your first visit! And what a prisoner to meet!"

Watching her drive away in her white Mini, I felt exhilarated. Who knows, there might be a few quid in it, as Charlie would say.

*

I didn't hear from Flan for several weeks, but then she called me at the *Express* one evening as I was leaving the Newsroom for a mid-shift drink, in the Wine Press, one of the numerous Fleet Street watering holes. "I'm just back from Parkhurst," she said. "I told Reg all about you and he'd like to see you. It's just a question of when."

"How soon are we talking about?"

"He gets seven visits a month. We have to choose a day and he'll let us know if it's convenient. Can you do next month?"

Under the nine-day fortnight system, I got five straight days off every four weeks, so I immediately told Flan I could.

"Okay," she said. "I'll try to fix a day in May."

"Lovely," I said. "He does know I'm a journalist, doesn't he?"

"Yes. Both he and Ron hate anything to do with newspapers because they feel they're never quoted accurately, but I've told Reg I've known you for thirteen years and you're okay."

"Thanks, Flan."

"I'll let you know as soon as I do," she said.

The following week she gave me a couple of dates, both of which fell on my days off. I picked one and, the following weekend, Flan phoned to say the visit was on. Reg had arranged for two VOs – one in her name, the other in mine – to be left at the prison gate.

*

I've tried to remember how I felt when that visit was confirmed, but I can't. I certainly wouldn't have been frightened – why would I be? The visit had been set up by one of Reg's closest and most trusted friends, who'd vouched for my integrity and no doubt Reg felt I could be useful to him in some way. I wouldn't have been fazed, either. From my days as a teenage cub reporter on the *Kentish Mercury* newspaper in South East London, I'd been accustomed to meeting famous people: I wrote a weekly record column and had met Cliff Richard, Frankie Vaughan and other British pop stars, as well as renowned U.S. singers, such as Peggy Lee. On the *Daily Sketch*, I'd chatted with Dudley Moore in his West End theatre dressing room, dined with Ginger Rogers at the Savoy, had lunch with Henry Cooper at Simpson's-in-the-Strand and entertained the 1969 Miss World, Eva Reuber-Staier, in a Fleet Street drinking club. As boss of Everest Books, I'd chatted one-to-one with Telly Savalas and Andy Williams in New York, Zsa Zsa Gabor at her Beverly Hills mansion, Gina Lollobrigida, at her house in Rome, and had dinner with Sammy Davis Jnr, at his favourite London club. And I'd met other international stars, such as Rod Stewart and Stewart Granger, in more social surroundings.

So no, the prospect of meeting one of Britain's most notorious killers did not bother me in the slightest. If anything, I was excited and looking forward to it. The only niggling worry was the travelling and what Reg would tell me to make the seven-hour, 200-mile round trip worthwhile. It was a long way to go for a chit-chat. I had to make sure I came away with some saleable copy to keep Reg happy, and, at least, cover our expenses.

I met Flan at Waterloo, well in time for the mid-morning train to Portsmouth. We'd then take the ferry to Newport, on the Isle of Wight, where we would be met by Ben, a taxi driver friend of Charlie Kray's, who would drive us to a pub for a bite to eat before taking us on to the prison. Reg did not want his visitors to be late, so Flan insisted we got to the prison at 1.30pm to ensure we were in the visiting room, in time for the 2pm visit.

Flan and I sat opposite each other on the train and, as it rattled through the Home Counties towards the South Coast, we reminisced about *Experience* and *Everest* and, our lives, generally. Flan is lively, engaging company, but she can talk the hind leg off the proverbial donkey and, after a while, I needed some quiet, and time to think. Obviously, I looked tense because, after twenty minutes or so, Flan broke the silence: "You're getting nervous, aren't you?"

I shook my head. "Not nervous. Apprehensive, maybe."

"I can understand that, but it'll be okay, Rob," she said. "He's looking forward to meeting you."

"And me, him," I said. "It's just that it's a bloody long way to go if we don't get anything."

"I'm sure you'll get something. Reg will be fired up. He won't stop talking."

"But about what?"

"He won't want to talk about the old days, that's for sure," Flan said. "He's got this thing about PMA."

"What?"

"Positive Mental Attitude. He's a strong, positive person and optimistic. He looks to the future, not back to the past."

"But that's what's interesting, Flan," I said. "The murders. The mayhem. How they got where they did. How and why they got nicked."

"You're not going to get him talking about all that in a couple of hours. Anyway, much of it was covered in *The Profession of Violence*."

I'd read the book written by a Sunday Times journalist, who was collaborating with all three brothers before their arrests. It was a best-seller, but I hadn't been impressed by it. Even the date the twins were born was wrong – an elementary mistake in any biography, let alone one about such high-profile personalities, and I wondered that, if the writer couldn't get the twins' birthdays right, what else was wrong?

"No, Flan," I said. "There's much more to be said. I mean, Reg has never talked about McVitie. Never admitted the killing."

Flan laughed. "I don't think he's going to confess that to you, Rob. Not when you've never met the man before."

I had to agree. At the same time, having travelled so far, I didn't want to sit there, talking about things that wouldn't interest the newspapers. Looking back – and in view of what happened over the next ten years – that was a mistake; I should have been concerned only with making a good impression, and winning Reg's trust. At the time, though, I feared the visit might be a one-off, and felt I had to make it count, with a headline-making exclusive story.

Flan and I sat in silence for ten minutes or so, then I took a writing pad from my briefcase, and wrote down a question in a blue felt-tip pen. It was just nine words, but I'd been pondering on it and was sure that, if it provoked a truthful answer, I'd have the scoop I wanted.

Flan was intrigued, and asked to see what I'd written. I handed her the pad. She stared at my question for several seconds, then threw her head back and guffawed.

"Jesus Christ, Rob, are you mad? You can't ask him *that*!"

"Why not? It's the great unsolved Kray mystery."

"Because it could kill the visit before it's started."

"That's a chance I have to take, Flan," I said, and I meant it. There were no guarantees that Reg would take to me and agree to see me again, so I had to make the most of our meeting. And if I got an answer to that question I'd be able to name my price with Fleet Street's Sunday newspapers.

I started writing more questions on my pad. By the time we pulled into Portsmouth and got the ferry, I had another eleven questions to take into Parkhurst's visiting room. I wondered what Reggie Kray would make of them.

*

With her colourful descriptive powers, Flan had painted a clear picture of the man I was due to meet. But, for some reason, I had not thought to ask her about the visiting conditions. Having never been in a jail before, I'm sure I was expecting a large hall, like I'd seen in James Cagney movies as a kid, with patrolling prison officers, watching every movement and listening to every word. But the venue for my face-to-face with one of the terrible twins was small, no more than thirty feet square, with just ten rectangular tables, big enough to seat four. And, although I was not conscious of counting them, I don't recall seeing more than three prison officers. What I *do* remember is being shocked by the deafening noise. I had not thought for a moment that the visit would be bedlam; that I'd find it hard to hear Reg speak above the raucous babble of wives and girlfriends and excited children. I wondered how we were going to have a conversation about anything, let alone something significant to provide enough copy for a newspaper.

At five minutes after 2p.m., Reg almost bounded into the room, the first of about a dozen Category A prisoners. He was always first in, and last out, Flan had told me. That's why she'd commandeered the table nearest the door. Watching him stride briskly, purposefully, towards us, in blue jeans, casual top and trainers, I was not surprised at how short he was: I'd seen photos of both Reg and Ron, next to prison officers, at their mother's funeral three years before. Nor was I surprised at how fit he looked. Flan had stressed that he was slim, well-muscled and looked younger than his fifty-one years. It was Reggie's voice that astonished me. Although I hadn't given it a moment's thought, I'm sure I would have expected him to speak like Charlie – not a baritone voice, by any means, but quite deep and rich and, well, normal, with no hint of a lazy Cockney accent. But when Reggie greeted me – "Hello, Robin, it's very nice to meet you, glad you could come" – his was quiet, thin and reedy, with, it seemed, the trace of an impediment that made him hard to understand.

"Hello, Reg," I said, holding out my hand. "Good to meet you, too. Thanks for arranging the visit."

Reg took my hand and crushed the tops of my fingers in the strongest handshake I could remember. He kissed Flan lightly on the cheek and we all sat down – Reg opposite us, facing the door – and tried to hear each other above the cacophony around us. Reg and Flan were clearly used to the noise, and children running around, but I found it hard to concentrate and kept leaning forward, towards Reg, fighting to pick up what was a barely audible mutter. He seemed to think we'd met before, but I told him I was a South Londoner and couldn't remember ever going to the East End. It wasn't the easiest of first meetings, particularly as I was eager to make a good impression, live up to whatever Flan had told Reg about me. It was very clear early on, though, that Reg saw me as someone who could be very useful to him. Having been introduced by Flan, I was coming from the right direction, as it were, and had a distinct advantage over other journalists who'd written to him over the years.

The constant maddening babble around us got on my nerves, but, as it didn't seem to bother Reg or Flan, I tried not to let it bother me. I was in "selling" mode – looking directly into Reg's eyes, smiling a lot, trying to be amusing and interesting, and, most important of all, going all out to convince him that I was someone he could trust, have confidence in, to deal with matters on the outside that were important to him and Ronnie.

Knowing that Ronnie had been transferred from Parkhurst to Broadmoor hospital for the criminally insane, in Berkshire, six years before, I asked how Reggie felt being separated from him.

"I welcomed the move," he said, surprisingly. "Actually, I encouraged it."

"Why's that, Reg?"

"You get a lot of young guys coming through, who'd want to make a name for themselves, fighting a Kray," he said. "I knew I could handle it, by turning a blind eye, but Ronnie was unwell and wouldn't have been able to control himself. He'd have got in loads of fights and probably ended up getting seriously hurt by guys attacking him mob-handed. Far better for him to go to Broadmoor, where he could be monitored and cared for."

Fascinated that Reggie's concern for his twin was so deep that he was prepared to be parted from him, I wanted to explore the subject, but Reggie was more interested in asking about me, and my job, and, more particularly, how I might be able to help him.

It gave me the opening I'd been waiting for. I reached into the inside pocket of my jacket. "I have some questions, Reg," I said. "Is it okay?"

"Yeah," he said. "Yeah, go ahead."

I took out the sheet of paper I'd ripped from my notebook and looked at the first of eleven questions I'd written.

I glanced around the room, made sure none of the visitors, nor prison officers, were eavesdropping, then leaned even closer to Reg. In no more than a whisper, I said: "Can you reveal where Frank Mitchell's body was taken?"

Frank "Mad Axeman" Mitchell was a mentally unstable criminal the Krays had sprung from Dartmoor Prison in 1966, and arranged to have murdered when he proved impossible to control. His body was never found.

Reg stared at me, looking puzzled, as if he wasn't sure he understood. Then he cocked an ear: "Eh?"

I glanced around the room again, embarrassed. But everyone was chatting among themselves and the children were playing noisily. Everyone was oblivious to what I'd said. I leaned towards Reg again. A little louder, I asked: "Can you reveal where Frank Mitchell's body was taken?"

The ear cocked again. "Eh?"

I took a deep breath. "CAN YOU REVEAL WHERE FRANK MITCHELL'S BODY WAS TAKEN?"

Suddenly, a deathly hush fell on the room. I didn't dare look around, but I could sense all eyes on our table. I stared at Reg, waiting for an answer, but he just looked at me, saying nothing. Finally, he shook his head. "I don't want to talk about that, Robin. Next question."

I looked at my list. The next question was: "And 'Jack the Hat' McVitie's?" but I didn't have the bottle to ask it. I waffled about something I can't remember now, and, somehow, we got over the awkwardness of the situation.

Reg didn't seem bothered, and for the next hour and a half, we had a pleasant, friendly chat. As Flan said, he was hyperactive, mentally alert, articulate and made it clear he was up for any idea I felt could make money. Reg was particularly keen for me to check out the position on royalties from *The Profession Of Violence*, as the solicitor he was using had not got anywhere. I promised to find out the author's agent, and contact the publisher.

On a more sinister note, Reg also asked me to get some newspaper cuttings on another prisoner, named Robinson, who had done something Reg did not approve of. Rather darkly, he said he wanted some information on the guy, "so that he would know he wasn't forgotten." Reg also asked me to send any books, and I promised to send some popular paperbacks, notably Sydney Sheldon's *Master of the Game*, which had recently been made into a TV series.

The visit was going so well that Reg was clearly disappointed as Flan signalled to a prison officer that we had to leave. There were still twenty minutes left of the two-hour visit, but we had to be at the prison gates at 3.45p.m. to meet Ben, who was driving us to the port to catch the 4p.m. ferry. I held out my hand to Reg, preparing myself for the bone-crushing handshake. "It's been a pleasure to meet you, Reg," I said. "Thank you for arranging the visit."

"Yeah, yeah," he said. "Thanks for coming. Now, don't forget those things I've asked you to do."

"No, I won't, Reg. I'll drop you a line, okay?"

"Yeah. Be hearing from you. Okay."

And then we were gone, escorted through one locked door then another and another, until we were outside the huge main wooden door. Walking down the long prison approach to Ben's waiting taxi, I was grateful not only for the late afternoon sunshine, but the deafening silence.

"So how do you think it went, Flan?" I asked.

"I can't believe you asked that question," she said. "I cringed, waiting for him to yell at me, 'Fuck off and don't bring him any more – he's a slag.'"

"But he didn't, did he?"

"No," Flan said. "But it could have gone the other way. Didn't you see how agitated he was when he sat down?"

"No," I said. "He seemed okay."

"He was very on edge. Didn't you see him rubbing his thumb against his forefinger of his right hand? He always does that when he's jumpy."

I shook my head. I'd been too concerned trying to hear what Reg was saying to notice anything else. "Anyway, did it go okay?"

"For a first visit, it was fine," Flan said. "The first thing he'll do when he gets back to his cell is write and tell Ronnie he's met you and that you're all right."

"Really?"

"I guarantee it. You're different to the type of visitor Ron usually gets. Reg knows he'll find you interesting."

"And useful?"

"Absolutely."

"He's certainly given me some jobs to do," I said.

"You got off lightly," Flan said. "I was surprised he didn't turn up with loads of papers. That's what he usually does if I'm on my own. He always has a list of things he wants me to do, people he wants me to contact."

"Like a secretary?"

"An errand girl, more like," she said. "You'll learn in time. Reggie Kray may be locked up but that doesn't stop him trying to live his life like a free man, earn money, one way or the other. He's very persistent. And very, very demanding."

"Thanks for the warning, Flan," I said. "By the way, is he really deaf?"

"In the right ear. From all the fighting – in and out of the ring."

"So, do you think he didn't hear my question about Mitchell?"

"Of course he heard it," she said. "Everyone heard it! He just didn't want to answer it. Until you bellowed it."

"It obviously didn't bother him too much."

"No. But it could have. I don't think it was a clever move. It could have

The questions the author wrote, en route to meet Reg.

Reggie Kray

My first meeting with Reg (Parkhurst 88)

(2)

1) Can you reveal where Frank Mitchell's body was taken?

2) And Jack 'the Hat' McVitie's.

3) Did you have a deal with an East End undertaker?

4) Do you know of any other people murdered by Ronnie — apart from George Cornell?

5) What have you been thinking about most during your 17 years in jail?

6) What effect has your absence from your twin had on you?

7) And Ronnie?

8) What did you do with your time on Maximum A?

9) What makes you think you might be paroled in 4/5 yrs?

10) Life in jail: have you any clout — or are you just "another prisoner."

11) What sort of things do you ask friends on the outside to do for you — if any?

12) What is the most important thing in your life at this moment?

gone the other way."

When I didn't respond, Flan said: "As it happens, I think it might have done you some good. Reg probably respected you for having the nerve to ask it."

"But we haven't come away with a story, have we? Not one that would be worth much anyway."

Flan smiled. "Don't worry about that. Coming down here you were concerned that the visit might be a one-off. Well, I'm sure Reg likes you and will want to see you again. Think of it long term. He's going to be inside a very long time."

She was right, of course. Asking about Mitchell was a stupid risk I shouldn't have taken. And yes, it could have killed the visit, and future contact. But I'd got away with it. Now, I had to look to the future and build a relationship. Who knew where it would lead.

Flan, however, was ahead of me. "Now you've met Reg, you've got to meet the other one," she said. "Fixing it will be easy now, but first you've got to meet Ronnie's wife."

I remembered that Ronnie had got married; it had been *The Sun* front page and a double-page spread in February. But I knew nothing of his bride.

"What's she like, Flan?" I asked.

"Lovely," she said. "You'll like her. Everybody does."

Chapter Three

HAVING been brought up to be polite and courteous, I wrote to Reg the next day, thanking him for the visit and promising to look into what he'd asked me to do. A few days later, in early June 1985, I received a letter, asking if I could see him the following week. Unfortunately, my shift pattern at the *Express* made that impossible, but I wrote back immediately, suggesting an alternative date and saying that I was prepared to stay at an hotel overnight, if he could arrange two visits on successive days.

I also addressed what had worried me at our first meeting. I made it clear that I wasn't backed by a wealthy company and able to write off hundreds of pounds as expenses; although I was a staff journalist with the *Daily Express*, I was seeing him as a freelance, in my own time, and whatever I paid out, generating business for each of us, my expenses must come off the top. I decided also to broach the subject of a book, giving his version of events that had led to he and his brothers being jailed for a total of seventy years. I told him I'd run my own publishing company, and I had high-level contacts in the industry, which made me the ideal person to write his story. And having worked with most of the tabloid editors, I was confident that a revelatory book would command at least £100,000 in newspaper and magazine serialisation. Posting the letter, I was quietly excited: thanks to Flan, I was close to being welcomed into the inner sanctum of the country's most newsworthy gangsters, and pulling off the biggest crime scoop of the century.

Reg seemed keen to see me, sooner rather than later, and wrote back, confirming the 15th. What he said, in the barely decipherable scrawl that would become so familiar over the years, was polite enough, but, even at that early stage, he clearly wanted to establish who was boss in the relationship. "*Please bring Rothman ciggarrettes (sic) and matches,*" he wrote. "*Also if Flanagan has not sent to me will you bring along papers on Robinson...*"

What Reg neglected to tell me was that he'd arranged for his brother, Charlie, to visit as well. I only learned this through Charlie, who rang, suggesting we travelled together. To be honest, I was disappointed. I liked Charlie enormously, and enjoyed his company, but I didn't want anyone else on the visit: I'd been looking forward to a one-to-one with Reg, so that we could get to know each other and, hopefully, progress the book idea.

*

By the time Charlie and I walked into the visiting room at Parkhurst, I'd convinced myself that a three-way visit was not such a bad idea. After all, how many journalists had sat down for a friendly chat with two of the Kray brothers? Apart from anything else, it would be fascinating for me to see how

Reg and his older brother were with each other. On the train, Charlie had told me he'd always got on better with Ronnie, who was more easy going and understanding of the problems Charlie faced, having been unjustly jailed in the McVitie case. Reg, on the other hand, was less tolerant and forever pestering Charlie – by phone and letter – to do things, or speak to people, on his behalf. Infuriatingly, however, I didn't have the three-way meeting I was expecting, because Reg came in with a fellow inmate he introduced as Steve Tully. He was a nice enough bloke – dark-haired, late twenties and good-looking in a rough and ready sort of way – but there was only one reason I was there, and it wasn't to have a chat with him. What made it worse was that, after introducing Steve, Reg left us to talk while he turned his attention to Charlie and proceeded to berate him, none too quietly, for, apparently, not having done what he'd been asked to.

It was embarrassing being party to someone so decent and gentle as Charlie being on the end of such a foul-mouthed tirade of abuse, but I tried to put it out of my mind as I made polite conversation with Steve. As it turned out, he was a most interesting young guy with an agile brain and a fascinating, if sad, story of his own. An only child, he told me he'd been put into care at the age of eight by a mother who didn't want him. Already criminally minded, he found a copy of *The Profession of Violence* – and was enthralled by the fearsome power the Kray twins held over people, and the glamorous, star-studded lives they seemed to lead. Even at eight, he knew he wanted to be a serious criminal. What he couldn't imagine was that, fourteen years later, having been sentenced to ten years for armed robbery, he would be in the chapel at Parkhurst, shaking hands with one of the twins he worshipped.

It was late summer, 1982, and Reg was in the hospital wing, acutely depressed, after trying to kill himself in Long Lartin Prison, in Nottingham. One Sunday, Steve spotted him in the chapel, where inmates gathered, not so much to pray, but to catch up on the latest prison gossip. He waited his moment, then went over and introduced himself. Reg took an instant liking to him and Steve was thrilled: he felt he had made it. The next step, he told me, was getting to know Reg, and he got the chance when the infamous twin was moved from the hospital to a cell in the prison's Category C wing – a few yards from Steve's.

Over the previous few months, Steve had been inspired in positive mental attitude by the so-called "Torture Gang" boss, Charlie Richardson, then into the seventeenth year of his twenty-five-year sentence. Charlie's philosophy was that if you really wanted something, you should go all out to get it, never taking no for an answer. Steve desperately wanted to be a top-line criminal, so he knocked on Reg's cell and asked: "Will you teach me to be like you?" Flattered, Reg had taken Steve under his wing, protecting him, I was sure, from sexually-motivated prisoners.

Dear Reg,

I would like to thank you for arranging for me to come to see you earlier this week with Flanagan. I don't know what I was expecting, but certainly I was surprised: you looked so fit and sounded so articulate and on top of things. I suppose I imagined that prison eventually killed a person's character. In your case that does not appear to be the case and I hope it stays that way.

I have done what you asked: the books are winging their way south to Mr Grace: and I've sent you a couple, too. That other thing – the thing you wanted to make sure was not forgotten! – is with Flanagan and she will bring it to you on her next visit. It seems the person in question was involved in that escapade with a woman, who was since been declared nuts!

For a first-ever meeting (I'm absolutely convinced we had never met before) I think we got on well, and I would most certainly like to visit you again. It takes time to understand and trust somebody and I would like to take the trouble to reach that sort of understanding. I get on well with Charlie and my wife are going to invite them over for dinner in the next few days, I'm dying to know what the latest is on the film.

As far as the royalties on The Profession of Violence are concerned, I am happy to get fully involved in this on behalf of you. Perhaps you can ask Charlie to get in touch as soon as possible if this is what you want. Solicitors are all very well, but I've been a publisher and know all the wrinkles.

Incidentally, I was reading the Guardian and Sun and saw something about your injunction. Thought you would appreciate the cuttings. No doubt you had more to say about the matter, but you know what newspapers are like – they cut everything down, don't they!!

Would it be possible for you to let Flanagan or Charlie know when it would be convenient for me to make another trip to see you, if only to have another casual and friendly chat?

Incidentally, I should have given Charlie that cutting you asked me to get, shouldn't I? I gave it to Flanagan and, of course, she hasn't been down. Shall I get another one and give it to Charlie?

Anyway, Reg, I've got to fly. Don't forget, if there is anything you would like me to do, and I can do it, I will. And I look forward to seeing you again when you feel it's convenient.

Yours sincerely,

5 June 85

Dear Reg,

At last I've got some idea of when I can come down to see you again! It has been difficult to come up with some dates, Reg, because a number of things have to be considered: e.g. accommodation overnight, days off from my work, my wife and dog who want to see the Isle of Wight etc. Now, though, I have a couple of suggestions.

1.David Hamilton, the BBC disc jockey, has a show on the island on Saturday week (June 15), and has offered to drive me down. If I took advantage of his offer, I'd be able to see you for a couple of hours that day.

2. I'm on holiday for a couple of weeks, starting June 24, and would be able to see you twice, as you suggested in your last letter, any time in that period.

Reg, the only reason I'm suggesting Saturday the 15th is that I really would like to see you again (there are lots of things to discuss) and would like it to be before my holiday. If you were agreeable to my coming on the 15th, I would be happy to come again during my holiday – it's not a question of one OR the other. It's both, if you would like.

I received a card about Krayleigh and phoned Jack Leigh. Unfortunately, I didn't get a call back, so there was nothing I could do. I was peeved to read it in the papers because I would have liked to have done the story first. Ah, well, c'est la vie!

I'm due to see Charlie at some point about a few matters and will you in about them when I see you.

I'm taking this opportunity of sending you Of Mice and Men. It's a classic, so you may well have read it. Take care of it, because it is a very old copy and I MUST have it back. It's a book I treasure. Take your time reading it because it is a marvellous story, beautifully told. I'm sure you'll enjoy it.

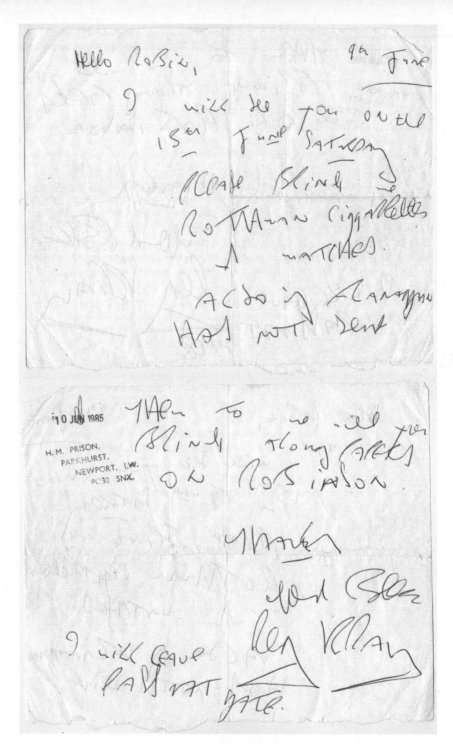

9th June Hello Robin, I will see you on the 15th June Saturday.
Please bring Rothman ciggarrettes and matches. Also if Flanagan
has not sent them to me will you bring along papers on Robinson
Thanks God Bless Reg Kray   I will leave pass at gate

Dear Reg,

Thank you for your letter, in which you suggested that I travelled to the Isle of Wight again to visit you. Yes, I'd like to do that, Reg, and I am only sorry I could not make it yesterday (Tuesday). I do a four-day week, but get a clear five-day break every third week. It makes sense to come down for two or three days, stay at a hotel and see you a couple of times.

Your true account of all the things that happened to put you where you are today is likely to be very valuable, not only to the newspapers and/or magazines, but also to a publisher. If you do want to consider "telling all", then I feel I am the man you should be talking to. My contacts in the publishing field are better than most and I would be able to advise you on the best course to take. But I don't know whether you want to do the ultimate first person story and all it entails. This is why it is important to have another meeting and kick the whole idea around.

I am up against it, at the moment, but I feel it worthwhile to invest some time and money, so that we can get to know each other. I want you to know, however, that when I come to the Isle of Wight, it is at my own expense - no big company is picking up the tab. If we do any business that brings in some cash, I feel it only fair that my travelling expenses come off the top. I don't mind breaking even, but I don't want to make a loss!

You have no need to worry about my integrity. I'm a very straightforward, honest bloke, as I'm sure Charlie has told you. There was a time when I could have written off thousands on a venture, but sadly, those days are gone.

My wife and I invited Charlie and Di to dinner last Monday but they had arranged to see the famous medium Doris Stokes at Croydon. No doubt we'll fix another date. It would be good to have them over 'cos Charlie and I get on well and Sue and Di hit it off, too. I'll be seeing them tonight at the charity function Flanagan has organised.

As they became friendly, Reg opened up to Steve about his recent suicide attempt, admitting he'd tried to kill himself because he believed all his family – mum, dad, Charlie and even Ronnie – blamed him for everything that had happened. Feeling it would be better for everyone if he were dead, he'd smashed his spectacles in half and sawed into one of his wrists. I'd heard most of the story from Charlie, who'd driven to Long Lartin, after learning what Reg had done. Nothing could have prepared him for what confronted him in Reg's cell in the hospital: the meticulous dresser, who always took a pride in his appearance, was lying on a bed, unshaven, hair uncombed and standing on end, and in clothes so creased they looked as if he'd slept in them. He seemed relatively together until Charlie asked him, for the third time, why he'd tried to kill himself, and then, close to tears, Reg had said he wanted to make life easier for the family – particularly their mother, Violet.

Charlie was told by the Chief Prison Officer that Reg had been found, covered in blood, and taken to the "Chokey" where he spent the maximum twenty-four hours in solitary, supposedly "for his own protection." But what that Prison Officer didn't say was that prison officers went into Reg's cell, mob-handed, and roughed him up before taking him there. It beggared belief that it took such extreme measures to control someone who'd lost so much blood, and I was thankful that Charlie did not know this at the time. He was angry enough that Reg had spent a day in solitary when someone could easily have kept an eye on him in his cell, and that the prison's top brass had suggested that Reg had probably only cut his wrist to cause trouble – or even to get himself certified insane so that he could be transferred to Broadmoor.

Listening to Steve, I did wonder if there was anything sexual in his relationship with Reg, though it certainly wasn't the moment to ask. However, when Steve told me he was being released in two months, I suggested we met to collaborate on a newspaper feature about what he and Reg called their "special bond". Steve liked the idea and promised to contact me after his release, in August.

Steve and I had chatted for nearly half an hour before Reg decided he'd humiliated his brother enough. He turned to me and calmly asked if my wife and I would be kind enough to invite Steve, to lunch or dinner when he was freed. I wasn't sure Sue would welcome an armed robber into our home, but I said we'd see what we could do, and changed the subject to a dear friend of mine, named Iris Burton, who, I felt, could be useful to Reg.

I met Iris when, as a nineteen-year-old, she joined the *Kentish Mercury* and we covered the Deptford and Rotherhithe areas together. More importantly, she was now Editor of *Woman's Own* and one of the most influential magazine journalists in the country. We'd remained close friends and Iris was fascinated that I'd met Reg Kray. When she said she'd like to meet him herself, I promised to ask Reg if he wanted to meet *her*. So, I brought it up on that visit. Reg immediately saw the value of meeting such a powerful publishing executive and promised to arrange a visit at a mutually convenient date. Iris had already expressed an interest in me writing an in-depth feature about Ronnie's bizarre marriage to a woman who had begun visiting the Krays in prison after reading a book about them, so as the visit drew to a close, it all seemed very positive. What I didn't care for, as we said our goodbyes, was Reg drawing me to one side and asking me to send ten pounds to an inmate at nearby Albany Prison.

When I didn't look too happy, he forced a weak smile. "Don't worry," he said. "Put it on the bill." Not wanting to spoil what was clearly a convivial start to our relationship, I said okay and made a note of the guy's name.

*

It was none of my business why Reg had steamed into Charlie so brutally, but I was curious, and on the train home, I decided to ask what it was all about.

"It's the bloody film," he said, wearily.

I looked puzzled. The only film I knew about was the one Charlie had mentioned when he was trying to squeeze a further advance out of me, and that was ten years ago.

"Roger Daltrey wants to do one," Charlie said. "He's been working on it a couple of years."

"Really!" I said, impressed. Daltrey, lead singer in *The Who* rock band, had been acclaimed for his role as high-profile villain John McVicar in the film of that name and I was sure that, if he was as committed to making a Kray film as Charlie said, he would have the clout to make it happen.

"How far's he got?"

"He's got a script," Charlie said. "Now all he needs is the money."

"So what's the problem with Reg?"

"What it always is," Charlie said. "He's impatient. He can't understand that things take time. Especially films."

"But why have a go at you?" I said. "It's not your fault."

"Try telling Reg that," Charlie said, forcing an ironic chuckle. "When things don't happen the way he wants, it's always my fault."

"But the money's nothing to do with you, Charlie," I said. "How can you be expected to raise the millions needed for a movie?"

"It's not only that," Charlie said.

"So what is it?"

"The twins," he said.

"The twins? What do you mean?"

"Two young brothers, Mike and Chris Harris," Charlie said. "Ronnie's told them they'll be in the film. Playing him and Reg."

"Are they actors?"

Charlie shook his head. "No. They're boxers. From Manchester."

"Cockney villains with a Mancunian accent," I laughed. "That's original."

"Reg and Ronnie want them in the film anyway," Charlie said. "That's what Reg was going on about. He can't understand why I can't get Daltrey to cast them."

"Jesus. The cast is the least of his problems."

"I've told Reg that," said Charlie. "But when you get to know him, you'll understand."

I think I'd got the picture already. When he was free, Reg got things done at his pace, by whatever means it took. Now, he expected his older brother to do the same. But intimidation wasn't in Charlie's nature, never had been, never would be.

"You've got to leave it all to Daltrey, Charlie," I said. "If he wants to make a film about the twins that badly, he'll do it. They should let him get on with it."

"I know," Charlie said. "But they always know best. Especially Reg."

Not for the first time, I felt sorry for Charlie. I had no brothers or sisters, but a part of me could imagine how emotionally crippling it was for him to be seen as such a feeble failure by such forceful, strong-minded siblings. The good news, though, was that it *did* seem that a film about the Kray twins was likely to happen. And from what Charlie told me about the script, it promised to be a profound, thought-provoking story, not one merely about murder and mayhem. The killings and the fear the twins instilled in people would be covered, of course, but, it seemed, Daltrey would concentrate more on the fascinating bond between the twins, and the power one had over the other.

"Have the twins met Daltrey?" I asked.

"Yeah. I took him and a film producer to Broadmoor. And we flew to Parkhurst."

"Flew?"

"Yeah," Charlie said. "Roger has a helicopter. He flies it himself. He got permission to land in the grounds of St Mary's hospital, near the prison."

"That's the way to do it," I said. "Beats the train, ferry and taxi."

"And cheaper, too," Charlie said, as always with an eye on the money. "Roger saved me a few quid that day."

"What do the twins think of the script, Charlie?"

"They think it's all right," Charlie said. "But they're more interested in the money. What they're going to get up front."

"What *are* they going to get?"

"Reg told Roger they want a hundred grand."

"What's that based on?"

Charlie laughed. "Not a lot. It just sounded about right to both of them."

"What about you?" I asked. "Are you part of it?"

"We're splitting it three ways," he said.

"Good for you, Charlie," I said.

And I meant it. With all the aggravation he was having to endure, he deserved a good pay day.

*

Reg's cheeky request for his mate in Albany still rankled and I decided to mention it to Charlie. He wasn't surprised, saying it was typical of Reg: he was always leaning on people to provide cash or gifts for so-called friends he was keen to impress. Although Charlie didn't spell it out, it was clear to me that Reg saw himself as a Godfather-type figure, with the power and contacts to make things happen; someone with a formidable image to nurture.

"You wouldn't believe what idiots he gets involved with," Charlie said. "I wouldn't give you two bob for them, but Reg is always on to me to do things, or get things, to make himself look big in their eyes. If someone he's palled up with is coming out, he'll get on to me to arrange a few quid for them, take them out for a few drinks or whatever, even though he knows I haven't got the money to do it. Nine times out of ten I'll never see the guy again. The twins have always led me a dog's life. When I do anything good for them, I never get any praise or thank you, but whenever anything goes wrong I always get the blame – even though it might not be my fault, or anything to do with me. Sometimes I get the impression that they feel it's my fault they're in prison."

Having witnessed the ear-bashing Reg had given him, I didn't doubt a word, and felt enormous sympathy for Charlie, who had always come over – to me, at least – as a genuine, genial, straightforward human being, who detested being tarred with the same brush as his violent brothers. And I have to be honest: it never occurred to me that some of the "things" he was asked to do on his brothers' behalf might be questionable, to put it mildly.

The following Tuesday, I received a letter – a few lines on each of four pages – from Reg, illustrating vividly his positive mental attitude. Though no invitation had yet been made, Reg wanted me to know that Steve would be pleased to have lunch with me and the family when he got out. And he was already thinking that Iris – whom he had elevated to "the Lady Burton" – might like to visit Ronnie with me "one day." Reg made no mention of the tenner, but I felt sure it would have crossed his mind to remind me.

*

Three days later, Flan brought Ronnie's wife, Elaine, to Beckenham, for my *Woman's Own* interview. I was shocked when I met her – but pleasantly so. I was expecting a loud, blowsy, in-your-face Cockney, but Elaine was quietly-spoken, very shy and not in the least full of herself, as some women might have been, having married a notorious gangster and been pictured on the front page of Britain's biggest-selling tabloid. She was a large, buxom lady, taller than I'd expected, immaculately made up, and smart in a blue dress and jacket. On being introduced, her face broke into a wide, warm smile, and I liked her

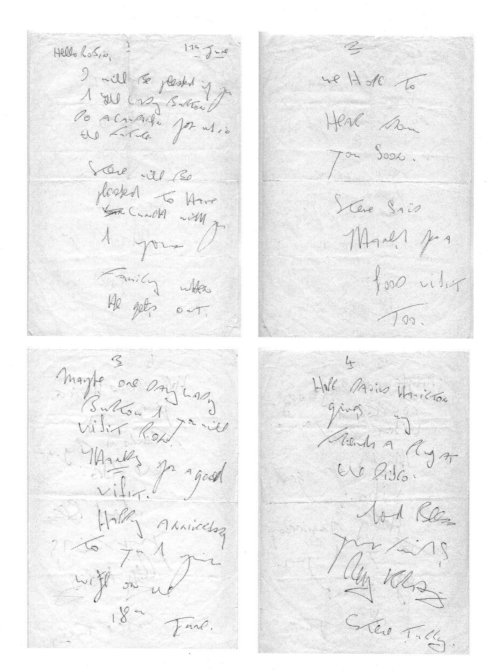

17th June   Hello Robin, I will be pleased if you and the Lady Burton do a campaign
for us in the future. Steve will be pleased to have lunch with you and your family
when he gets out. We hope to hear from you soon. Steve said thanks for a good visit
too. Maybe one day Lady Burton and you will visit Ron. Thanks for a good visit.
Happy anniversary to you and your wife on the 18th June. Hope David Hamilton
gives my friends a plug at the Disco. God Bless. Your friends Reg Kray Steve Tully

on sight. Flan had told me she'd met Elaine through Charlie, who'd described her as "a lovely lady" and, if first impressions were anything to go by, I thought he was spot-on.

Over the next hour or so, Elaine told me all about her "romance." It all began, she said, when she wrote to Reggie in the Spring of 1983, after reading the book about the twins. It was a warm, friendly letter in which she told Reg, among other things, that she'd gone to the same primary school – Daniel Street – as he and Ron. Reggie was so taken with the letter he invited Elaine to Parkhurst and when he saw her, he, like me, was pleasantly surprised. The twenty-eight-year-year-old, well-educated, modest typist, wasn't like the blonde glamour-model types that usually wrote to him: she had two children – Andrew, aged twelve, and Debbie, aged eleven – and, indeed, looked more "mumsy" than sexy. In fact, Reg thought, she was the perfect lady to visit Ronnie, whose life he was forever trying to make more comfortable and interesting. After Elaine went home, he'd written to Ronnie, saying he was asking Charlie to take "a lovely, good-natured woman" to Broadmoor; he was sure Ronnie would like her as much as he. Charlie did as he was told, and, sure enough, Ronnie was taken with Elaine as much as his twin: she reminded him of his beloved mother, who'd doted on him and Reg in the same way Elaine cared for her own children. And Elaine liked Ronnie, too: his gentleness and old-fashioned courtesy was something she'd never experienced, and she told him she would visit him whenever he wanted.

Throughout that summer of 1983, Charlie drove Elaine to Broadmoor many times and she became a good friend to Ronnie, someone he could rely on; she seemed only too pleased to run around and do things for him. Eventually, Charlie persuaded Flan to relieve him of his duty, and, over the next year, the two women became close friends. Elaine began travelling to Broadmoor on her own – once in the week, and on Saturday – and, after each visit she would get off the train at Waterloo, take the underground to Mile End and walk round to Flan's home, near Victoria Park, where Flan would cook her something to eat while Elaine told her about the visit.

In the third week of November the following year, Ronnie asked Flan to take Elaine with her when she visited on Saturday. Knowing Flan was taking her ten-year-old son, Elaine was confused. "Why does he want me there as well?" she asked.

"I've no idea," said Flan. And she hadn't. Ronnie had just told her: "Bring Elaine."

When they arrived, four of Ronnie's pals had arrived unexpectedly and Elaine and Flan, and the little boy, had to wait in reception until they left. When they finally got to see Ronnie it was gone 3p.m. They chatted about this and that for half an hour or so, then Ronnie suddenly blurted out: "Well, Elaine, are you going to marry me, or what?"

Elaine was shocked. She looked at Flan, not knowing how to respond.

"You've got to answer, Elaine," Ronnie said.

Elaine looked at Flan again. "I don't know. What shall I say, Flan?"

"What you asking her for?" Ronnie said, impatiently.

Finally, Elaine said yes. Ronnie smiled and gave her a gentle hug and peck on the cheek. It was a romantic moment, but all Flan could think of was headlines "and a few quid". She couldn't wait to get out and call *The Sun* from the phone box across the road from the main gate. As it was Saturday, she had to wait until the next day to speak to one of her Picture Desk contacts, but, of course, the paper loved the story and published it on Page One the following Monday morning, with an exclusive interview with Elaine across the centre pages, under the headline, "*Why I Fell For A Kray.*" Not surprisingly, *The Sun* also got the exclusive rights to the wedding in Broadmoor, the following February. Elaine made the most of her time in the spotlight, insisting that the paper hire her a white fox stole to wear over a striking electric blue suit, to give the occasion what she called a "Hollywood glamour touch."

There were two reasons why Ronnie married Elaine - one for the money a tabloid would pay for the exclusive story of the wedding, the other because he loved the idea of someone 'mumsy' taking in little luxuries and generally running errands for him

*

On the Monday after interviewing Elaine, I wrote to Reg assuring him that I'd make it clear in my feature for Woman's Own that Ronnie was caring and considerate, not only to Elaine, but her children, too. It was time, I said, for people to see there was another side to the so-called "monster." Aware that Reg's first concern would be money, not image, however, I warned him that magazines did not pay nearly as much as newspapers. But there would certainly be some cash in it for Ronnie and Elaine.

I dressed up the piece the best I could and Iris Burton felt it would work as a double-page spread, with new photographs of Elaine and her children. But it contained no revelations that would be picked up by other publications and promote the magazine, so it was no surprise when Iris said she'd pay only £500. I didn't commit myself, just said I was visiting Ronnie with Elaine the following week, and I'd see how they felt.

That first meeting, in Broadmoor's vast visiting hall, was an experience I'll never forget. Flan had described, graphically, how hugely different the twins were, and she was so right, not only in looks, but in demeanour, too. While Reg was hyperactive, eager to start the visit, and make the most of the allotted two hours, Ronnie didn't show up until at least five minutes after all the other patients had filed into the hall and were chatting to their visitors. And when he did, he sauntered past the dozens of formica tables, head high, back stiff, as though he owned the place.

Flan had told me there were two reasons he was always the last patient to arrive: he didn't like walking in with – and being jostled by – other patients, many of whom could behave unpredictably, and he liked to make a grand entrance that befitted his status as Broadmoor's most celebrated resident. Sometimes, Flan said, she sat on her own for as long as fifteen minutes, and would glance at an orderly, point to her watch, and ask: "Does Ronnie know I'm here?" She always got the same answer: "Yes, he's been getting ready since eleven o'clock!" Then, a few moments later, she'd hear the familiar sound of Ronnie's freshly-polished shoes on the wooden floor, and know that "The Duke of Broadmoor" – as one of the tabloids had dubbed him – was on his way. I never got around to asking Ronnie why he was always late for visits, but from the look of the impeccably-dressed gentleman strolling towards Elaine and I that summer afternoon, I felt sure that it was a strong desire, if not a craving, to be noticed. He imagined all eyes on him and he was positively basking in the impact he believed his arrival heralded.

As Flan had predicted, he was wearing an exquisitely-tailored dark blue double-breasted suit – one of the many outfits provided, free, by a friend of Flan's, Barry Scott - a wealthy tailor-cum-jeweller, from Neasden, in north-west London, she'd met in the late seventies. Barry was happily married, but enjoyed the London nightclub scene with Flan and her modelling mates. He revelled in being among glamorous "faces" and when Flan suggested he made a suit for Ronnie Kray, Barry said Yes immediately. Not surprisingly, Ronnie was thrilled, and, for the last four years, Barry had been going to Broadmoor every autumn to measure Ronnie for two suits, so that they would be ready to wear in the new year. Barry also provided shirts, gratis, and although I could see only the collar of Ronnie's crisply-ironed white shirt, I took Flan's word that Ronnie's monogram *RK* would be on the pocket. Completing his sartorial elegance was a pair of gold cufflinks – again, courtesy of Mr Scott – and a grey silk tie, one of many clothing accessories from Barry's shop bought by rich admirers, desperate to win favour and be honoured with a Thank You card, or letter, in Ronnie's inimitable scrawl.

There were several things I might have expected Ronnie Kray to say on meeting me for the first time, but what he *did* say would never have crossed my mind. He'd barely shaken my hand and sat down when he said, in the same, reedy voice as Reg: "Not a lot of money, Robin." I was shocked. I knew we were going to talk about the *Woman's Own* offer, but I thought he might have said "Hello" first! However, as I would quickly learn, that was Ronnie: he, even more than Reggie, was not one for small talk when money was on the agenda.

I explained that, traditionally, magazines had never paid as much as newspapers because the competition was not so fierce. But it cut no ice with Ronnie. "Then leave it, Robin," he said. "Okay?"

"I could go back and try to squeeze a bit more," I said.

"No," Ronnie said. "It's not worth it."

My first thought was to say that I'd spent a couple of days on the project and needed to get something for it – as did Elaine – but there was something in Ronnie's look, as much as his tone, that made me feel it wise to say nothing; to just agree and spend the visit, getting to know something about the man. Which I did – up to a point. Unlike Reg, he was subdued and quiet, clearly more concerned with having a leisurely chat over his favourite John Player Special cigarettes and cans of Barbican non-alcoholic lager. However, he was very much like Reg at our first meeting in that, in the two hours we chatted, he never swore once – not even "bloody" – nor raised his voice.

I found him warm and welcoming, polite, well-mannered and very courteous, not only to Elaine and me, but also to the hospital staff who came to the table with refreshments. I saw or heard nothing that made me think, yes, this man was once one of Britain's most dangerous psychopaths who had shot rival gangster George Cornell dead in the Blind Beggar pub in Whitechapel in 1966. I found him easy and charming company, and interested in what I was doing, not only on the *Express* but in my spare time, too.

All the time we chatted, I was also very aware of Peter Sutcliffe, "the Yorkshire Ripper," at the next table – only a dozen feet or so away – cheek-to-cheek with his wife, Sonia, reading the Bible to each other. Would I find him such easy and charming company, too, I wondered?

Towards the end of the visit, I mentioned the Richardsons, two equally infamous South London brothers, and my fascination with Charlie Richardson's South African mining enterprise, and the murder of his partner, Thomas Waldeck in 1965, a crime that led to the Richardsons' downfall. I was working as a sub-editor on the *Daily Sketch* at the time and, before starting my evening shift, had located Sheila Bradbury, wife of one of the two men involved in the murder. Chatting to her in her basement flat in New Cross, I'd persuaded Sheila to tell me about the night her husband, John, drove the killer to Waldeck's home in Johannesburg and waited while he shot the man dead on the doorstep.

"I know the name of Waldeck's killer," I told Ronnie. "I'm trying to find him. To get him to do a story: 'How I got away with murder.'"

Ronnie shook his head. "Don't do that, Robin," he said, quietly.

"Why?" I said. "It's a great story, if he'll talk to me. Valuable, too."

Ronnie took my hand and squeezed. "I'd rather you leave it alone. Forget it."

"I can't, Ronnie," I said. "I'm a journalist. We can't turn our backs on good stories."

As I shook my head again, he squeezed harder, gripping my fingers tightly, as Reg had in Parkhurst. "Leave it alone, and I'll make it up to you, Robin."

I found myself staring into Ronnie's black eyes and heard myself say: "Okay."

Beckenham,
KENT

Monday, June 24, 1985

Dear Reg,

Firstly, apologies for not getting back to you sooner.
I wanted to firm things up with Iris Burton about the 7th
July before confirming with you and she was out of town
for a few days. I have spoken with her now, however, and,
unfortunately, the 7th is not on. The following Friday,
July 12, would be far better. Is it a problem for you to
arrange this date instead of the 7th, Reg? I hope you can
arrange for us to visit on the 12th because my wife will
come down with us and we'll stay overnight somewhere. Let
me know soonest because Iris will have to make her own
arrangements with Woman's Own.

Talking of the magazine, Elaine came round to our flat
last Friday and I had a long chat with her about her
marriage to Ronnie. I have some interesting words on tape
and I'm convinced there is a nice piece to be written.
They don't pay enough to buy a new Ferrari, but they'll
definitely be something in it for Elaine. We might also
get a spin-off for a newspaper and, who knows, another
Breakfast TV spot. From my point of view, I'm happy to do
a piece that puts Ronnie in a good light because, from
what Elaine says, he is a very caring man, not only to her
but also to her children. Perhaps it is time for the
public to think of the Kray Twins in a term other than
"monsters."

Flanagan jetted off to Los Angeles this morning to
celebrate her boyfriend's birthday. She has taken
Mitchell's dog with her, which seems to indicate that he
won't be coming back. I'm not sure how this affects Flan:
on the surface, she is quite hard, but underneath she's a
marshmallow. It would be nice for love to come into her
life, but somehow I don't think it is going to come from a
bloke 6,000 miles away!

I enjoyed meeting Steve Tully. I can see why you two
are friendly, and I must repeat my offer to him to give me
a call to arrange lunch or dinner. I would like to speak
to him a bit longer about the special bond between you
both. From my brief chat with him, I detected, like you,
that he has a sharp, incisive brain that could be put to
very good (straight) use on the outside.

Chapter Four

MONEY had always meant everything to the twins. Before their stupidity in believing they were above the law, they had earned lots of it through terrifying intimidation, but now, locked up, they needed the help of someone with a business brain, initiative and contacts. Ideally, that person would have been their older brother, but having been robbed of nearly seven years of his life, Charlie was more concerned with having a good time. Even now, ten years after being released from prison, he was always scratching around for cash and relied, in the main, on the hard-working Diana. They were now living in a three-bedroomed maisonette she'd bought in the more respectable part of Upper Norwood, in South London and socially, Charlie got by on what he could scrounge from people eager to be seen with one of the Kray brothers. He was a party animal, the archetypal Champagne Charlie, and his greatest strength was that he got on with everyone he met. He could put people, if not a deal, together, and the brothers had him to thank for introducing them to Wilf Pine, one of the few people equipped to earn them money – and withstand their unpredictable mood swings.

Charlie had taken Wilf to Broadmoor in 1980, a year after Ronnie was transferred there from the Isle of Wight. Ever since he'd learned of Wilf's Mafia connections in New York, Ronnie had been pressing Charlie to introduce them, but Wilf wasn't keen to go, and all the time Ronnie was in Parkhurst, the strict Category A restrictions meant he didn't have to. Now Ronnie was in Broadmoor, however, Wilf had no excuse, so Charlie took him that summer.

"You took your fucking time," were Ronnie's words of greeting.

Not sure if it was a joke, Wilf didn't respond, and there was an awkward silence until Ronnie started laughing, then held out a welcoming hand. He thanked Wilf for trying to help with a film deal in New York, then excused himself to talk to Charlie. For the next fifteen minutes, Wilf listened, embarrassed, as Ronnie laid into his brother, berating him for supposedly not doing what he'd been told to. Charlie tried to explain, but, every time, Ronnie talked over him. Finally, Ronnie turned to Wilf. "Sorry about that, Wilf," he said. "Charlie and I had a few things to sort out." Then, typically, he cut to the chase. "We do okay, but we always need cash. Charlie says you're a clever bloke. Is there any way you can make us some money out of our name?" Unaware that he was there as a source of income, Wilf didn't know what to say, but he could see the possibilities in such an infamous name. He said he'd give the matter some thought and speak with Charlie.

"No," Ronnie said. "Don't contact Charlie. Now that you're on my visitors' list you can come here again, any time you want."

Once outside, Charlie looked at Wilf and said: "Now you can see what I've been putting up with all my life. But it's you I feel sorry for now. Once Ronnie gets into you, you're trapped."

That night, Wilf listed some ideas he thought might make the twins money. T-shirts with the twins' name on them was an obvious one, but photographs on postcards and china mugs could work too, such was the public's fascination with the growing Kray legend. Ignoring Ronnie's order to go back to him, Wilf contacted Charlie, saying that he had spoken to several print firms about merchandising the Kray name and wanted to go to Broadmoor with Charlie to discuss his plans with Ronnie.

But Charlie didn't want to know. "Leave me out of it, please, Wilf," he said. "This is your problem now."

So, Wilf went to Broadmoor on his own and outlined his plans. Ronnie saw the potential, but didn't want to meet printers, advertising executives and publicists. "I'm not some puppet sitting here for people to gawp at," he said.

"But people who'll be involved in the projects will want to know that they have your blessing," Wilf said.

Ronnie saw the sense in that and that night wrote to Reg explaining everything. So the "cottage industry" flourished. Ronnie badgered Wilf to visit Reg, but Wilf refused: Charlie had told him that if you got involved with both, one would play you off against the other and drive you barmy, and Wilf heeded the warning. Incensed at what he considered an insult, Reg started writing to him, not so much asking him to do certain things, but *telling* him. Wilf reacted badly to that and during one of his weekly visits to Broadmoor, Ronnie told him that the twins had had a blazing row over him.

"Why?" Wilf said. "What have I done?"

"It's because you refuse to go to Parkhurst," Ronnie said. "He said he won't be bothering with you any more, because you're *my* man."

And Wilf was. He visited Ronnie more often than anyone – including Charlie – and they became so close that Ronnie invited him to sit in on three hearings to assess his mental state. Not that the panel of professionals ever got any joy from Ronnie. He'd dress up for each hearing – insisting Wilf did, too – but it was always a waste of time. Ronnie would listen to what the assessment board had to say, but when asked for his comments, he would thank them, politely, for their time and tell them there was nothing he had to say. The hearings Wilf attended lasted only minutes, indicating that Ronnie was happy in Broadmoor and did not want to say or do anything that might risk him being sent back to prison.

It took Wilf two years to go to Parkhurst and, when he did, he disliked Reg so much he decided he'd visit only when necessary. The feeling was mutual: Reg had no time for anyone who didn't do what he wanted. Over the next three years they had a frosty relationship and only tolerated each other at all for Ronnie's benefit.

Reg didn't like idle chatter that was non-productive, either – as he made clear to me in a letter, on Tuesday, 4 July. He was happy to see me on Friday week, he said, if I felt we weren't wasting our time. Obviously, he didn't view

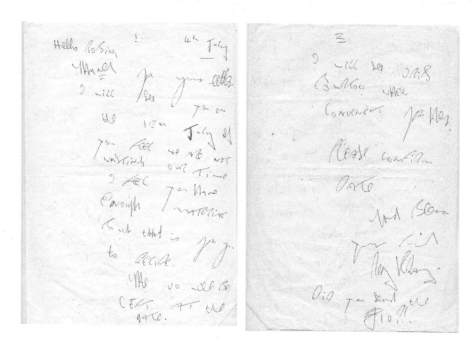

4th July Hello Robin Thanks for your letter   I will see you on the 12th July if you feel we are not wasting our time. I feel you have enough material but that is for you to decide.   The VO will be left at the gate. I will see Iris Burton when convenient for her.   Please confirm date. God Bless Your friend Reg Kray Did you send the £10?!

Iris Burton as a waste of time, because he was still keen to see her "when convenient for her." And this time there was a reminder about the tenner! Whether or not I was a time-waster was playing on his mind because, a few days later, he cancelled the Friday visit, saying: "I've changed my mind, Robin. Unless there is a reason to see you, I will leave it till another time as there is no point going over the same things again. I do not like repeating myself and I need the VOs."

The letter, and its arrogant tone, offended me and Sue had to persuade me not to reply in kind; after all, I was the one spending time and money on travelling. And I was the one being messed about. I decided to put the proverbial ball in Reg's court by asking him to specify what relationship he wanted with me, and how he saw it working. I reminded him that collaborating on a book – with or without Ronnie – was the best way to earn money, and to achieve that, I was prepared to visit him regularly to build the vital trust between us. We might be able to earn modest amounts from newspapers, as well, I said, but that would not be the aim. I urged Reg to think it over and let me know where I stood.

Beckenham,
KENT

Monday, July 8.

Dear Reg,

Good grief! Our July meeting has been on and off more times than a hooker's drawers!

I got your last letter, saying you would be happy to see me on Friday, but, took you at your word that you didn't like repeating yourself, and made other arrangements. Also, I told the guy who was loaning us a house on the island that the trip was off.

I think you should tell me how you see our relationship. From my point of view, I am happy to come to Parkhurst to get to know you better and vice-versa. I would like to work with you and your brothers (or you alone, if you prefer) to produce a worthwhile book, TV interview etc, which could earn us all a substantial amount of money, and this will be possible only if we both trust each other. Such trust isn't gained overnight and I am prepared to work at it by coming to see you and talking, in the strictest confidence, about everything and anything. Along the way, we might be able to make some money, but that wouldn't be the main aim of the game.

From your last letter, it seemed you felt a meeting was desirable, only if we had some definite business. And this is why I feel it best if you tell me exactly what your feelings are. I know I can be useful to you. I am also trustworthy: if you tell me something is to go no further, it won't. If you ask me to try to do something, I will try to do it.

Having said all that, I understand your position over the V.O.s. You have a number of people you want to see for specific purposes and I can see why you would want to save the V.O. for them, rather than for someone who is coming for a general chat. Why don't you think it over and drop me a line, outlining your feelings. Then I'll know where I stand. Certainly I don't like messing you about when you're stuck there, not knowing what's going on...

Paul Goodrich has been down to our flat again and we seem to be getting on okay. He's a very straight guy, I've found, and calls a spade a spade. Whether we'll be able to make his stories of Richard Harris work financially remains to be seen. But certainly he and his girlfriend Sally are pleasant company.

Take care of yourself and I look forward to hearing from you at your convenience. Again, sorry about this Friday – it's just one of those things that didn't work out.

But the Iris Burton visit will definitely be on... when she gets back from her hols.

Sincerest wishes,

PART OF A LETTER *9th July* Thanks for your letter received today. When you last saw us it was with a purpose and it came to nothing. So I can too get despondent, but as from now I would like our relationship to be on a basis of friends and then we know how we stand. Enclosed copy for you to read and then you will know why campaign is important. I'm waiting for phone call being made to you about the visit. Being friends does not stop you from deducting expenses on future business visits.

God Bless Reg   PS I have just changed my mind Robin. Unless there is a reason to see you on the 12th July I will leave it till another time as there is no point in going over the same things again I do not like repeating myself and I need the VOs.

Beckenham,
KENT

24 July 85

Dear Reg,

I've been away from the Express for a few days – hence the delay in getting back to you with news of the other cuttings. I'm in today, so tonight I'll have another go at our library. I does appear, however, that they can find no trace whatsoever of Messrs Mecca (Mulla?) and John Hall.

On McVicar, Screen International have promised to send me the relevant details, but so far – zilch. I shall chase them up later today or tomorrow. Someone somewhere has got to have this information. I'll also track down McV himself – he should know the answers!

Did you receive the big batch of cuttings? Were they what you wanted? Should I try something different? Incidentally, which twin was it who copped Mandy's left hook?!

I had lunch with someone yesterday who is coming to Albany to visit a friend who was nicked in Operation Snowball (cocaine smuggling). Apparently there's a helicopter service from Battersea. I'm going to look into that 'cos that would save one hell of a lot of travelling.

It's better to leave my next visit until Iris Burton gets back from her holiday; then we can kill two birds with one stone. Unless, you want, or need, to see me before then, that is.

I got a terrific card from Steve. How did he know my wife Sue simply adores badgers!!? I'm dropping him a thank you note because it was a very considerate thought. He really does seem like a good bloke.

I didn't have long to wait: two days later, Reg replied, informing me, bluntly, that he wanted our relationship to be based on friendship, not business. But, "being friends," he added, "does not stop you from deducting expenses on future business visits." I didn't know what to make of that: being entitled to claim business expenses when I was visiting as a friend didn't make sense. I could only put his muddled thinking down to not wanting to commit himself to working with me on a book. As it turned out, I was more right than I could possibly have imagined.

A month or so before I met him, Reg had been so moved by a TV programme about Julia Maguire, a four-year-old girl in need of a liver transplant, that he was backing a fellow prisoner's idea to raise money for the hospital treating the child. The idea was to ask prisoners in jails around the country to paint pictures, which would then be auctioned and the proceeds given to the Addenbrookes's Liver Transplant Fund, a charity set up by Julia's father, Peter Maguire, a civil servant from Gosport, Hampshire. It was a very good story that I could unquestionably have written for the nationals and made some money either for the Maguire charity, or for Reg personally. But he never brought it up either during my visit, or in his letters. Far more significantly, however, he also failed to mention that he'd invited the TV journalist who'd made the Maguire programme to the prison and made the same suggestion to him about writing the twins' autobiography that I'd made in my letter.

*

Reg's last letter put the block on our relationship for a while, but, then, surprisingly, I received an encouraging one towards the end of July that helped restore my faith in him. He seemed to have changed his mind about me being purely a friend because he wanted to see me to "join" him in an idea "that will be a bestseller." It didn't sound as if he was planning the "tell all" autobiography I wanted to ghost, but I was reasonably optimistic, because, at that time, any publication with the Kray name on the cover would have massive potential. Three days later, however, I had to curb what enthusiasm I had when Reg wrote again, asking to see me at the end of August "to discuss a project which can be started without delay." I was confused and not a little concerned. If he had an idea "that will be a best seller," why not see me as soon as possible? If he wanted to discuss a project "which can be started without delay," why didn't he want to see me until the end of the following month?

I suspected Reg was bullshitting me, but, on Tuesday, 13 August, he wrote again – his first letter on lined paper – asking to see me the following week, to discuss "what I have in mind." I was delighted, too, that he confirmed a visit for Iris Burton and I for the second Wednesday in September – the first date Iris could make. In addition, I was pleased that Steve Tully was being released on Friday 23 August, and would be getting in touch about the article we were

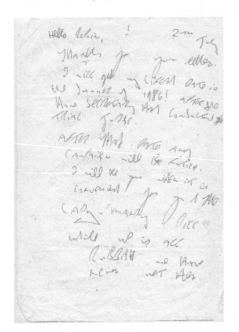
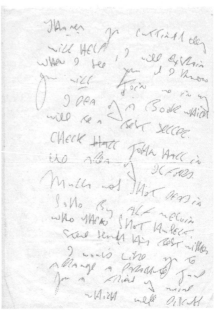

PART OF A LETTER   27th July   Hello Robin,   Thanks for your letter.
I will get my Lifers Date in the summer of 1986! After the Home Secretary has
consulted the trial judge. After that date any campaign will be futile. I will see you
when it is convenient for you and the Lady. Mandy Rice write up is all rubbish we
have never met her.Thanks for cuttings they will help, I will explain when I see you
and I know you will join me in my idea of a book which will be a best seller.
Check John Hall in the area of Ilford. Mulla was shot dead in Soho by Alf Melvin who
then shot himself.Steve sends his best wishes. I would like you to arrange a
parachute jump for a friend of mine which we'll discuss.

31st July   Hello Robin,   Thanks for your
letter. Can you come to see me the end of
August as I wish to discuss a project with
you that can be started on with out delay.
God Bless   Reg

Beckenham,
KENT

12 August 85

Dear Reg,

Apologies for the lack of contact last week: I've had conjunctivitis and it puts one out of the game for a while. It's more or less cleared up now, thank goodness.

I have spoken to Iris and the earliest she can get down to meet you is Wednesday September 11. I know this may sound a long way off, but she is committed until then. I have stressed the need for a definite arrangement – remembering the cock-up last time – and she says she has put it in, not one, but two diaries. So it is ON – if it's okay with you.

In your last letter you said you'd like me to pop down sometime this month. I'm off next Tuesday and Wednesday – the 20th and 21st – and would be able to make it one of those day if it was very important. But obviously it makes sense to leave it until the 11th September. I'll leave this to you. If you would like me to come next week, I shall do so.

Still no joy on the Hall or Mulla cuttings. Were they definitely in the papers, Reg? The file on Billy Hill is big, though, and I'll be sending you some of these later this week.

I haven't spoken to McPherson, the solicitor, because I wanted to see the contract and neither Charlie nor Laurie O'Leary have given me it yet.

I've written an article for Woman's Own on Elaine's marriage to Ronnie and I think she'll be pleased with it. You and Ron, too. I'll send a proof as soon as I get one. Not a lot of money in it, unfortunately, but Elaine should pick up a couple of hundred.

That letter to the Home Secretary: I haven't done it yet, but I have plans to give it some detailed thought later this week. It is not a letter that needs to be rushed, is it?

Like you, I thought we had a good meeting last Saturday and I look forward to bringing Iris Burton down on the 12th – assuming that's okay with you.

Take care… and keep your spirits up. Please pass on my best regards to Steve, and remind him to give me a call.

13 August Hello Robin,   Thanks for your letter   Steve goes out for good on Friday
He will be in touch with you when he has settled down. Could you visit me on
Wednesday the 21st August to discuss what I have in mind. I will also see you and
Lady Burton on the 11th September   On both days VOs will be left at the gate
This McPherson phone number   Please confirm day of 21st August   Steve sends
his best wishes   God Bless   Your friend   Reg Kray

going to write about their "special bond." So, after all the frustrating on-off visits, and Reg's concerns at wasting time with me, it looked as though I was getting somewhere and that I would, at last, capitalise on my entrée into the Kray circle.

I arrived on time for the afternoon visit, but, after twenty minutes or so, Reg asked me to go to a phone-box outside the prison and make a call for him to Fred Dinenage, a presenter at Southern Television, who was most famous as one of the stars of the children's TV programme *How!*. After spending four hours getting to the prison, the last thing I needed was to go through the rigmarole of being let through God knows how many locked doors, walk four hundred yards down the road, to phone someone I didn't know, about something that had nothing to do with me, then go through the whole tedious process to get back in and try to pick up where I left off. But what was the alternative? Tell Reg I didn't want to do something he clearly thought crucially important? I did say I wasn't happy; that surely, I could make the call after our visit. But Reg said it was too important to wait and insisted I went.

It took the best part of half an hour before I was back in the visiting room. Reg was sitting where I'd left him and, although he was grateful I'd made the call, he was barely communicative and had clearly gone off the boil. We had over an hour left on the visit, but we both knew it wasn't going to prove productive. We sat in virtual silence for long moments, then Reg said: "I'm sorry, Robin, this isn't a good visit. I want to end it now." He was very polite. He didn't raise his voice. But he was terminating the visit. And I saw red.

"So, that's it, is it?" I said, none too quietly. "You got me down here to run a fucking errand for you. Now I can go home, eh? I'll tell you this, Reg – I don't give a fuck who you are, I'm too long in the tooth to be treated like a fucking idiot. I don't need it." And I got up, walked over to one of the prison officers, and asked to be let out while Reg was escorted back to his cell.

The journey home was thoroughly miserable and I spent most of it trying to convince myself that my outburst was justified, and that it hadn't killed our relationship, but, by the time I reached Beckenham I'd convinced myself it had.

*

I didn't expect an apology, but, on Friday morning, I got one. Reg sent me a scrappy note, scribbled on a piece of paper, just three inches square, torn from a bigger sheet, saying: "Hello, Robin. Sorry for last visit. VO enclosed. I'm sure we'll have a good visit on the 11th Sept. and Iris too. Thanks. God Bless. Your friend Reg."

Staring at his hurried scrawl, I was angry that he couldn't be bothered to write a more conciliatory note, but outweighing my fury was a feeling of immense relief that I hadn't blown it; that I was still in favour - and that, at last, Iris was going to meet the man I'd told her so much about. I threw myself into my shift at the *Express*, buoyant, and rang Iris during the evening to confirm that 11th September was definitely on.

Infuriatingly, three days later, it was off again. In a letter, oddly stamped 22 August and 24 August, Reg told me it would be *"beneficial"* if Iris and I now saw him in the first week of October, *"any date at your convenience"*. He went on: *"You will think I am messing you and Iris about – but I assure you it is not the case. I will send you both a fresh visiting order. By the time October gets here we will have a good visit. Please do not take offence at this change in dates and I hope Iris will also understand."*

Well, actually, I *didn't* understand. I *did* think he was messing us about. And I *did* take offence. What else was so important, so vitally pressing in his miserable bloody life that he couldn't set up a visit with one of the country's most prominent magazine journalists, and stick to it? He was, after all, desperate for media backing for his campaign - spearheaded by Flanagan - to persuade the Home Office to give him a parole date, once he'd completed his thirty years - and, if Iris felt Reg was justified, she was in an exceedingly powerful position to help.

*

That last Friday in August, Steve Tully walked out of Parkhurst, wearing one of three new suits that Reg had organised – free of charge – courtesy of Barry Scott. Steve spent the weekend enjoying freedom with his girlfriend, Patricia, at his flat in Bow, East London, then late Monday morning, he set off in his white Peugeot for Broadmoor, excited at the prospect of meeting the other half of the legendary twins. Unfortunately, he got lost in the Berkshire countryside and ended up having to ring the hospital to say he could not make the 2 p.m. visit.

Relieved that, at least, Ronnie would know why he hadn't made it, Steve returned to the East End, with the intention of calling Broadmoor the next day to rearrange the visit. However, someone from the hospital called that evening, saying Ronnie wanted him to visit at 9a.m. the next morning. Steve went to bed early, with the alarm set for 6a.m. The next morning, fearful of getting lost again, he took the Underground to Waterloo, got a train to Crowthorne, and then a taxi to Broadmoor. He was there fifteen minutes before the scheduled visiting time, but when he said he was there to see Ronnie Kray, he was told he wasn't on the visitors' list. He explained about the evening phone call and asked them to check. They did, but returned, saying Ronnie didn't want to see him.

Steve remembers the episode well. "I was gutted, and walked away, wondering why. I got the answer a couple of weeks later when I went to Broadmoor with Charlie. Ronnie said he'd been so disappointed I hadn't turned up for our visit, that he'd decided to teach me a lesson. He told me that if I

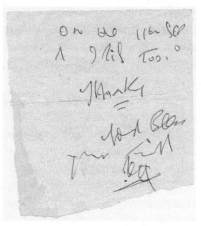

22 *August*   Hello Robin,   Sorry about last visit.   VO enclosed.   I'm sure we will have a good visit on the 11th Sep and Iris too.   Thanks   God Bless   Your friend   Reg

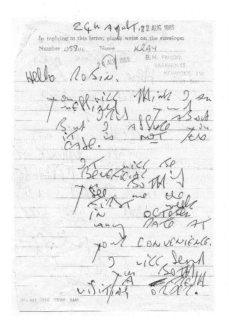

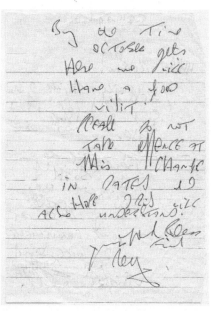

24th *August*   Hello Robin,   You will think I am messing you and Iris about but I assure you it is not the case.   It will be beneficial if you both see me the first week in October any date at your convenience.   I will send you both a fresh visiting order.   By the time October gets here we will have a good visit.   Please do not take offence at this change in dates and I hope Iris will also understand.   God Bless   Your friend   Reg

promised to be somewhere at a certain time, I had to make sure I kept that promise, no matter what the circumstances. I tried to explain about getting lost, but it didn't cut any ice. He felt I was out of order and wanted me to know that he didn't like being let down. It was a harsh lesson, but one I've never forgotten."

I grew to like Steve. I never got around to writing about that "special bond" but we did spend many hours talking about the three years he and Reg were together – an intense, often tempestuous time when Steve experienced aspects of Reg's personality that not only illustrated how different he was to Ronnie, but what a handful he must have been to deal with on a daily basis.

At the start of that relationship, however, Reg was far from the ruthless, feared gangster. Released from hospital, on to the volatile C-Wing, he found life among 120 of the country's most notorious criminals overwhelming. He was still paranoid and vulnerable from his suicide attempt and unable to cope with the dangerous, often explosive, mix of IRA killers, mass murderers and armed robbers on the Wing. He stayed in his cell all day, hunched in a chair, the curtains pulled across the barred window, blocking the light. Steve was one of a handful of fellow prisoners he would allow in the cell, but Reg was so paranoid he sometimes thought that even he was plotting against him. Reg lasted just two weeks before it became clear C-Wing was too much for him, and he was moved back to the hospital. However, Reg missed his young friend so much, he regularly bribed an orderly to smuggle him confidential letters. Someone in authority must have monitored the friendship and been concerned because, while Reg was in hospital, Steve was transferred to nearby Albany Prison. Astonishingly, the move lasted less than two weeks. First, Steve went on hunger strike for ten days, then smashed up his wing, causing £10,000 of damage, and, rather than risk him wreaking havoc at another prison, he was moved back to Parkhurst. He was punished with six months loss of remission, but hailed a hero by fellow prisoners, who felt he scored a moral victory over the prison system.

Early in 1983, Reg was allowed back on to C-Wing, and resumed his relationship with Steve – one that now clearly did not concern the prison hierarchy. Despite the intensity of their friendship, Steve is adamant that it wasn't sexual. He admits Reg found him attractive and came on to him late one wintry night, but insists he resisted the advance and left Reg in no doubt he wasn't that way inclined.

"I was asleep on my front, in my cell, when Reg came in. When I came to and realised what was happening, I got off the bed immediately and glared at him. I said: 'Reg, I asked you to educate me, not fuck me.' He looked very embarrassed and said: 'Oh, I'm sorry. I'm sorry.' And that was that, really. He didn't say anything else and never approached me like that again." But Reg most certainly took him under his wing, and, for that, Steve was very grateful, because, being a fit, good-looking twenty-four-year-old, he would, unquestionably, have been a target for older prisoners. "Being so close to Reg offered me invaluable protection, no doubt about it," he told me. "And, for him, I must have been a godsend. Having tried to kill himself, then losing his mum he was in a terrible state and I'm sure he saw me as someone he could get close to and mould – someone who could, perhaps, ease his torment."

Obviously, Steve was relieved to walk out a free man that August Friday, but the picture he painted of Parkhurst life – at least on C-Wing, and later, the more relaxed, B-Wing – didn't strike me as particularly stressful. Indeed the days seemed positively leisurely, and the nights more like a rowdy evening at the local pub. For Reg and Steve, a typical evening would be to have dinner – duck, rabbit, spaghetti, even pheasant or Lobster Thermidor, bought through trading tobacco on the black market – between 6 p.m. and 7 p.m. round a big table in Steve's cell, to background eighties' music, often Richard Clayderman, on a record player. Then, four or five invited guests would crowd into the cell and drink from a bucket of "hooch" – homemade alcohol, made by fellow prisoners from potato or fruit peelings, mixed with yeast, then fermented on the hot radiator pipes under the floorboards in the cells. Less than a pint was enough to get one drunk, but, able to afford more than other prisoners, Reg and Steve would buy a bucket, holding eight pints, for £5. Every night, they and their "guests" would drink solidly before collapsing in their respective cells at 9 p.m. "bang up" time.

"Every night was party night and Reg loved playing host," Steve told me. "We looked forward to those evenings, especially Fridays when it became something of a ritual for us to have the IRA boys in for a sing-song. I wouldn't say they were impressed with Reg's reputation, but there was definitely a mutual respect, and never a hint of trouble between them."

Looking back on his friendship with Reg, it is the intensity that Steve remembers most: the closer they got, the more overbearing Reg became. The only person he allowed into the relationship was Ronnie, who would write to both of them, addressing the letters, either, Dear Reg and Steve, or Dear Steve and Reg. Each of them wore an amethyst ring, and an amethyst stone round the neck, and Reg guarded their triangle of love and friendship jealously. Patricia's brother, who was also serving time in Parkhurst, was friendly with them, but was quickly pushed away if Reg felt he was getting too close. "You can be our mate," he'd tell him, "but you can't be in this relationship."

With Patricia, it was even worse, particularly when she came on a visit and Steve returned to the Wing on a high. Reg would be uptight and distant, jealous that Steve had enjoyed the company of someone other than him; that it was a woman no doubt made it worse. Once, in the middle of an emotional chat about her, Reg said something that prompted Steve to say: 'Well, what about you and Frances?'

Steve knew that mentioning the name of Reg's late wife, Frances Shea, who committed suicide in 1967, aged just twenty-three, was a no-go area, but it slipped out in the heat of the discussion and, without warning, Reg threw a right-hander, lifting Steve off the cell floor. "It didn't hurt physically," Steve assured me, "but it did, emotionally. I was shocked – I couldn't believe he'd done it. I went back to my cell, disappointed in him. I brooded on it and slowly the disappointment turned to anger and I went back to Reg's cell. I held out my hand, in a peaceful gesture, then, as he held out his, I whacked him hard in the ribs. Then I ran back to my cell and slammed the door. Nothing was said the rest of the evening and night, and, the next day, Reg was all smiles. Everything was forgiven, but Reg's intensity and jealousy did make me appreciate, in a small way, just what pressure Frances must have been under."

It was not always such strong passion that would make Reg snap. Once, he got so angry that Steve didn't see his point of view, he smashed an enamel mug and held the jagged edge to Steve's throat, his face contorted in a vicious, twisted grimace. Steve froze, staring into Reg's eyes, almost daring him, but, after a few seconds, Reg came out of his fury and pulled away. Steve said nothing, just walked off and wandered around the wing, brooding for a couple of hours, until he felt Reg had calmed down. Then he went into Reg's cell and held out his hand. Reg shook it. That was the end of that row. But there would be many more – thankfully, none so violent.

Beneath this selfish, ruthless streak, Reg did have a softer side. But what generosity or kindness he showed was rarely unconditional: he'd always have an eye to the future, anticipating what a generous gesture might reap. One Sunday, for example, he and Steve were sitting around, reading the papers when Reg spotted a feature about the model, Vivienne Neves. She had been struck down with Multiple Sclerosis, and the story was publicising her appeal for the MS Society. Reg saw the potential immediately. He told Steve to read the article, then said: "Right – I'm going to show you what we can do. We're going to write a joint letter to the paper and send some money for the charity."

"What good's that gonna do?" Steve wanted to know.

"Wait and see," said Reg.

The following day, Reg posted the letter, enclosing five pounds from each of them. The following Sunday, the paper ran a story, saying that help for Vivienne Neves's appeal had been received from "a surprising quarter" – one of the Kray twins. Reg was not surprised. "I've learned how to use the media to my advantage," he told Steve. "The papers love hardened criminals helping worthy causes."

The cynic in me wondered whether these good-natured acts were aimed at increasing Reg's chances of a release date, but Steve shook his head. "Reg was very much against anyone doing anything to influence their chances of parole," he told me. "Of course, he wanted to be a free man, but he accepted his lot and never once lapped up to authority to curry favour."

*

No matter how much Reg yearned for his freedom, he was thrilled for Steve when his release date arrived. And, according to Steve, he asked for some advice before his pal left the prison that last Friday in August. "He admitted he hadn't had sex since he was arrested," Steve told me. "And he asked me whether he should have sex with a younger man.

"I just said: 'You've got to do what you want to do, Reg.' What else could I say? I'm heterosexual, with male desires, but if I'd done seventeen years, and had another lot in front of me, who knows how I'd react? What I do know is that I'd do what suited me, without worrying what other people thought, or said. So that's the advice I gave Reg. I couldn't say: 'Don't do this or that, because everyone's going to think you're a poof.' And it wasn't for me to say: 'Go ahead and have sex with whoever wants it.' So, I bounced the ball back into his court. I heard he went into a sexual relationship a few months after I left and I don't think he gave a monkey's if anyone thought he was a poof. He was very much his own man."

*

Iris Burton is one of the most relaxed and phlegmatic people I've met and when I told her that Reg had put back our meeting again she was as understanding as I expected her to be. "It must be dreadful, trying to run your life behind bars," she said. "Let's wait and see. If I can go in October, I shall."

I was steaming, though, and didn't reply to Reg. This clearly bothered him because, two weeks later, he wrote asking me to confirm that Iris and I could visit in the first week of October. "I have a lot to talk to you about," he said. He repeated that it was "beneficial" that we both wait until October and asked me to confirm that 8 October was convenient for Iris and I to visit. "If not, any date will do as long as I know in advance," he said. "It will not be a waste of time."

Not surprisingly, Iris was unable to arrange a visit at such short notice, but said she could make Friday, 1 November. On 25 September, Reg wrote, saying he would send two VOs, and asking for my phone number.

The visit never happened. Iris was mildly disappointed not to meet Reg, because, like millions of others, she was fascinated to know what a so-called "monster" was like, face to face. And, obviously, as a journalist, she would have revelled in a sensational exclusive for her magazine, but Iris had so much going on in her life that she quickly forgot about Reg Kray.

I was far from happy, however. And puzzled. Iris was a very well-connected journalist – later head-hunted to become Editor-In-Chief of *Prima* and *Best* magazines – who was prepared to sit with Reg and listen to anything he had to say. Had she been given the opportunity to see for herself how seventeen years behind bars had changed him, who knows, she might have used her considerable influence to back his Release Campaign. But, for reasons I never

2nd Sep   Hello Robin, Thanks for your letter and I wrote you a previous letter saying I will see you and Iris some time in October when it is convenient to you both.
Please confirm a day by letter. I will send you a VO. I have a lot to talk to you and Iris about. It is beneficial you both wait till October. God Bless Your friend Reg Kray

16th September   Hello Robin, Enclosed VO, hope you and Iris can visit me in October. Can you both make it on the 8th a Tuesday. If not any date will do as long as you write to let me know in advance. It will not be a waste of time. Hope to hear from you soon. God Bless Your friend Reg Kray

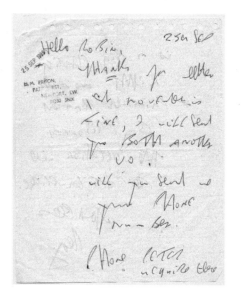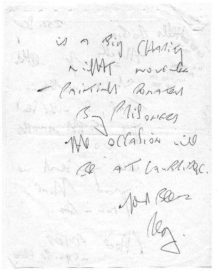

25th Sep Hello Robin, Thanks for letter 1st November is fine, I will send you both another VO. Will you send me your phone number. Phone Peter McGuire there is a big charity night November – paintings donated by prisoners. The occasion will be at Cambridge. God Bless Reg

found out, Reg chose to miss the opportunity.

As 1985 drew to a close, he was more concerned that I make contact with Steve Tully, who was organising "a big charity night" in the East End, for a Liverpool boxing club that had been destroyed in a fire. The event was held in Bubbles, a wine bar, in Mile End, a few days before Christmas. Two of the men there, Jack Leigh and Paul Goodrich, had formed a company earlier in the year with Charlie and the Kray twins. They called it Krayleigh Enterprises and I'd seen a brief BBC TV news item about it, featuring not only the gentlemen themselves, but also Ronnie's wife, Elaine, acting – in the literal sense – the role of notepad-holding secretary in the company's offices in Mile End Road. The company's business cards boasted that it offered security to eminent and/or wealthy personalities, and claimed that, among its clients were film stars and "Arab noblemen." I didn't know Mr Leigh, but Charlie had introduced me to Mr Goodrich: a tall, fair-haired, well-built heavyweight in the Billy Walker mould, but without the Blond Bomber's warmth and charisma.

The basic idea, of course, was sound, because, in 1985, the bodyguard business was nothing like it is today. But, as with everything with Charlie, he – and, no doubt, his partners – had not thought through the mechanics of how to get business, much less consider the negative effect the names of two convicted

28th Nov Hello Robin, Will you send me the old cuttings on Duff which related to his being bared from East India Hall Poplar. Steve said you wished to see me but I have not heard from you. Charlie was supposed to phone you. God Bless Reg Kray RTO Steve is organising big charity night at Bubbles Wine Bar East End for Liverpool kids. I am helping him. Date is 12th or 16th Dec. Check with Steve.

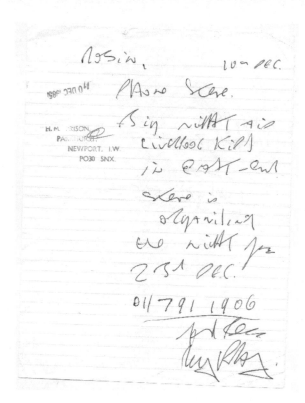

10th Dec   Robin,
Phone Steve. Big
night aid of
Liverpool kids in
East End.
Steve is organising
the night for 23rd
Dec. God Bless
Reg Kray

murderers on the letterheads might have on prospective clients. With some pride, Krayleigh boasted that it "looked after" Richard Harris. Goodrich did, indeed, work for the actor for a while, but the employment had more to do with Harris's dear friend, Bobby McKew, than Krayleigh. Bobby, a genial Irishman, much respected in the higher echelons of London's underworld through his connection with Billy Hill, a highly successful criminal who masterminded several big money robberies and controlled most of the city's top nightspots in the fifties. Bobby had introduced Charlie to Harris, who agreed to take on Goodrich as his "minder." The liaison might have led to more work with the showbiz world, had Goodrich not let himself down while "looking after" Harris when the actor was appearing on the London stage. The two had been drinking in Harris's hotel suite most of the afternoon when Elizabeth Taylor – in London rehearsing for the play *Little Foxes* - arrived to have dinner with the actor. Motioning towards Goodrich, who was leaning against the patio doors, Harris said: "Liz, I'd like you to meet my minder, Paul." As Ms. Taylor offered her hand, Paul promptly fell back, crashing through the patio doors on to the balcony. As he struggled, unsteadily, to his feet, Ms Taylor gave Harris a cheeky smile. "Sorry?" she said, sarcastically. "Just *who* is looking after *who* here?"   It was this lack of professionalism that made me fear that Krayleigh was doomed. And in fact the company quickly folded.

Until that noisy night in the Mile End Road, Mike and Chris Harris, the Manchester twins Ronnie and Reg wanted in the film, had viewed Charlie as their mate – a friendly, affable uncle-like figure, who regularly rang their home to invite them to functions, always at no cost to them. This night was no exception and Mike and Chris had travelled south, looking forward to an enjoyable night. When Charlie greeted them at Bubbles, however, he was not as friendly as usual and asked for thirty pounds to get in. Shocked, the twins explained that they'd been invited as guests, but Charlie insisted on being paid. Not having the money, Mike and Chris would not have got in that night, had Charlie's partner, Diana, not intervened and told Charlie he was out of order expecting them to pay when they'd travelled more than three hundred miles. The twins found it disconcerting that for once, Charlie seemed interested only in their money, not their company. It was a side they'd never seen before.

I didn't hear from Reg any more that year. Sue and I got a Christmas card from Ronnie – it arrived in early November! – but not from Reg. Obviously, he felt I still had my uses though: why else would he ask me to contact Steve? But he was clearly disappointed he'd got no return on the time he'd spent with me. Come to that, so was I. And I hadn't even had a thank you for the tenner I'd sent his mate in Albany!

Chapter Five

GIVING Reg my phone number was a mistake. With no one to consider but himself and nothing to occupy his mind but how he could make money, he'd think nothing of ringing me the moment he was cleared to make calls, shortly after 8 a.m. I'd told him I was a night worker - after my shifts as a sub-editor, I didn't get to bed until 3.30 or 4 a.m. - but it cut no ice: Reg would have been awake for three of four hours and, if there was something on his mind, he'd want to discuss it. If I was slow coming out of a deep sleep, he'd order me, to "speak faster, because my units are running out." One Sunday, when I was more groggy than usual, and explained I'd had a very late night, he was particularly irritable. "Suppose you were out enjoying yourself. Wish I could have been out enjoying myself!" I wasn't the only one to suffer, however; Flanagan had it worse. As the twins' errand girl, before and after Elaine, she was regularly expected to get out of bed and make notes of tasks Reg deemed important, and names and numbers of people he wanted her to contact. Sometimes she'd get so angry she'd stop him, in mid-sentence, and say: "I *have* got a son to look after, and work to do, you know!" But it never cut any ice with Reg; he saw Flan as his personal skivvy. And, in a way, she was.

"If he gave me ten jobs, I would try to do seven," she told me. "I'd go to see people to get money and to shops to ask for free food and sports gear." Reg clearly expected freebies because of his name and reputation and, for whatever reason, many shopkeepers obliged. Charlie Magri, the former champion boxer, who ran a sports shop in the East End, was one. He provided a number of trainers and track suits, free of charge, over the years before running out of patience with Reg's arrogance. Even then, Charlie didn't turn his back totally, telling Flan that he would supply some sports gear for a charity auction and allow Reg to have some of the proceeds so that he would have enough money to pay for what he wanted.

For all his charming courtesy, Ronnie was no less demanding. Once, before his marriage, Flan and Charlie bought him two silk shirts, costing £40 each, at Asser and Turnbull, the eminent Piccadilly shirt-makers. On the next visit, they opened the box, proudly, sure that Ronnie would be thrilled. But he took one look and shook his head. "You can take them back," he said. "I want them monogrammed. On the pockets." Charlie, who could never understand why Ronnie wanted to wear such expensive shirts, was furious and, once outside, fumed: "You take them, Flan. After that, I'm not running around after him any more." Flan took the shirts back, got them monogrammed and, a couple of weeks later, took them to Broadmoor – with some smoked salmon bagels, with cream cheese, which she thought Ronnie would love. He didn't. The shirts were fine, he said, but he didn't want cream cheese; next time Flan came, would she make sure the bagels came with lemon instead. One might wonder why Flan didn't chuck them in his face.

In the summer of 1986, Reg called out of the blue, bubbling with excitement over a new young prisoner, who had replaced Steve Tully in his affections. His name was Peter Gillett. He was 25, short and blond. And, according to Reg, had a great singing voice. "He's really got something, Robin," he enthused. "I'm going to make him a star."

The two had met the previous November, shortly after Gillett arrived at Parkhurst to serve the last two years of a five-year sentence for armed robbery. Reg spotted him walking along a balcony with a group of other inmates and was immediately attracted by his boyish good looks. He held out a hand in greeting: "Don't I know you?"

"No," Gillett replied, with a cheeky grin. "But I know all about YOU!"

Reg laughed and invited Gillett to his cell for a cup of tea. There was a sign on the door, Familiarity Breeds Contempt, a warning to inmates to keep their distance. But this clearly did not apply to the new arrival. Gillett was drawn to Reg because he considered him a genuine top criminal, not like other "plastic gangsters", who thought they were great when they were not, and Reg quickly took to the fit, finely-muscled young man, who was clearly impressed by his attention. Over the next few months, the friendship deepened to the point where Reg openly described Gillett as his "magnificent obsession," and they started making plans to live together should Reg be released – even if the younger man had got married and had a wife!

Reg was fired up about his latest venture, insisting that his protégé would be big news and I should "make the most of it." Certainly, I could see the news potential in a Kray twin promoting a fellow prisoner as a pop star, and I was looking forward to meeting Gillett. Who knows, if I asked nicely, he might give me a song, and I'd be able to judge his talent for myself. However, Reg asked me to visit him with Charlie, and remembering how Reg had laid into him on our previous visit, I feared the worst when Reg's letter accused him of being "too lazy" to send some newspaper cuttings, and for not asking me something – and Reg didn't let me down. No sooner had he introduced me to Gillett and got us talking, than he turned to Charlie and started haranguing him the way he had before. Gillett, like Tully, was articulate and likeable, and we chatted like old friends, but, again, I found it embarrassing hearing Reg belittle his brother so aggressively. What Charlie had done to upset him must have meant a lot to Reg because, the following week, he wrote to me, saying he no longer wanted Charlie involved in his plans for Gillett, and nor did he want Wilf as manager.

Apart from the time he'd insisted on me making that phone call, Reg had never pressured me as he had others, but when I mentioned that my wife had met a well-known record plugger, Golly Gallagher, at Samantha Fox's 21st

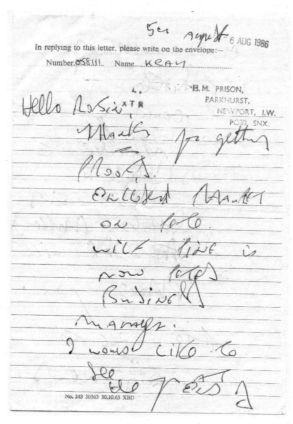

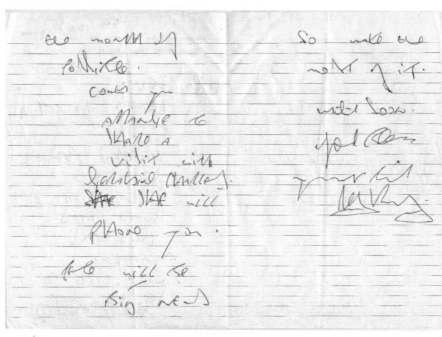

5th August
Hello Robin,
Thanks for getting proofs.
Enclosed pamphlet on Pete.
Wilf Pine is now Petes
Business Manager.
I would like to see you at
the end of the month if
possible.
Could you arrange to share
a visit with Geraldine
Charles. She will phone
you.
Pete will be big news so
make the most of it.
Write soon.
God Bless
Your friend
Reg Kray

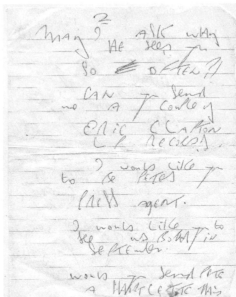

15th August Hello Robin, Thanks for your letter. Geraldine will be phoning you with a message late next week. Charlie did not send either Ron or I the cuttings by your son in fact does very little for me if anything at all. May I ask why he sees you so often?! Can you send me a couple of Eric Clapton LP records. I would like you to be Petes Press agent. I would like you to see us both in September. Would you send Pete a short letter this address because you need to be on his record sheet to get visit. Wish your son luck for his career from Ron, Pete and I. Write soon. God Bless Your friend Reg Kray

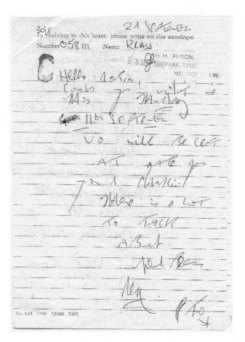

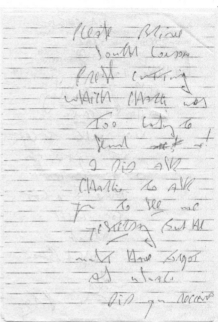

2 September Hello Robin, Could you visit me this Thursday 11th September
VO will be left at gate for you and Charlie   There is a lot to talk about, God Bless Reg PTO Please bring South London Press cutting which Charlie was too lazy to send me! I did ask Charlie to ask you to see me yesterday but he must have forgot as usual. Did you receive my last letter?! Phone to confirm you will be here on Thursday.

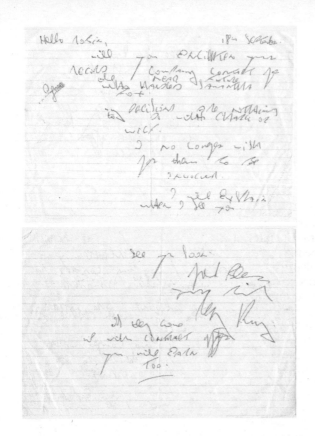

18th September Hello Robin, Will you enlighten your record company contact for the near future who handles Samantha Fox Decisions are nothing to do with Charlie or Wilf I no longer wish for them to be involved   I will explain when I see you See you soon   God Bless Your friend   Reg Kray   If they come up with contract you will earn too.

birthday party, Reg saw the potential immediately and leaned on me to make contact. I didn't know at the time, but Golly had met the Kray twins in the mid-sixties when, as a seventeen-year-old, he had been taken on as disc jockey at a club, near his home, in Aldershot, Hampshire. The twins were there with Laurie O'Leary, who owned the club, and Ronnie was so taken with the dark-haired, good-looking teenager that he gave him two hundred pounds to get himself kitted out for his new job.

It's just as well Golly didn't mention this connection when I called him, because, if Reg had known, he would have demanded his phone number and started pestering him. As it was, Golly said nothing, just agreed to listen to Gillett's tape and discuss its possibilities – or otherwise – with the renowned music publisher, Deke Arlon. That was enough to fire Reg's enthusiasm, and when I told him that Golly was working on Samantha Fox's first record, he seemed to think he'd cracked it, expecting me to have news when I visited him later that month. He was clearly living in the past when he and Ronnie - through one means or another - made things happen at their pace, not other people's, and he became ridiculously paranoid over what, at the moment, didn't amount to anything. "Keep everything strictly confidential," he ordered, quoting a Sicilian bandit who supposedly once said: "I know my enemies, but God protect me from my friends."

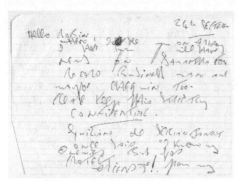

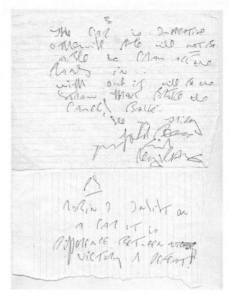

24th September Hello Robin, When I see you on Friday I hope you will have news on Samantha Fox record business man and maybe Chegwin too. Please keep this strictly confidential. Guiliano the Sicilian bandit once said "I know my enemies but God protect me from my friends! The car is imperative otherwise Pete will not be able to cram all the plans in.
With out it will be the straw that broke the camels back. See you Friday.
God Bless Your friend Reg Kray

PS Robin I insist on a car it is difference between victory and defeat!

What I didn't know then was that, despite sacking Wilf, Reg had written to Broadmoor, wanting Ronnie to ask Wilf to use his music business contacts to help Gillett.

"Reg thinks Pete's a brilliant singer," Ronnie told Wilf on their next visit.

"Reg wouldn't know a bloody good singer if he hit him in the face," Wilf said. But he promised to get in touch with Fred Dinenage, to try to get Gillett featured on his *Southern Television* evening show, *Coast to Coast*. Fred saw the news value and Wilf was encouraged enough to ask a publican friend, Frank Doyle, to allow the TV company to use his large, rambling pub – the Olde Mill in Holbury, 13 miles from Southampton – to film Gillett performing at a supposed audition for a recording agent, while on a four-day home leave.

Then Reg wanted Wilf to arrange for a white Rolls Royce to pick Gillett up on the day of his release. Originally, Dinenage had agreed to lay on a car, but his bosses had overruled him. "*Please arrange a Roller,*" Reg begged. "*It would mean everything to me.*" Behind Wilf's back, however, Reg was asking *me* to arrange a car, too. He was obsessed with an expensive vehicle, writing before our scheduled 26 September meeting: "*…a car is imperative…without it will be the straw that broke the camel's back.*" And, in case I hadn't got the point, he added a PS: "*Robin, I insist on a car. It is the difference between victory and defeat.*"

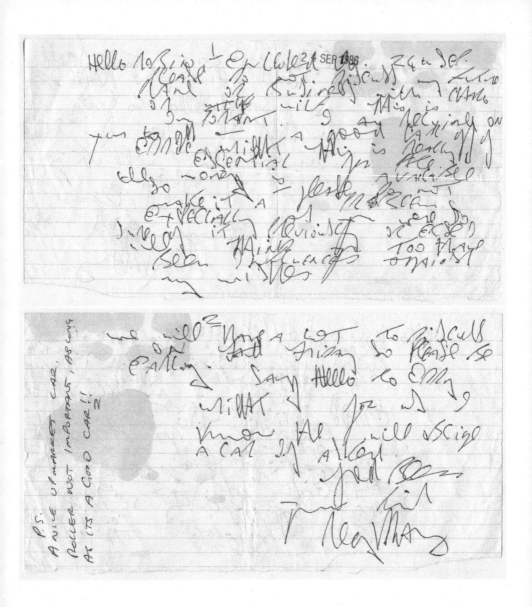

24th Sep Hello Robin, Enclosed VO Please do not discuss my future plans or business with Charlie or with Wilf This is important I am relying on you to get a good car off of Eddie Wright This is really essential for Pete The money is available so please do not make it a problem especially as you were so sure of it previously or else I will think you too have been influenced against my wishes We will have a lot to discuss on that Friday so please be early. Say hello to Eddy Wright for us I know he will oblige a car if asked God Bless Your friend Reg Kray
PS (From Peter Gillett) A nice up market car, Roller not important, as long as it's a good car!!

If I'd known Wilf was on the case, I wouldn't have wasted time on the car. As it was, I said I knew someone who ran a top-of-the-range car showroom, in Ilford, Essex, and I'd ask him. The guy was Jason Wright, youngest son of Eddie Wright, and nephew of former British lightweight boxing champion, Joe Lucy. I'd met Jason through his girlfriend, Samantha Fox, whom Sue and I had got to know through a company we'd launched, offering free holidays to celebrities, in return for travel articles for provincial newspapers. We'd arranged for David Hamilton to go to Singapore, Bob Monkhouse to Mauritius and Gloria Hunniford to the Seychelles – and Sam was one of a number of celebrities we'd invited to generate publicity at an hotel opening in Paphos.

Reg said he'd known the Wright family in the East End and - as though he was back in his influential heyday - told me to ask for a Mercedes for the day. "*I'm relying on you to get a good car off of Eddie Wright,*" he wrote. "*This is really essential for Pete. The money is available, so please do not make it a problem especially as you were so sure of it previously or else I will think you too have been influenced against my wishes…say hello to Eddy (sic) Wright for us. I know he will oblige a car if asked.*" Jason, who I learned much later, was only an employee of the showroom's owner, Richard Clemence, did not "oblige" Reg with a car.

Sam also introduced us to Suzanne Mizzi – a relatively new Page Three Girl, who asked me to be her Press agent. Reg Kray's pop protégé and a topless model was a natural for *The Sun,* and Suzanne was delighted when I suggested she met Gillett at the prison gates and drove with him to his "audition." But, astonishingly Reg wouldn't hear of it. "*I don't want some model stealing my boy's thunder,*" he snapped when I outlined the idea that Friday. There was, as they say, no answer to that.

Worried that Reg was losing the plot, I phoned Dinenage and was shocked to hear that Reg had been ringing him continually, with one cheeky demand after another. Fred said he was complicating matters so much that he was in danger of forcing the programme's bosses to pull the plug. Furious, I wrote a blunt, no-nonsense letter to Reg, but it had to be, if I was to get through to him that he was jeopardising the project.

"If certain things seem harsh on paper, put that down to circumstances," I wrote. "If we could meet face to face, on our own without prying eyes and eavesdropping ears, I would probably be able to explain my feelings better."

I also had to try to convince Reg that it was madness not to use Suzanne to get Gillett in *The Sun.* Dinenage was most disappointed we weren't using her and I urged Reg to reconsider his decision. It did cross my mind to ignore him and use her anyway, but feared that, even if *The Sun* gave the story a good show, it would destroy our relationship, given that we'd discussed the subject so much. I did tell him, however, that he was throwing away a heaven-sent opportunity and I hoped he didn't regret it. I posted the letter, praying that Reg would stop playing the prima donna and see sense. Surprisingly, he didn't react

Beckenham.
KENT

29 September 86

Dear Reg,

I felt you would like a progress report, following our visit. There is a fair amount I want to say, Reg, so I shall try to keep the letter strictly to the points that concern everyone involved. If certain things seem harsh on paper, put that down to circumstances: if we could meet face-to-face, on our own, without prying eyes and eavesdropping ears, I would probably be able to explain my feelings better.

1. I had a long chat with Fred on the phone this morning. Everything from his end is fine – but, honestly, mate, he does not need any further complication in what should have been a very easy project. He is providing this marvellous opportunity (a) because it is a nice little story; and (b) as a favour because he's impressed with your desire to help someone get back on the straight and narrow. But, make no mistake, if one makes too many demands, one runs the risk of him pulling the plug. In fact, Fred made it clear that he has kept all the niggling problems away from his bosses, because, if they thought things were getting difficult, they would not be keen to go ahead.

So, having said that, here's the picture: a backing track, as previously agreed, is by far the most ideal way of approaching the performance. If, as you made clear on Friday, this is out of the question, then an unaccompanied guitar is the solution. Session musicians, my friend, are out of the questions. From Fred's point of view, the original idea of a backing track is the most favourable because he is worried that the performance might be less than satisfactory with just a guitar. But I have made clear your feelings and he understands that the final decision is yours.

2. The car. Yes, originally, Fred did say he would provide a vehicle, but his bosses have said this is out of the question. However, he is arranging for £100 in cash to be made available on the day, which can be used to hire a car. With this in mind, I have phoned a few companies to fix one up. I was pleased to discover that Avis have introduced a special low-cost weekend hire that works out at £36.25, petrol included. This will leave Suzanne £64-odd for other things. As requested, I did ask Wrights of Ilford for a "cheapish" Merc, but they only sell cars.

3. Suzanne. We have covered this one, Reg, but I would
be failing in my duty, as a friend, if I did not say again
that you are making a HUGE mistake taking the view you
are. Fred was most disappointed because, from his point of
view – and his bosses' – she would have turned the whole
thing into an Event that would generate a great deal more
publicity and interest and help people to remember it. He
also thought it was a master-stroke because she is …a
girl.

From my point of view, I know she would have made the
difference between a back of the paper, ordinary picture
and, perhaps, Page One. After all, you've only got to look
at the papers to see the space given to girls. Anyway,
you've made the decision; the only reason for mentioning
it is that I want you to know that you are definitely
throwing away a heaven-sent opportunity and I hope you
don't regret it.

4. It was news to me that I could not do anything for
the morning of departure. In making people aware two days
before, one runs the risk of them doing something before
the event on their own. I have got to say a certain
amount, if not all, haven't I?

5. The relationship. I will be speaking to the people
mentioned previously during our conversation and need to
know from you the bottom line because I cannot get
involved in it unless it is going to prove financially
worthwhile. And you need to know that the figure you
suggested does not impress me. I could do it the way you
want, but I'm not going to be treated like some minion who
needs the work. You and I need to do something together
and this is probably it, but you have got to appreciate
that it is not the world-shaker you seem to think it is.
Personally, I think five is top whack (I might be wrong!!)
and if that is the case I'd be happy with one – i.e. 20
per cent. If the figure was three, I'd be happy with a
monkey. You're paying for my skill here because what I've
got to deal with is pretty good, but nothing to set the
world on fire. What can I say to make you have faith in me
to do the best?

Well, Reg, I think that's covered everything. I hope
you're well and that you'll be able to drop me a line in
reply to this rather long letter. You don't know me that
well, but I'm the sort of bloke who is prepared to work
hard to make things happen, provided I'm treated well –
and I don't mean only moneywise.

Yours sincerely,

as badly as I feared, although he was immovable on Suzanne. *"With all respect,"* he wrote, *"we agreed it was a good story before there was any mention of Sue, and that is the way I still see it."*

He seemed more keen to tell me that Gillett had decided to sing one of the songs – *Masquerade* - that Reg had written, boasting that *"it should be easier now to pull a crowd and create even more interest."* It beggared belief that he kicked a cast-iron certainty of a *Sun* exclusive - possibly a front page one - into touch. But that was Reg: he always knew best.

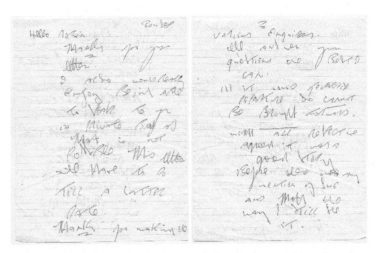

30th Sep Hello Robin   Thanks for your letter   I also would really enjoy being able to speak to you in private but as that is not possible this letter will have to do till a latter date.   Thanks for making the various enquiries.   Will answer your questions the best I can.   (3) it would jeopardise departure so cannot be brought forward.   With all respect we agreed it was a good story before there was any mention of Sue and that's the way I still see it.

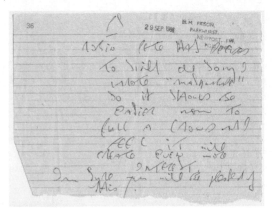

PART OF LETTER
PS   Robin Pete has decided to sing the song I wrote "Masquarade" so it should be easier now to pull a crowd and I feel it will create even more interest.   Im sure you will be pleased of this.

Beckenham,
KENT

1 October 86

Hi Reg,
    Blimey! You're getting somewhat prolific in the letter-
writing stakes…two long ones in two days! Great stuff.
    I know about Chris, and with a name like Peacock he'd
better not try to ruffle too many feathers. I'll be going
over with him, so don't worry about anything.
    In thinking about the car, I had a thought: driving
licence! Is there one in existence? If there isn't, no car
I'm afraid. Please advise soonest.
    Point taken about the departure date. Naturally, it can
wait until afterwards.
    Definite interest on two fronts on the record side – not
only Samantha Fox's plugger, but another chap I mentioned to
you, who handles several big stars. I need tapes, however. I
will talk about this at a later date.
    Yes, extremely pleased about Masquarade. So you can see
some sense at times, eh?! That will make a big difference, I
feel, and I shall deal with it tomorrow. One way and
another, I believe we'll get all we aimed to achieve from
this little exercise – without giving you an ulcer!
    Rest assured I shall ring those numbers. Whether they
act on it or not will be up to them, of course.
    That's all for now, but that licence thing needs sorting
out pronto.

Sincerely,

Incredibly, given all the angst, everything turned out well. At one minute past eight, on 3 October, Gillett walked out of the prison to be met by Southern TV reporter Christopher Peacock and a cameraman, Roy Page. Peacock, who was expecting a tall, burly gangland figure, was surprised by the rather angelic-looking guy, who looked about twelve.

"Peter Gillett?" he ventured.

"That's me," Gillett said, with a cheery smile.

"Reg Kray's friend?"

"Yep," Gillette said, cockily, then pointed to a white Rolls Royce, fifty yards away. "That's the car Reg laid on for me."

Page then filmed Peacock interviewing Gillett in the back of the Rolls. For a wannabe gangster who knew little about life outside the humdrum town of Crawley, being treated like a celebrity was the highlight of his uneventful life, and he revelled in telling how he'd become like a son to the legendary killer.

2nd October   Hello Robin,   Thanks for your welcome letter so glad all is going well. Baby Farris leaves (cannot decipher) United States Texas on the 14th October so I visualise he will become an American citizen!   Pete and I are really excited.
His licence has been registered at Swansea.   What about Sue Mizzi taking back to the gate Pete at the end of his 4 days home leave, enlighten Fred and the media! She took Pete on a tour of the East End at my suggestion and request because us East-Enders stick together!   I will return the compliment to Sue at a latter date! Knowing you Robin you could soon put this into action!   Take care of Pete!!!!! God Bless   Your Friend   Reg Kray   Phone number address where Pete will be staying at Crawley

After that, it was on to Holbury, where Gillett was filmed performing at the supposed audition, in front of a supposed agent. It was all a pathetic sham, but Gillett lapped up the attention and Messrs Peacock and Page delivered an entertaining four-minute story that went out on TV that evening.

Surprisingly, I received another missive from Reg that Friday, suggesting that Suzanne drove Gillett back to prison after his home leave, having taken him of a tour of the East End. He wanted me to "enlighten" Fred and other media, saying the tour was his idea because Suzanne was from the East End, and "East Enders stick together." Knowing this would annoy me, he tried a none-too-subtle piece of soft-soap – *"knowing you Robin, you could soon put this into action"* – but it didn't wash with me. It was all too late in the day and, anyway I wasn't going to revisit the idea, only for Reg to change his mind again.

No sooner had Gillett returned to Parkhurst than Reg was on to me again, anxious to know which papers had covered the story. I'd given it exclusively to *The Sun*, who'd sent one of their top reporters - a likeable young woman, named Shan Lancaster - to the Isle of Wight to work with me. She and photographer Roger Bamber produced a prominent page lead, with a photo of Pete, but that wasn't enough for Reg; he now wanted the paper to run a piece, saying his pretty pal was back in Parkhurst – so that *"he isn't deprived of his fan mail."* I wrote back, making it clear I wouldn't embarrass myself by trying to use *The Sun* as an advertising vehicle for his mate.

On the business side, he thanked me for speaking to my record business

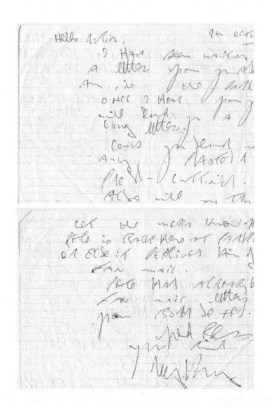

9th October Hello Robin,
I have been waiting for a letter from you as I am in the dark. Once I hear from you I will send you a long letter.
Could you send me any photos and press cuttings. Also will you try to let the media know that Pete is back here at Parkhurst or else it deprives him of fan mail. Pete has already had fan mail letters from both sexes. God Bless Your Friend Reg Kray

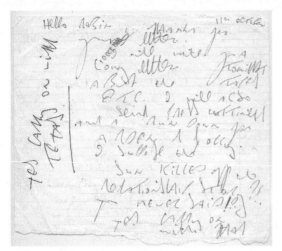

11th October Hello Robin, Thanks for your letter.   I will write you a long letter tonight about the tapes etc.   I will also send press cuttings and a run down for Arden and Golly.   I suppose the Sun killed off the relationship story you never said!? (Yes carry on with Texas) Yes carry on with that other story that's why I told you the departure date of 14th October. Pete send you his best wishes. Will you get us all the cuttings and photos from the Sun.   God Bless   Your Friend   Reg   I will write tonight   PS   Robin just received your other letter just use discretion on our relationship story longer article

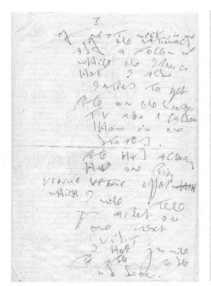
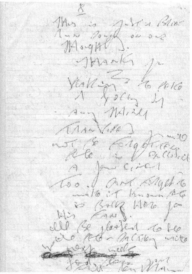

UNDATED   PART OF LETTER … next week, in one of the nationals also a follow up while the Iron is hot. I also intend to get Pete on the London TV area and Carson show in the States. Pete has already had one big venue offer which I will tell you about on the next visit. I hope you will be able to see us soon. This is just a brief run down on our thoughts.   Thanks for speaking to Deke and Golly if any thing transpires you will not be forgotten. Pete is enclosing a few lines too. Don't forget to make it known Pete is back here for his fans.   Will be pleased to see Pete – Daltrey write up next week. God Bless   Your friend   Reg Kray

Beckenham,
KENT

13 October 86

Dear Reg,
    Thanks for your two letters. To put your mind at rest, I
have asked Roger Bamber, the Sun photographer who went on
the story, to send me a selection of snaps.
    The chances of a national newspaper inserting a piece,
saying Pete is back inside are virtually nil, Reg. As you
know, space is at a premium and there's no story value and
the papers will not take too kindly to being used as an
advertising service for a prisoner! What we could do,
however, is try to come up with another story, such as a
record company's interest in him, which would give us the
chance to say: "Pete is back in Parkhurst." Once I get the
tape to Arlen or Golly we might be able to get a story off
the ground.
    May I suggest you try to get hold of a book called
Compulsion. The author is Meyer Levin and the book was made
into a film, starring Orson Welles as the famous lawyer,
Clarence Darrow. It tells the true story – in novel form –
of Loeb and Leopold, two teenagers in the twenties, who
murdered a 14-year-old Jewish boy in what became known as
the "kill for a thrill" murder. The reason I'm mentioning
this is because I've had an idea concerning the film being
made of your life. You can bet your boots that when the film
is released, The Profession of Violence will be given a new
lease of life – with another up-date and new jacket. But you
won't receive a penny. A novel, based on the screenplay,
however, could sell even better, especially if it was a
powerful book, rather like The Godfather. One could try to
write and sell such a book independent of the film company,
but it would be far better to tie in with them on it. How do
you feel about the idea? And should I write to Daltrey
direct if you think it is an idea worth pursuing.
    Anyway, please try to get Compulsion and you'll see
exactly how the story was turned into a marvellous piece of
faction.

contacts, promising that *"if anything transpires, you will not be forgotten."* Which, bearing in mind, all the running around I'd done, and money I'd spent, was mighty big of him! If he was to be believed, however, he didn't need my help, for he boasted that he intended getting his "magnificent obsession" on the *London Tonight* TV show – and the famous Johnny Carson show, in the U.S. Just why a TV programme, majoring on news in the capital, or an American chat-show, would be interested in an insignificant hoodlum on the Isle of Wight, he didn't say.

Equally pressing for Reg was for me to refute a big story *The Sun* had run – shortly before Gillett's home leave – claiming they were gay. In the brief time I'd known him, Gillett had come over as a healthy heterosexual, constantly boasting of his sexual prowess with women, so I had no qualms about trying to set the record straight. On my next visit, I spent the whole time talking to him and Reg about their relationship, and wrote an article, which I thought might appeal to *The Sun*, as a follow-up to its 'gay' story. As agreed, I sent the article to Reg for approval and he was happy with it, although he did not want to be described as a "bully," nor that he didn't know what Grace was. And he didn't want me to plug *The Sun*.

*

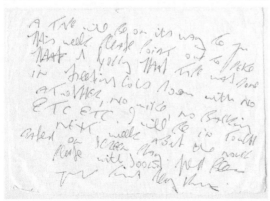

15th Oct Hello Robin, Thanks for letter. You did not say if Deke and Golly will write to the Home Office to get Pete an Home Leave?! Also are you doing anything with that large article or not?! Also what about Texas?
A tape will be on its way to you this week. Please point out to Deke and Golly that tape was done in freezing cold room with no atmosphere, no mike, no backing etc etc I will be in touch next week about the novel based on screen play. Please write soon
God Bless Your friend
Reg Kray

It all sounds like a cosy homosexual affair. But Pete
and Reg laugh at suggestions that they are gay.

Pete, a healthy heterosexual, with scores of female
conquests to prove it, says: "Often in life, two people click -
and Reg and clicked. People think it's a father and son relationship. But it's not.

"We are just two guys who, despite the difference in
age, like each other's company and think and feel the same about
nearly everything."

Millions throughout Britain were convinced Reg Kray
had turned homosexual when fellow prisoner Bill Bailey revealed
Reg's close friendship with Pete to the Sun earlier this year.

But, speaking for the first time about the allegations,
Reg says that Bailey had a strong, and vindictive, motive for
making the slur.

"He was a raving poof who got the hump because I turned
down his offers," Reg said angrily. " He then made an approach
to Pete, offering him £100 worth of dope in return for oral sex.

"When Pete told him where to go, Bill decided to get
his own back by telling everyone on the outside that Pete and I
were a couple of old queers.

"It didn't bother me because I've lived with people
saying bad things and lies about me for nearly 20 years. But I
was very concerned about the effect the allegations would have
on Pete."

Reg need not have worried. When Pete saw the story
of the alleged affair on the Sun's front page, he burst out
laughing. And he started mincing about the prison, hand on hip
and lips pursed, asking prisoner officers in an effeminate voice
if they wanted a date.

"I camped it up so well that when I threw myself open
to be searched, the screws left me alone," he chuckled.

m/f

Even Reg joined in the send-up. He arranged for a copy
of "Gay News" - the weekly paper for homosexuals - to be sent
to Pete at Parkhurst. Pete promptly sent it along to his cell,
with the words "Piss-taker" scrawled across the front page.

But the two men are pleased something worthwhile came
from Bailey's outburst. The article gave them the idea to
write a song about it, which Pete aims to record when he is
released next May. The song is called Spiteful Words.

Both men, however, appreciate why people who do not
know them are doubtful about their relationship. After all, on
the face of it, they have little in common except their lack of
freedom.

At 53, Reg is 27 years older than Pete. And, these
days, what sort of man buys a fellow male a necklace chain for
his birthday - engraved With Affection - without it being some
sort of homosexual offering. ?

To those who know Reg Kray well, though, such a generous
act will come as no surprise. True, he has a reputation as a
ruthless gangster, whose uncompromising methods of persuasion
ended in murder, and a minimum 30-year jail sentence.

But there is another side to his personality that, in
the eyes of the Press and public, has always taken second place
to the violent aspect. Even today, long after their reign of
terror, Eastenders remember how he and twin brother Ronnie were
always eager to help deserving charities, digging deep into
their pockets to take care of children and old people.

Pete Gillett, it seems, has seen this side of the
mobster at close quarters.

And he says: "Reg is one of the kindest, most gentle,
people I've ever met. In prison, he gives everything away. When
he heard me sing, the first thing he said was, 'I'm going to
get you a guitar.' And he did.

"I've always been very headstrong - a bit of a jack
the lad who always thought he knew best.

"Well, Reg has clamed me down and made me respect other people's views. He's the only person I've ever taken notice of."

The feeling is mutual. Before Pete arrived at Parkhurst Reg was a 40-cigarettes-a-day chain smoker. Now, thanks to Pete's keep-fit approach to life, he has not touched or wanted, a cigarette for over seven months.

"Pete makes me feel young again," Reg said, with unashamed joy. "He gave me the incentive to start weight training again - and even got me onto a football pitch for the first time in 15 years. I celebrated that remarkable feat with a goal from one of Pete's corners. And he got one, too. We even play padder (wooden racquets) tennis together.

"Since he came here, I've become a different person. He has so much vitality and lust for life. He sets a fast pace and we're a good team."

Both of them believe they were destined to meet and become friends.

"Even before I was sentenced I had this feeling I was going to go down," says Pete. "And I knew I was going to meet Reg Kray. I was sent to one prison - then, lo and behold! - I was transferred to Parkhurst.

"When Reg started talking to me it was as if we had known each other 100 years. He seemed to know all about my past, even before I told him. It was weird, but exciting, too.

"I'd never had many friends on the outside. And in his hey-day Reg was always too busy ducking and diving in some business or other to find time to develop a friendship with anyone other than his brother.

"I honestly believe that when I walked through that prison door, Reg saw me as the friend, the playmate, he'd never had as a kid."

m/f

"The morning after my arrival he flew into my cell, asking if I wanted a cup of tea. Then we started nattering. That night, there were about seven or eight of us chatting in my cell, but the next day Reg said he thought there was only me and him.

"He admitted he was so interested and fascinated by me, as someone fresh from the street, that he was oblivious to everyone around him. And before anyone says, nudge, nudge, wink wink, Reggie fancied me, I've got to say there was not one sexual overtone or undertone to anything he said. Nor has there ever been."

For his part, Reg is the first to admit that the odd friendship has affected him in a way that would astonish all those who view him only as the vicious bully, who, with brother Ron, made even hard men walk in fear.

He said: "Every morning I get up at 7.40 and either wash in my cell or take a shower downstairs. Then I take a jug of tea and some breakfast - cornflakes or whatever - to Pete who is normally still sleeping in his cell.

"We don't have to get up till 9 a.m., so I think it's nice for him to be able to sleep in late every morning. There's no point in both of us getting up if one of us doesn't have to, is there ? And I think it's good if I can make Pete's term in jail as pleasant as possible."

Making Pete happy, it seems, is very important to Reg. Last Christmas, shortly after they met, for example, Reg invited Pete to Christmas dinner in his cell to share in a turkey he had managed to acquire.

"As we were about to tuck in, Pete suddenly suggested saying, Grace," said Reg. "I'd never said it in my life - I didn't really know what it was - but it was important to Pete, so I took pleasure in letting him say it. It was beautiful."

m/f

As one might expect in such a close relationship, there are no secrets. They receive around 60 letters a week between them and every day at 10 a.m. they read them all.

To Reg, it was important for Pete to know *everything* about him, so he insisted the young man read The Profession of Violence, the best-selling book about the rise and fall of the Kray brothers.

"It is a very good book in many ways, " says Reg. "But there are several blatant lies, particularly about my marriage to Frances (she later killed herself), and I wanted Pete to know the truth - not just what the public thought of me.

"It's pointless having a very close friend if he doesn't know you inside out, is it? So, over the months we've known each other, I've explained in detail to Pete the whole truth about the past.

"It is the first time I've done that. But Pete has good values and principles and has proved to me he can keep secrets. I trust him implicitly."

Finding someone he feels he can confide in means a great deal to the man who was convicted on some of his crimes on the evidence of so-called friends.

With a rare smile, he says: "Thanks to Pete I no longer have the need for that profound philosophy, 'I know my enemies, but God protect me from my friends.'"

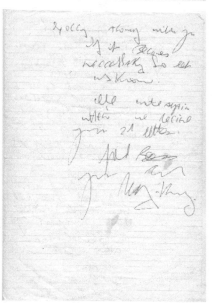

21st Oct   Hello Robin,   Thanks for your letter. Go ahead with Texas. You cannot be getting all my mail as I said this in previous letter.   Would you need to see me for book based on the screen play or could you just get on with it?!   You are right about Deke and Golly. Just hope you keep interest alive and hope they like the tapes using there imagination for a bleak room where tape was done.   I could see either Deke or Golly along with you if it becomes neccessary so let us know.   Ill write again when we receive your 2nd letter.   God Bless   Your Friend   Reg Kray

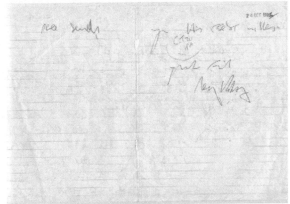

24th October Hello Robin, Thanks for your letter. Also the write up. Enclosed it back to you. I will put a line through each part I want cut out. I have my reasons. My heart does not beat a little faster when I see a male! Does yours?! I told you I am not gay! Plug the sun if you wish. But is it necessary?! I thought Id made it clear I did not fancy Pete no more than you do I just like him as a person I hope my little complaints meet your approval I do have some dignity. Hope to hear from you soon. Pete sends you his best wishes. Your friend Reg Kray

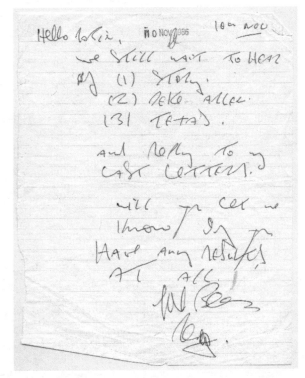

10th Nov
Hello Robin,
We still wait to hear
Of (1) Story
(2) Deke Arlen
(3) Texas
And reply to my last letters.
Will you let me know if you
have any results at all.
God Bless
Reg

During that summer, Charlie admitted to Sue and I that he'd fallen out of love with Diana – and in love with her cleaner, a thirty-five-year-old mother of three, named Judy Stanley. When we met her, we failed to see what Charlie saw in her: she was nowhere near as attractive or classy as Diana, and had none of the *joie de vivre* that made Di such enjoyable company. But Charlie was smitten, there was no doubt about that, and began an affair behind Diana's back. To be fair to him, he and Diana had reached an unspoken understanding that each of them was free to have flings with other people, provided they were discreet and did not get heavily involved. What a result for Charlie! He could have his cake and eat it: he could continue to treat Di's maisonette as his home, while going off in search of female company, with her blessing, if not her encouragement. Whether Diana would have taken such a liberal attitude if she'd known that the man she called her soul-mate was betraying her with – among others – an employee of hers is open to question. Charlie dreaded the thought of hurting Diana, but Judy became like a drug to him; he had to see her as often as he could, and, towards the end of the year, the strain of having such an all-consuming affair so close to home began to show.

*

Since the twins didn't seem interested in writing their autobiography, I suggested I collaborated with them on a novel, based on the screenplay of the film. If the movie *was* made, it would give *The Profession of Violence* a new lease of life, but a novel might sell even better, particularly if it was similar to *Compulsion*, a book based on the famous Loeb-Leopold murder case, in Chicago, in the twenties. The book had made a profound impression on me as a teenage reporter, and I urged Reg to try to get it from the prison library, so that he'd understand what I was talking about. I quickly got the impression he didn't want to be bothered because, a week later, he wrote suggesting I got on with the book without seeing him. He was more concerned that Deke Arlon and Golly Gallagher liked Gillett's tape, saying he'd see them on a visit, if necessary.

The last letter Reg wrote that year had a sombre and, I mistakenly thought, a defeated tone. Upset that I hadn't told him what Deke and Golly thought of the tape, or whether *The Sun* were interested in the story of his relationship with Pete, he asked: "*Will you let me know if you have any results at all?*" We were both disappointed – he at seeing his dreams for his protégé's pop career disappearing, me at having spent so much time, effort and money for nothing. And then, a few weeks later it became clear why Reg wasn't interested in writing a book with me. I was shocked - and bitterly disappointed - to read in *The Times* and *Sun* that he and Ron were doing a book with someone else.

Fred Dinenage.

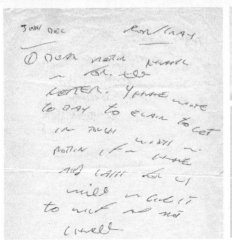

30th Dec Ron Kray (1) Dear Robin Thank you for the letter. I have wrote to day to Elain to get in touch with you Robin if you have any cash for us will you give it to Wilf and not Charlie Will keep in touch God Bless Ron PTO Thank you for getting in touch with Brian Hitchen for us

Letter from the author to Ron Kray

14 January 87
Dear Ron,

Thank you for agreeing to see young Rob and myself last Monday, and I am most sorry the weather made it impossible for us to get there on
time for a full visit. As they say, better luck next time.

With the snow as thick as it is, I think that the next time, Ron, cannot be next Monday as we both hoped. Far better, I think, to wait and see how the weather turns out. Apparently, the Big Freeze is going to continue for some time yet. I shall liaise with Elaine on this.

In the meantime, a bit of news: Rob has, indeed, managed to stall everyone on the Billy Webb aggro. He spoke to Webb himself and, it seems, the gentleman is writing you another letter. Expect it soon. Rob managed to impress on him the stupidity of stirring things up for Reg at such an important time, so let's hope Billy sees sense. It is possible, of course, for Rob to be asked to produce some sort of piece, but you can be assured it will not be anti-Kray.

Can I ask you, Ron, to give some thought to things you would like to talk about when we next meet. Make some notes even. As you will appreciate, I need some good stuff to make it financially worthwhile for everyone. I'm not necessarily talking about sensational revelations, as I made clear on Monday.

One other thing: I've tried, without success, to contact Lennie Peters. But I'll keep trying.

Take care and God Bless.

Bickley,
KENT

22 January 87

Dear Reg,

Well, the date is drawing on when you are due to be
given a date for your eventual release, and I sincerely
hope the news you get will be encouraging.

One of the main reasons for writing, Reg, is to say
that it wasn't until I'd spoken to Charlie that it dawned
on me that you have to pay for stamps to put on your
letters. For some reason – don't ask me why! – I thought
the prison paid for them! What is the best way to get some
stamps to you? Is it best to send them on envelopes
already stamped, or should I send some individually? I'd
like us to keep in contact generally, and, naturally, I
don't expect you to have to pay when it's so hard for you
to get hold of cash.

As you probably know, I went to see Ronnie with Elaine
last week. God, what a murderous journey. We finally
arrived at 3.10 for a 2 p.m. visit! Ron was concerned at
Billy Webb making himself busy again, but my son, Rob, who
you met, has managed to stall the Sun on doing a story.
Webb wanted to stir things up for you, hoping to
jeopardise your parole chances.

One other thing, Reg: knowing how keen you are on
physical exercise, I wonder whether you would like to see
a video of a truly amazing feat a friend of mine pulled
off for his 50th birthday. I'm enclosing a cutting of a
story I did about Ken Heathcote's superhuman effort, which
explains all about it. Charlie has got the video at the
moment. He could hardly believe it. If you yourself would
like to see it, please let me know and I'll send it. Tell
you one thing – it would certainly cause a lot of interest
at Parkhurst. I shouldn't think anyone inside could do
what Ken did – even if they were half his age!

How is Pete, by the way. Any news form Wilf on his pop
career prospects? If he can spare a few minutes, I'd love
to hear from Pete.

Dear Ron,

I got your letter this morning and felt you would appreciate a reply by return of post.

Firstly, I hope things are well with you and that you are in good health.

Secondly, I gave Elaine £300 out of the £500 I received from the Sun for the divorce story. She was well pleased because it will enable her to pay off a few debts and get her phone back on. As far as a longer article is concerned Elaine does not feel she has got enough to say. She felt it would be a waste of everyone's time.

That was a couple of weeks ago and since then I've had another thought. Even though her thoughts and plans might not be strong enough for a national paper, they might interest a woman's magazine. If you remember, you put the block on the previous Woman's Own article I did because you felt £500 was not enough. Well, circumstances are different now, and Elaine could well do with some money. I have had a word with a woman journalist I know and asked her if she would have a chat to Elaine, with a view to writing a sympathetic piece on a woman's angle. I dropped a note into Elaine's flat late on Sunday night, asking her to ring me on Monday to set up a meeting, but so far I haven't heard from her.

The Sunday People promised her £100 for talking to them about the divorce, but she hasn't received this. I have chased this up, but the paper has told me Elaine must speak to the reporter involved. Typical case of passing the buck, eh?

The Sun were interested in my Hale and Pace story, but decided not to run it for some reason. Now that they have their own series, however, it might be worth having another go. I have passed on the information to Rob, who is now working on The Star.

The Sun were going to do a You The Jury on whether the Kray twins should be released. Sadly, that hasn't appeared yet. If I get word on it, I'll let you know.

If you have any ideas on how we can all make a few quid, let me know and I'll do my best to make it happen. Haven't heard from Reg in ages. No doubt he took my last letter too much to heart! Take care.

Bickley,
KENT

Dear Ron,
Well, were you pleased with the Sun's effort? Certainly the paper itself was. The Editor, Kelvin Mackenzie, whom I first spoke to about the vote, was delighted. He said the response was the best they had had, except for the ones on child abuse and capital punishment. I'd dearly love to know what Reg thought. It can't do his parole chances any harm, can it? As I said to Charlie this morning, you ought to try to capitalise on the Sun's article by stepping up the campaign, perhaps with a good letter to Maggie Thatcher. I did write one for Charlie about a year ago, but the more the merrier, as they say. You have nothing to lose and everything to gain.
Elaine is a mystery, Ron. I put a note through her door, saying I have come up with an idea how to earn a few quid, but haven't heard a dickie bird. Very puzzling…
Thanks for you last letter, offering to let me know as soon as you yourself hear from Elaine.
Take care,

29th Jan Ron Kray
(1)   Dear Robin
Could you please write to me and let me know what is happening about Elain and the write up   If there is to be one or not and when and what paper and if I will be getting some cash out of it
God Bless
Your friend   Ron Kray

The author's letter to Reg, after discovering that the twins had agreed a publishing deal for their autobiography

Bickley,
KENT

31 January 87

Dear Reg,
    As you can imagine, it came as great shock to me to read in the Times and the Sun that you had agreed a deal for a book, and had, in fact, chosen a writer to do it. I thought I had paid my dues enough to be well in the frame for that.
    I would be grateful if you could write and tell me whether what I read was true, so that, if necessary, I can concentrate my mind on other things. I thought that by running around speaking to people, making phone calls, writing letters to companies, etc I was proving to you that I was to be trusted. I also thought that, as someone who'd actually run a publishing company, I would be the best person to speak to about a book. It does seem as though you have taken the very first deal that came along and all I hope is that you don't live to regret it, like The Profession of Violence. There are not many people to be trusted in this world and I honestly believed Charlie had impressed on you that I was someone you should.
    It does seem, Reg, that you were happy for me to try to interest Fleet Street in the pro-Kray stories, but as soon as a good deal comes along I'm rowed out. Perhaps you could let me know why you took this attitude because I certainly think it was unjust.
    Can you remember that tenner you asked me to send to that bloke in Albany. You said: "Put it on the bill." What bill, Reg?
    On a more pleasant note, I wonder if you got my last letter, in which I said I would send some stamps. I expressed my best wishes in relation to the release date. Despite my feelings of rejection right now, I still do hope you get the news you are hoping for. Who knows, you might even let me know what it is as soon as you get it.

Take care.

Chapter Six

MY mind reeled with mixed emotions: disappointment at not being asked if I'd like to write the book; and blind fury at not even being told anything about it when I'd spent nearly two years talking and writing to the twins. My first thought was to demand to see Reg – now in Gartree Prison, in Leicester – and have it out with him. But when I calmed down and realised that it would be a waste of time and money, I did what I always did when I was angry and needed to make a point: I wrote a letter.

Firstly, I asked Reg if what I'd read in *The Times* and *The Sun* was true: if it was, I wanted to know why he hadn't had the courtesy to tell me: surely I'd done enough running around for him to warrant that? And as someone who'd not only made a living from writing, but had run my own publishing company, did he not think I was the ideal person to talk to about a book? He was happy for me to use my contacts to get inconsequential, pro-Kray stories in the papers, I fumed, but as soon as a worthwhile, money-spinning deal came along, I didn't rate even a chat. I was boiling mad, and, reading my letter today, I'm surprised it doesn't reflect that. I've often wondered whether it would have changed things had I insisted on confronting Reg, or written a meatier letter, slagging him off for mugging me off, as they say in the Mile End Road. As it was, I kept my letter to the point, limiting my anger to a comment that I hoped he and Ronnie would not regret their decision, as they had with *The Profession of Violence* – and a sarcastic aside about that tenner Reg had "nipped" off me. Reminding him that he told me to 'put it on the bill,'" I asked: "What bill, Reg?" Not surprisingly, I never got a reply to that letter – let alone the ten quid.

Although I'd lost touch with Elaine, I still went to Broadmoor and, during one visit, Ronnie brought up Hale and Pace, two comics who'd made an impact on the entertainment scene, following a Christmas special the previous month. Ronnie hadn't seen the act, but had been told that, in one of their sketches, the duo seemed to be taking the mickey out of the twins. Dressed in dinner jackets and dickie bows, they played The Two Rons, stone-faced, supposedly frightening, nightclub "heavies," also known as The Management - a very funny skit, which most people assumed was based on the twins, because, in their stilted conversations, one would keep grunting: "I do Ron, Ron." The phrase was a play on The Crystals' hit record *Da Doo Ron Ron*, but Ronnie thought that Hale and Pace were having a pop at them, and he wanted to have a pop back at them in the paper. Despite the huge money the pair must be earning, Ronnie was sure they didn't donate as much to charity as he and Reg, and he wanted to challenge them in a newspaper to see who donated most. Knowing *The Sun's* appetite for bizarre Kray stories, I tried it on the Editor, Kelvin MacKenzie, but, for once, he wasn't interested. Much to Ronnie's disappointment, I dropped the idea, for, apart from anything else, why would two emerging showbiz stars be inclined to reveal what they did with their money, and so publicise the Kray twins.

Ronnie clearly thought I was still trying to place an article about his marriage, because he wrote, wanting any money – if there was any – to go to Wilf, not Charlie. Obviously, his long-suffering older brother was out of favour – again! Worried that none of Elaine's friends knew where she was, I drove to her Shoreditch flat one Sunday night after my *Express* shift and dropped in a note, asking her to call me the next day. She didn't – and a few weeks later I learned that she'd wanted to be on her own because she was desperately unhappy and depressed, and planning to divorce Ronnie.

Who knows about that bizarre marriage? I don't believe it was merely a ruse to squeeze a wedding day cash bonanza out of *The Sun*, because Ronnie did tell me – and other friends – how much he enjoyed seeing Elaine and her children. And there was a time, the previous year, when they had even looked into the practicalities of having a baby.

I was sad for Elaine, but she needed money and the divorce was a good story, so, with Elaine's permission, I sold it exclusively to *The Sun,* which the paper ran as its Page One lead. Elaine's share of the fee paid most of her debts.

For Ronnie, a divorce was hardly likely to bother him. He'd miss Elaine's willingness to run around for him, but there were numerous pals, as well as sycophants, only too keen to do whatever he wanted. Sexually, he was enjoying relationships with other patients – and, I'm told, a good-looking male member of staff. The lust for young men that had been so evident before his incarceration was still strong – as Steve Tully discovered on a visit that summer. They were chatting over a couple of cans of Barbican when Steve became aware of Ronnie staring at the next table, where a young guy, in his late teens, was sitting with an older man and woman, probably his parents. After a while Ronnie looked at Steve and nodded towards the boy. "Isn't he lovely?" he whispered. Then he looked over to the refreshment bar and motioned the owner, Ken, to come over. Very quietly, Ronnie asked for some flowers and chocolates to be taken to the young man. Ken, clearly acquainted with this impromptu generosity, nodded, knowingly, and went back to the bar.

A few minutes later, Ken took Ronnie's gift to the table and obviously told the young man who had sent them, because he and the older couple immediately looked towards Ronnie's table. "It was so comical," Steve remembers. "The three of them wondering what it was all about, and Ronnie leering, like a hungry wolf, a silly grin on his face. In that instant, I knew that all the stories I'd heard about Ronnie's fascination for young boys were well founded."

Just why Ronnie was allowed to indulge in such extravagances on credit is a mystery. In theory, he was buying goods on the basis that he would settle his account in due course, but the bill was allowed to mount up. Ronnie's debt was over £1,000 at the time, but that was nothing to what it rose to later.

*

One might wonder why I didn't cut my losses with the twins, or, at least, with Reg, who was clearly interested only in what suited him. That I swallowed it – or wiped my mouth, as he would say – was due entirely to a journalistic sixth sense that, with the twins certain to be newsworthy for the foreseeable future, I'd be foolish to let my pride kill off what might still prove to be a profitable relationship.

That instinct proved right, a few weeks later when Kelvin MacKenzie, told me how surprised he was by the voting in the paper's *You The Jury* feature, which had asked: "*Should the Krays be freed?*" Kelvin said that, apart from capital punishment and child abuse, the response was higher than any other issue *The Sun* had featured – which made me think it might help Reg's chances when the parole review panel considered his case in March. Not wanting to set myself up for a knock-back so soon after my angry letter, I wrote to Ronnie, suggesting that his brother capitalised on *The Sun* publicity by asking Prime Minister Margaret Thatcher for help. I didn't hear anything, but keeping lines of communication open did benefit me at the end of March when Charlie called to tell me that Reg had been told his plea for a release date had been thrown out and the parole panel would not consider the case again for four years. It was hugely disappointing for Reg, but a good story, nevertheless. *The Sun* ran it as the Page Two lead, under the headline: *Reggie Kray is 'shattered' by ban on parole.*

The author's *Sun* exclusive on Reg's reaction
to the Home Office rejecting his for parole.

LAW AND ORDER ++ LAW AND ORDER ++ LAW AND ORDER

REGGIE KRAY IS 'SHATTERED' BY BAN ON PAROLE

Reggie Kray . . . "no longer a threat"

Brother plans appeal

By ROB McGIBBON

JAILED gangland killer Reggie Kray was "shattered" last night after learning his hopes of parole had been dashed again.

The former East End mobster, now 53, had set his heart on being given a release date after serving 18 years behind bars.

But the Home Office have told him a parole review panel has thrown out his plea—and will not consider his case again until 1991.

Reggie, who is now in Gartree Prison, Leics, has not been given reasons for the decision. He and his twin brother Ronnie—now held in Broadmoor top security hospital—were both jailed for life in 1969 with a recommendation they should serve 30 years.

Reggie may now take legal advice in a new bid to have his case reviewed—and his other brother Charlie is planning to ask Premier Margaret Thatcher for help.

Threat

Charlie, 60, said last night: "Reg is choked—he is no longer a threat to anyone.

"But he thinks the establishment is determined to break him and Ronnie until they become cabbages.

"I want to know how they can justify keeping him in jail after so many years.

"Dennis Nilsen murdered 16 innocent young men, but got a shorter sentence.

"And the spy Anthony Blunt—the biggest traitor of all—was not even arrested. How many lives was he responsible for?"

When told of Reggie's blow, twin Ronnie said: "I'm not surprised—they want to crucify us."

Ronnie has told friends he will never be freed from Broadmoor.

Reggie was jailed for the murder of John "The Hat" McVitie, and for being an accessory to the murder of George Cornell. Ronnie was jailed for both killings.

Charlie Kray . . . anger

Another *Sun* exclusive

Hurd to probe murder bail

By DAVID KEMP

HOME Secretary Douglas Hurd yesterday ordered a probe into how Winston Silcott was freed on bail while accused of murder—then went on to kill PC Keith Blakelock.

Mr Hurd will investigate

● The bail laws that allowed Silcott to be freed pending trial on a charge of murdering boxer Anthony Smith in a nightclub. He was later found guilty.

● Judge Robert Lymbery's decision in granting that bail.

● The material Judge Lymbery was given to help him make up his mind.

Silcott was on bail when he led the mob who hacked PC Keith Blakelock to death in the Broadwater Farm riots, at Tottenham, North London.

Reasonable

Mr Hurd said: "Obviously the decision in the end turned out to be wrong and it is perfectly reasonable for us to find out how that came about."

Judge Lymbery has already defended his controversial bail decision. But some ministers and MPs think that he—and not the laws—may have been at fault.

Speaking on BBC TV yesterday, Mr Hurd said that a judge did not have to grant bail "under these circumstances."

He pointed out that the judge is allowed to take into account the seriousness of the offence, the character and background of the defendant—and the possibility of another offence being committed.

Mr Hurd said the question was what went wrong in this case which was held in private.

Beast On Bail—See Page 9

Judge Lymbery . . . decision   Douglas Hurd . . . probe

IF BREATHING BECOMES AN EFFORT PUT DO-DO INTO ACTION.

STEP 1	STEP 2
Do-Do opens up the upper airways and clears the catarrh.	It prevents the build up of more congestion.

If you're suffering from breathlessness and wheezing brought on by bronchial catarrh, don't worry.

Help is at hand in the shape of Do-Do.

You see, Do-Do is a small, effective tablet that really gets to work on your blocked upper chest.

With an eye on a follow-up story I worked in that Charlie was writing to Mrs Thatcher for help, and got together with him to decide what to write on his behalf. Convinced Reg was no longer a threat to society, Charlie wanted to ask Mrs Thatcher to visit Gartree to see for herself that his brother was a changed man, so I wrote suggesting this. We never found out what she thought of the idea, because no one at Downing Street acknowledged receiving the 1,500-word letter.

While discussing the letter, Charlie mentioned that he had been approached by Ian Paten, a commissioning editor at Grafton Books, who was keen to republish the 1976 *Everest* edition of *Me and My Brothers*. Always looking for quick cash for little effort, Charlie saw the proposition as a way to squeeze another advance, this time for nothing more than signing a contract. With *Everest's* liquidation, rights to the book had reverted to Charlie, and he could do what he wanted, but he was keen to know what I thought. Unfortunately, I could see an insurmountable problem: since the twins had now confessed to the Cornell and McVitie murders, most of the lies Charlie had told in the book made it worthless. Grafton would need to be told the truth, and once they were, they wouldn't want to know; no publisher would. Seeing the easy money vanishing, Charlie was deflated, but brightened when I said I had an idea. "Why don't we rewrite the book?" I said. "From start to finish. Treat it as a new project. Tell the truth about where you were the night McVitie was murdered. Explain how you came to be jailed for a crime you didn't commit. We could ask for a sizeable advance – certainly more than I paid you in '76."

Charlie's bright-blue eyes lit up. "Do you think they'd go for a new book?"

I laughed. "Of course, they will."

And I meant it. I was sure Grafton had approached Charlie because they wanted a Kray book of their own, to rival the twins' own story, due to be published the following September. We were bound to get a good deal, particularly if we could guarantee delivering the manuscript in time for the publication to cash in on the huge publicity the twins' book would get. On reflection, I should have approached other publishers and tried to secure a better deal, but Charlie felt confident in Ian Paten and, when I met him, so did I. Everyone was happy: Ian couldn't believe his luck at hooking a Kray brother; Charlie was thrilled at getting some upfront money, and by the prospect of revealing how and why his life had been destroyed. And I had the chance to write my first book.

I was somewhat daunted by the enormity of what lay ahead. Getting the material out of Charlie wasn't a worry: we'd always got on well and, provided he told me the truth – which, he assured me, he would – I was sure I'd have enough for what Paten required. It was writing the manuscript and meeting the autumn deadline that concerned me. Although being a sub-editor wasn't the most demanding job in the world, it did take up most of the working week. Was I being naïve, promising to deliver 100,000 words in five months when I

Part of Charlie's letter to Margaret Thatcher

The Rt. Hon. Margaret Thatcher,
Prime Minister,
10 Downing Street,
London S.W.1.

Cantley Gardens,
Sylvan Road,
Upper Norwood,
London S.E.20.

22 March 87

Dear Mrs Thatcher,
I do appreciate that the plight of jailed criminals will not be your top priority at the moment, but a recent Home Office decision, concerning my brother, Reginald, leaves me no alternative but to seek your help.

I'm not the world's greatest letter writer, but I have what I feel are sensible, constructive and justifiable points to make, and I would urge you, busy as you are, to take the time and trouble to consider them.

Hopefully, you will share my view - one shared by many hundreds of thousands of people throughout the country - that the treatment of Reginald gives cause for immense concern, and needs examining from the highest level.

So many outrageous things have been said and written about Reginald that, in all honesty, it is difficult to separate the fact from the fiction. But now that the Home Office has ruled that his case will not even be considered again until 1991, I feel it is vitally important that the lies should give way to some truth.

It IS a fact that, as young men, Reginald and his twin brother, Ronald, frightened innocent people into paying money for "protection." It IS a fact that the violent lifestyle they both led ended in the murder of two gangland figures, for one of which Reginald was convicted.

But, Prime Minister, it is fiction to suggest that in the 19 years he has been denied his freedom, Reginald is "still a threat," and has not changed.

One of a long-serving prisoner's greatest frustrations is that the Home Office is not obliged to give reasons for refusing parole. I have always wondered why this should be so. Surely, it is in everyone's interests for an inmate to know why it is felt unwise to allow him to rejoin society.

In Reginald's case, for example, WHO is saying he is "still a threat."?

WHAT justification is being offered to support such a weighty and damning statement ?

WHY can't Reginald be told the reasons for his continued incarceration ?

I, members of my family, friends, publishers, journalists - even a noble lord - have spoken at length with Reginald over the years and, without exception, all agree that the Reginald Kray of yesterday is not the Reginald Kray of today.

/continued

GANGLAND killer Reggie Kray's brother, Charles, has written to the Prime Minister, urging her to visit Reg in prison.

Charles, 60, wants Mrs Thatcher to see for herself that the former East End mobster is a changed man, who should qualify for parole.

The decision to write to Downing Street follows a Home Office move to turn down Reggie's request for parole and not consider his case again until 1991.

In his 1,500-word letter, Charles says that after 19 years behind bars, Reggie is no longer a threat and should be given the chance to prove that on the outside.

"I'm not trying to paint a picture of a saint, but I am trying to convince you that Reginald is no longer a sinner," Charles tells Mrs Thatcher.

"And as he comes up to his 20th year in jail, I would urge you, most seriously and strongly, to make an exception in your role as Prime Minister and go to Gartree Prison to see for yourself.

"Talk to Reginald for half an hour or so. Hear what he has to say about life today and what he has done for other people while he has been in jail. Ask him what he would be doing if he were to be freed.

"I don't know what image you have of the Kray family in general, and Reginald in particular, but I am convinced it would not be the one you would see."

Charles argues that because the Krays' 1968 trial was "a big political event" a Prime Ministerial intervention 20 years on would be "most appropriate."

And in a cheeky pay-off, he says that "as a devoted Tory, Reggie would be delighted to see you on a visit."

In his emotional plea for compassion for his brother, Charles likens Reggie's plight to that of John Profumo, the former War Minister who was at the centre of the 1960s sex and spy scandal involving Christine Keeler and Dr. Stephen Ward.

"The worlds of Mr Profumo and Reginald were vastly different, of course," says Charles. "But in some ways what happened to them was strikingly similar.

> "Both men outraged society. Both men's lives were in tatters as a result of society's demand for justice. Both men were banished – Reginald to prison, Mr Profumo to the relative obscurity of non-public life.
>
> "Both men, in their own ways, took their punishments on the chin, not showing remorse or regret for what they had done necessarily, but accepting that they had done wrong and deserved to be punished.
>
> "Mr Profumo has won back some of the public's lost respect by working with deprived people in, ironically, the East End. Reginald, too, has won respect in jail by being a model prisoner and going out of his way to encourage young offenders to change their ways.
>
> "If Mr Profumo has earned the right to regain a respectable place in society after so long in the wilderness, is it not reasonable to ask that Reginald be given the chance, now that he is approaching the winter of his life?"
>
> After sending his letter, Charlie said, yesterday: "We were all so choked at the decision not to review Reggie's case for another four years, I had to do something. It took me three days to write my letter and all I hope is that Mrs Thatcher has the chance to read it.
>
> "Perhaps she took it it Moscow with her and read it over a large vodka," he joked.

hadn't even started interviewing Charlie?

In the end, it was my wife, Sue, who convinced me to take on the project. Since I'd joined the *Express*, she'd been working part-time with handicapped children, while helping me run the company offering free holidays to celebrities. However, she wanted me to ghost Charlie's book and said she would transcribe my taped interviews with Charlie and type my longhand manuscript on to a typewriter. So, full of confidence and optimism, Charlie and I signed the publishing contract on 28 April and, three or four times a week for the next two months, Charlie would come to our new home, near Bromley, to tell me his remarkable story. He'd usually drive from Diana's maisonette himself, but sometimes he'd be dropped off by a friend he'd known for years, John Corbett, a tall, dark, languid, very personable guy, in his mid-twenties.

Charlie introduced John to Sue and I as a friend, but I got the impression they were business associates, too, because every time John drew up, they would talk earnestly in the car for ten minutes or so, before Charlie would come to the house to start work. At that time, I had no reason to think that

Charlie was anything but straight; on the contrary, I believed that, having been so devastated by his prison sentence, he wouldn't do anything to risk going back inside. And although I never saw any evidence of any money, I assumed that whatever he was up to provided a legitimate income.

It was a warm summer in 1987 and Charlie and I worked mostly in the garden – which explains why, on several of my tapes, the eloquence of his recollections is often punctuated by the cheerful chirping of sparrows, blackbirds, thrushes, robins, chaffinches, and the occasional coo of wood pigeons and doves.

At the time, playing everything by ear, I had no idea what ghost-writers should expect from their subjects, but over the next twenty years, I would meet dozens of celebrities and villains, and learn that Charlie was in a different class. He did not have an inflated ego and think he was special. He was always on time, having done his homework on what we were to cover. He did his best to remember what I needed to make the narrative a page-turner, never pontificating, or rambling, on stories that were interesting to him, but to no one else. And he was always, but always, charming to Sue, whose coffee he adored, and he insisted on mentioning her in his acknowledgements in the book. He was a joy to work with – a ghost-writer's dream.

Charlie had promised to tell the truth, and I was certain he would. We'd spent so much time together, I was sure I knew the man and genuinely believed he was ready – indeed, eager – to tell his story, no holds barred. We had this understanding that everything he told me on tape would be true and for the book; if he wanted to tell me something not for publication, we'd turn off the tape recorder and he'd tell me in confidence.

Charlie often stayed for dinner and one night, after a particularly relaxing couple of hours, he brought out a selection of photographs he wanted us to consider for the book. Looking at the smiling faces of his family brought back happy memories and Charlie was in his element, reliving the captured moments of his life. But, then, he came across a particularly lovely picture of his mother, laughing, without a care in the world, and it seemed to bring into focus all that his family had lost. He started to weep, quietly. Sue, who was sitting beside him, hugged him until his tears stopped, and I poured him a large brandy and coke.

*

Obviously, to millions who never met Charlie, he was the murderous Kray twins' older brother, and every bit as wicked as them. As he'd explain to anyone willing to listen, this was the cross he'd had to bear since their convictions, in 1969. Just how heavy that cross was didn't hit home to me until one afternoon that summer after I arrived at the *Express* for my afternoon shift. One of my colleagues, a burly, likeable, but strongly-opinionated Scotsman, named Bill Montgomery, who knew I was ghosting Charlie's story, asked how it was going.

"Extremely well, thanks," I said. "We've just done a few hours in the garden."

"In the garden?"

"Yeah, Charlie loves the sun. We always go in the garden when we can."

"At your place?"

"Yeah."

"You allow that man in your house?"

"Of course, I do," I said. "We're working together."

"But he's one of the Krays, Robbie," Bill said. "They murdered people, for God's sake."

"Charlie didn't," I said, quietly.

"He did his brother's dirty work," Bill said. "Got rid of McVitie's body after they killed him."

"No, he didn't. Charlie had nothing to do with McVitie's murder. He was fitted up."

"That's what *he* says," Bill scoffed. "How do you know he's telling the truth?"

"How can you be so sure he's not? You've never even met the man."

"And I don't fucking want to."

"Because he's a Kray?"

"Yeah," Bill said. "If you want to put it that way. They're all fucking gangsters."

"Charlie wasn't a gangster, Bill. The twins were the gangsters."

"They're all the same, Robbie," Bill said. "All the same."

I didn't want to waste time having a row with a man with a closed mind, so I forced a smile. "Let's agree to disagree, Bill. Let's leave it there."

And we did. We never spoke about Charlie - or his book - again. But that conversation played on my mind and brought into focus the enormity of Charlie's torment. If a seasoned sub-editor, responsible for writing headlines and editing reporters' copy in a national newspaper, believed he was every bit as nasty as the twins, what price the paper's millions of readers? If a journalist with forty years' experience detested him so vehemently, without having met him, what hope did that give Charlie?

Personally, Sue and I were convinced that being so candid about the night McVitie died, and how lying to protect the twins had destroyed his life, would do much for Charlie's self-esteem and public image. Confident that Ian Paten would be as pleased with the manuscript as Charlie was, we posted it on Friday 9 October, then flew to Tenerife to switch off. It was a winter break we've never forgotten because, in the middle of it, the English weather turned out windier than the BBC forecaster predicted and we knew nothing about The Storm of the Century until we read about it while sunbathing by our apartment pool.

Chapter Seven

I'M bound to say Charlie's autobiography was better than the twins' *Our Story*. But it really was. Charlie told his story with candour, heart-on-the-sleeve emotion, and produced an absorbing read, which is why it was reprinted nine times within months of its publication, in September, 1988. The reason for its success was due, in no small part, to Charlie's wonderful performance at Grafton's pre-publication sales conference, at The Belfry Golf Club. After mingling with guests before dinner, Charlie took part in an informal question and answer session and won the reps over with his warmth, openness and wide, welcoming smile. I don't know what those reps were expecting, but it was clear from their expressions that the quietly-spoken, gentle-natured charmer was nothing like the hard-nosed, thuggish image the Kray name had conjured. He was a revelation to those reps and gave them the incentive to push his forthcoming autobiography as hard as possible.

The twins, on the other hand, didn't have a clue what the book game was all about. They had a monumental opportunity to produce not only an explosive bestseller that would eclipse the Pearson biography they hated so much, but also a publication that would be taken seriously as a significant historical document. But they blew it. They thought only of the money they could make, not what they could say to the millions who saw them only as vicious murderers. If they had been even remotely clever and forward-thinking, they would have produced an explicit, revelatory tome that would have put right all the facts *The Profession of Violence* got wrong – their dates of birth, for a start! As it was, *Our Story* was a thin, poorly-written chronicle of events, with little style and substance. The first-person story of the country's most infamous killers should have been a four or five-hundred pager, packed with anecdotes of London gangland only the twins could reveal. But it was less than half that – and contained none of the detail the publishers had a right to expect for its £100,000 advance. How they let the twins and Fred Dinenage get away with it was – and still is – beyond me. I've spoken to Dinenage about his handling of the twins and he said he should have pushed them more. You bet he should.

I didn't write to either Ronnie or Reg about their book. And they didn't offer me their views on Charlie's. I did hear from some of their visitors, however, that the twins disapproved of Charlie banging on about getting ten years for something he didn't do, while they were serving thirty years. The fundamental difference they refused to acknowledge was that they were locked up because they were guilty, whereas Charlie was innocent.

Who knows, if the twins and Fred Dinenage had produced the book their story warranted, Roger Daltrey might have been able to raise the money to produce a film to rival *The Godfather*. The Who's singer acquired an option on the rights to *The Profession of Violence*, courtesy of an informal agreement, signed in 1979, between film producer Don Boyd and John Pearson, and had

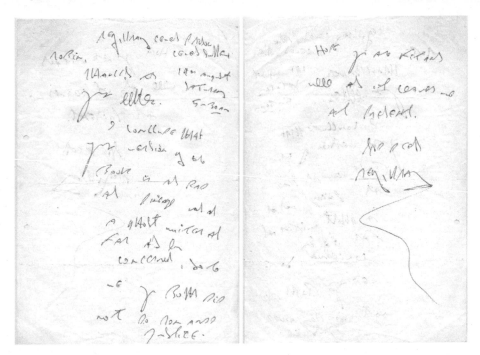

McGillary Lewes Prison   Lewes Sussex   19th August   Saturday   5-30AM
Robin, Thanks for your letter. I conclude that your version of the book is as bad as
Dineage was as a ghost writer as far as Im concerned so to me to you both did not
do Ron and I justice. Hope you are fit and well as it leave me at present.
God Bless   Reg Kray

set his heart on producing a film that would be taken seriously. Dealing with
the twins' unpredictable, and often unreasonable, demands proved too much
of a headache however, and when an actor/producer, named Ray Burdis,
offered to buy the rights from him, Daltrey accepted. Ronnie, Reg and Charlie
were hugely disappointed, because they liked Roger and the type of film he
wanted to make, but in the end, they didn't care who made it, as long as they
all got a big chunk of money.

Also disappointed were the Harris twins, from Manchester, whose dream
of appearing in the film died with Daltrey's. Ronnie and Reg did keep in touch
for a while, but when Mike and Chris got involved with girls, they were phased
out. "I think they felt betrayed, as we weren't readily available as we had been,"
Mike told me. "When we did suggest visits they were always too busy. They
had high expectations for us and when it became clear they couldn't hold our
interest as intently as a girl's body, they seemed to realise they had lost their
power. We were no longer useful."

Charlie and his brothers needed someone experienced in contract
negotiation, and they had the ideal man in Wilf Pine, who, by now, was

handling Ronnie's financial affairs and – albeit reluctantly – some of Reg's.

Burdis and his partner in Fugitive Films, Dominic Anciano, had persuaded a public company, named Parkfield, to finance the film – to be called *The Krays* – and at the end of May, 1989, Wilf and Charlie were invited to a meeting at its offices, near Heathrow, with Burdis, two senior Parkfield executives, and Jim Beach, manager of the rock group, *Queen*, and a partner in Fugitive Films.

Wilf was to talk for Ronnie and Charlie, and took Charlie with him. Not wanting Wilf to represent *him*, Reg had sent one of Peter Gillett's friends, Nick Treeby, who had visited him in Parkhurst. Wilf was happy with Treeby, who he considered a genuine and likeable guy, and a good businessman, but was dismayed that Treeby had brought Gillett, who was considered an embarrassment by the underworld elite. Having managed successful bands for over twenty years, Wilf knew his way around big business boardrooms, and he was confident of Treeby, who knew enough to follow his lead and not make a fool of himself. But Wilf and Charlie were worried that Gillett's cocksure arrogance and naivety might let them down.

For half an hour or so, the wannabe gangster said nothing, just listened as Wilf – briefed on the finances of the movie business by Hemdale creator John Daly – stuck out for the best possible upfront deal. When the Parkfield bosses seemed to be prevaricating, Wilf decided on a bluff. "Well, gentlemen, why don't we leave you to mull it over. Let us know what you think and we'll have a further meeting."

"No, no," the chief executive said, hurriedly. "We want to put this to bed today. We want to do a deal."

At that, Gillett rose from his seat, glared at the two executives and announced, with all the eloquence he could muster: "I've got a message for you from Reg. If I'm not in the film, there ain't gonna be no fucking film."

Charlie, whose financial future rested on the meeting, almost jumped out of his chair; Wilf restrained him; Treeby looked down, embarrassed. Wilf snapped: "Peter. Sit down. Just sit down."

"All I'm saying is if I ain't got no part in the film…"

"Why don't you and Nick go and have a cigarette, or something," Wilf told him, stiffly.

To Wilf's and Charlie's relief, the two of them left the room. Once the door closed behind them, the chief executive looked at Wilf. "Okay, tell us what you have in mind."

"I'll be honest with you," Wilf said. "One figure and one figure only. And I'm not moving off it."

"What is it?"

"Two hundred and fifty thousand."

In 1989, that was a lot of money, particularly when the film script could have been written from information in the public domain, without needing the Krays' approval.

The two executives talked quietly among themselves, then asked Wilf and Charlie to leave them alone for a few minutes. Once outside, Charlie's quiet demeanour and genteel manner disappeared. "Where's that jumped up little cunt. I'm going to fucking…"

"Charlie," Wilf said, putting his arm round him. "Let it go. Please."

Suddenly Gillett and Treeby appeared. Gillett strutted over to Charlie and Wilf and started talking at them.

"Do you mind, Peter," Wilf said. "We're talking." They then ignored Gillett until he got the message and swaggered back to Nick.

A few minutes later, they were all called back into the boardroom. As they filed in, Wilf drew Gillett to one side: "Please keep your fucking mouth shut," he said. "Don't mention that thing again. Just sit there and listen. Don't say a word."

Within minutes, the £250,000 – less £25,000, to be paid on the film's release - was agreed and a letter of intent signed. Neither Gillett, nor Treeby, knew the figure Wilf had asked for, until he told them when they left.

"That's fucking great," Gillett said. "Wait till I tell Reg. He'll be pleased with what we done today. Good boy, Nick."

Charlie and Wilf stared at each other in disbelief, then left the building, making sure they went in the opposite direction to Reg's trusted representative and his mate. When they reached the Prince Albert, in Egham, Charlie was still steaming over Gillett's crass behaviour, and it took several large ones to calm him down.

*

Although no one mentioned it to me, Ronnie was being visited regularly that year by a bubbly blonde, named Kate Howard, who had been 'passed on' to Ronnie after visiting Reg, in Parkhurst. She was a kissogram girl, in her early thirties, and Ronnie was so smitten that, one morning in June, he told Wilf he wanted to marry her.

"But you're already married," Wilf said.

"Elaine and I haven't had contact for nearly two years, so I'm going for a divorce on the grounds of irretrievable breakdown," he said. "Anyhow, the marriage was never consummated," he added, with a chuckle.

Until then, Ronnie had not discussed the matter with anyone, except his solicitor, Stephen Gold. Now that divorce proceedings were going to start, however, Gold advised Ronnie that it was unlikely he'd be released to attend the hearing, in Portsmouth, and he should ask Wilf to give evidence on his behalf. Wilf agreed and, several weeks later, testified that Elaine had refused to have any contact with Ronnie for the last two years. Since she'd failed to respond to the legal papers, the judge granted the divorce – but warned that he had taken an unusual step and the case must not set a legal precedent. I never got a chance to ask Elaine why she didn't go through with the divorce *The Sun* had splashed so prominently; sadly, she fell ill and died not long afterwards.

*

For Charlie, his share of the film deal meant he could do what he'd always done best – party! Even after paying everyone who'd lent him money against his share of the film, he still had more than he'd had in his life, and he wasted little time spending it – mainly on Judy. Throughout her married life, her idea of an exciting night out was going to the local *Berni Inn*, but, now, Charlie introduced her to the West End high life – cocktails at five-star hotels, dinner at fashionable restaurants and nightcaps in Mayfair clubs before falling into a taxi for the twenty mile drive to South London. He would take her shopping, too, and being one who liked to give, more than receive, he delighted in surprising Judy with gifts he'd been unable to afford before.

It was good to see Charlie so happy after the miserable time he'd endured, though Sue and I did often wonder what Diana would have thought, had she known that Charlie had broken their pact of not getting "heavily involved" with someone else. Although he was seeing at least four other women – far more glamorous and sexy than Judy – it was clear that Charlie had fallen for Di's cleaner in a big way and was spending as much time at her home in Sanderstead, as he did at Diana's. It was none of our business, however, so we said nothing, just made sure we saw as little of Judy as possible.

*

Watching *The Krays* being filmed, in the Rotherhithe area of South East London, was exciting for Charlie, but the more he saw, the more he told me he feared the outcome. Having read the script, he knew the film Burdis and Anciano were making was nothing like the one Roger Daltrey had had in mind, but he wasn't prepared for the appalling inaccuracies: there were so many he felt the scriptwriter was talking about other people, not him and his brothers. Having paid Charlie £5,000 on top of the advance to be "technical advisor," one would have thought the film-makers would have been keen to capitalise on his knowledge, to make the movie authentic. But all he was asked to "advise" on, he told me, was the look of the house the Krays had lived in, and the décor in their clubs. He couldn't help feeling that the producers had missed a great chance: there were so many dramatic incidents that *had* happened, there was no need to exaggerate anything. By sticking to the facts, they could have made a spectacular, compelling movie that would have been taken seriously, as well as good box office. As it was, they made a ludicrous one that appealed only to those who bought into the myth that Ronnie and Reg were Britain's answer to Al Capone.

What angered Charlie most was the way his mother was portrayed: she never swore in her life – not even 'bloody' – but, early in the film, she is heard yelling 'Bollocks' to a doctor treating one of the two-year-old twins for a double hernia. Charlie confided in me that even Billie Whitelaw, the actress playing Violet Kray, knew the scriptwriter had got it wrong. She asked to have a quiet word with Charlie and, over a cup of coffee in her trailer, admitted that she knew the portrayal of Violet was inaccurate.

"Unfortunately, I have to say what's in the script and play the part to suit the director," she said. Charlie told Billie he understood, and it was enough for him to know that she was aware that his mum was nothing like the person the public was going to see.

The only aggravation for Charlie, as he enjoyed the movie windfall that summer, was Reg. He'd promised Peter Gillett a part in the film, but had been told the young man needed an Equity card. He'd asked Charlie and Wilf to pull what strings they could, but they hadn't bothered; neither liked Gillett and didn't want anything to do with him. Now, Reg had turned to Joey Pyle, arguably the top man in London's underworld and long-time friend of all three Kray brothers. But he, too, disliked Gillett and had done nothing about it. Reg was constantly on the phone, wanting to know what was happening, but the three of them passed the buck, hoping the problem would go away.

*

Bobby McKew was everything Charlie would have liked to be – a serious, respected underworld figure, but also an intelligent, well-connected businessman with all the social graces, and always welcome in the highest circles. Bobby adored the old charmer, too, and, in the seventies, had boosted Charlie's income by arranging for him to have the T-shirt franchise during fellow Irishman Richard Harris's run in the musical, Camelot, at London's Apollo Theatre. Charlie had never forgotten that much-needed favour.

Being a significant part of London's clubland, Bobby saw a lot of the twins in the sixties, but, until now, had no desire to visit them, especially Reg, whom he'd never liked. However, when Charlie invited him to go to Broadmoor, with him and one of the film's producers, Ray Burdis, Bobby felt it might be interesting to see Ronnie again. They all had a pleasant enough afternoon, but, as his visitors prepared to leave, Ronnie asked to speak to Bobby on his own. Once outside, Charlie couldn't wait to ask Bobby what his brother had said.

"He told me he remembered me as someone who had a lot of contacts," Bobby said. "He wanted some machine guns, pistols and grenades and wondered if, with my Irish connections, I could get them for him. He had a list of all the people who'd helped put him away, and wanted them to know how grateful he was."

Charlie didn't know whether to laugh or cry.

A few weeks later, Wilf was on a visit to Broadmoor when Ronnie brought up his favourite subject, which, after pretty young boys and money, was what he would do if he was released. Knowing Ronnie's passion for travelling, Wilf prepared himself for the usual stuff about a world cruise, but Ronnie had been daydreaming about having a party – a big party, with lots of guests.

"I'm sure you'd have the biggest party imaginable," Wilf said. "Everyone would come."

"No, no," Ronnie said quickly. "I'd want *you* to arrange it. I'd be the surprise guest of honour."

Wilf frowned, not understanding.

"I'd tell you who to invite," Ronnie said. "But no one would know I was going to be there until I arrived."

"Ok…ay," Wilf said, still not sure where Ronnie was going.

"We'd need a ballroom," Ronnie said. "A ballroom with big doors. At the appropriate time, when everybody's there, I'll come in and you'll introduce me."

"You won't *need* an introduction," Wilf said. "They'll all be cheering. It'll be great."

"Not exactly," Ronnie said. "Because when I tip you the wink, I want you out of there, as quick as you can. And shut the doors behind you."

"What for?"

Ronnie spread his arms wide, each fist clenched. "Because I'll have a hand grenade in this hand and hand grenade in the other, and I'm going to blow us all up. We're all going to go together."

Wilf started laughing loudly.

"You think it's funny?" Ronnie said, offended.

"I think it's fucking brilliant," Wilf humoured him.

"I'm not joking, Wilf," Ronnie said. "That's what I'd like to do."

Wilf was still smiling to himself as he walked to his car. Would he have found Ronnie's fanciful daydream so funny, I wonder, if he'd known about his pal's whispered conversation with the genial Irishman?

*

Predictably, Ronnie couldn't wait to give away his share of the film deal. Much of it went to other patients in Broadmoor - £100 in this envelope, £200 in that one – but he was so moved by a letter from a window cleaner, in Blackburn, that he told Wilf to send him a cheque for £10,000.

"It was by no means a begging letter," Wilf told me. "The guy was just one of hundreds who wrote to Ronnie, and he just happened to mention that he couldn't work because he'd fallen off his ladder and broken his back. Ronnie replied to every letter he received, but only if he thought it was genuine. If he felt someone was trying to have him over, he always had the means to give them a problem, but if anyone was genuinely in need, Ronnie would help. He loved receiving letters where people talked of everyday things, and got to know many families by letter over the years. He always seemed interested in how they were getting on. The window cleaner's letter seemed genuine, but I still went to Blackburn to check, before handing over the cheque."

Such generosity did not surprise Wilf, who told me that, in less than a year, Ronnie gave away more than £60,000 – including £10,000 to him as a thank you for handling the film negotiation. One wonders why he didn't use some of the cash to settle his canteen account, which had now risen to a staggering £7,000!

Reg gave away a chunk of his share, too - £50,000 to Gillett, to put down as a deposit on a house, in Crawley.

*

Later that summer, Wilf was in bed, recovering from a heart attack, when his wife, Ros, took him up a letter from Reg addressed: "To you, one of the three stooges." Reg went on to say that he'd asked him, Charlie and Joey Pyle to get an Equity card for Gillett, but none had done so. "I'm writing to you waste of time people that I've arranged it from in here," Reg continued. "I don't need stooges like you three. So, fuck you…"

Steaming, Wilf was thinking about how to reply, when the phone rang. It was Joey, equally angry.

"Did you get a fucking letter this morning?" he asked.

"Yeah, I got a fucking letter," Wilf said. "Who the fuck does he think he is?"

"What are you going to do?"

"I don't know," Wilf said. "I'm thinking about it."

"Call me when you've thought. We can't let this go."

"Too right."

Wilf was still wondering what to do when the phone rang again. It was Charlie - beside himself.

"Did you get a letter? Reg's calling us the three stooges."

"I know," Wilf said. "Joey's been on."

When he put the phone down, Wilf asked Ros for a writing pad. Not one to mince words, he began, "Dear Reg," then cut to the chase. "Who the fuck do you think you're talking to? How fucking dare you, you fucking liberty-taking…" And so it went on. When he finished, he read his diatribe to Joey and Charlie, who found it hilarious. Then, after photocopying it, Ros posted the letter to Parkhurst.

Feeling better, a few days later, Wilf visited Ronnie. Typically, Ronnie asked about his health, but there was still only one thing on Wilf's mind.

"I had a letter from your Reg," he said. "Joey got the same one. And Charlie."

"Yeah, I heard," Ronnie said. "Reg's had a right go about that. Don't take no notice."

"*Take no notice*!" Wilf said, handing Ronnie his own letter. "Read that."

Ronnie read the letter, slowly. Finishing it, he said: "Fucking hell, Wilf – don't send *that*!"

"I've already fucking sent it," Wilf said, "That's a copy for you. So there's no misunderstanding, when he tells you."

Ronnie laughed. "Oo,oo…even I wouldn't strong it that much with him."

"Fuck him," Wilf said.

The next day, Wilf received another letter from Reg. "Bloody good letter that. You'll have to forgive me, it was one of those bloody days, mate. We're okay, aren't we? Anyway, best wishes to Ros and your family."

Wilf chucked the letter in the bin.

*

Neither Wilf, nor Joey or Charlie, gave a toss whether Peter Gillett was in the movie, but since Reg had got him an Equity card, they felt it only right that Charlie should do all he could to get the young man a part they felt he deserved. Which is why, in a scene where one of the twins has an altercation with a young thug beside a car, Gillett is seen being knocked out. As Charlie said to me after watching the scene: "It couldn't have happened to a nicer bloke!"

*

Early that November, Ronnie married Kate Howard, in Broadmoor's chapel, and, a few days later, Wilf rang me, asking if I would write the story of the "romance" for one of the tabloids. He put me in touch with Kate, and Sue and I had dinner with her – no expense spared, courtesy of Ronnie – at a Chinese restaurant, near her home, in Maidstone, Kent. Kate was a dream to interview and, between the three of us, we got together a cracking two-parter for *The Sun,* which Kelvin MacKenzie felt was well worth what we'd asked for.

The following week, I wrote to Ron, saying how much Sue and I liked Kate, and that she wanted us to visit together. We never managed to, which is a pity because we would have liked to have seen Ronnie and Kate together. We did see a lot of her on her own, however, and even signed an agreement to be her public relations representative. My first suggestion was for Kate to be photographed wearing colourful outfits associated with some of the countries Ronnie longed to visit. I hoped a Sunday paper, and magazine,

Bickley,
KENT

22 November 1989

Dear Ron,

I gather from Kate that you and Reg had a good visit yesterday. I'm so pleased for both of you; it must be bloody awful to build yourselves up for a meeting after so long, only for it to go wrong, like last time.

Ron, thanks a million for your kind gesture in paying for the Chinese meal Kate, Sue and I had on Monday. Once I knew it was on you, I looked on the wine list for some vintage Dom Perignon, but couldn't see any – so you got off lightly with a couple of bottles of Chablis! When you're released, you'll both have a meal on me.

What a delightful and charming young lady your wife is: never short of something to say, always ready to see the funny side, and intelligent, too. Both Sue and I took to her on our first meeting and I'm sure all of us can enjoy a worthwhile relationship.

From where I'm sitting, it was one of your better moves to part company with Mr Treeby. To deal profitably with the media you've got to know the people running things, and how they think. Nick didn't. That's why he made a fool of himself and ended up with nothing to show for his efforts.

Kate said it might be a good idea for me to share one of her visits, so I'll arrange something with her over the next couple of weeks. In the meantime, I'm reading Charlie Smith's sad story and will tell him my views when I come to see you.

Take care, Ron, and thanks again. Your kindness was very much appreciated.

Yours sincerely,

would run them as an amusing picture spread, but, even if they didn't, I was sure they would enhance Ronnie's room. He loved the idea and willingly gave Kate the money. A Fleet Street pal took lovely photographs of Kate in Russian, Indian and Chinese outfits, but, unfortunately, we didn't strike lucky with any of the papers.

Kate loved the photos. So did Ronnie. But they both wanted some more formal, high-quality ones taken, so I suggested I approach the Queen's cousin, Patrick Lichfield, an accomplished photographer I'd met a few years before.

"But he's a Lord, isn't he?" Kate said. "Surely he won't take pictures of a

28th Nov 1989   Ron Kray   Dear Sue   Thank you so much for the food.   It was most kind of you   I am very great full to you May God Bless   Friend   Ron Kray Thank you (Ronnie is referring to some cheese and home-made pickled onions Sue sent him, via Kate.)

Kray twin's wife."

"That won't bother him if he's going to be paid his going rate," I said.

"What do you think that is?" she asked.

"I've no idea," I said. "I'll find out."

So I did. And when I told Kate that Lichfield would cost £2,000, she was thrilled.

"That's fine," she said. "Ronnie wants him to do it and two grand won't be a problem."

Despite her overtly cocky attitude, Kate seemed in awe of meeting titled Royalty and although Lichfield did his best to put her at ease, Kate was plainly nervous. Indeed, when she saw the photos he'd taken, and didn't like some of them, she refused to tell him.

"But you're the paying customer, Kate," I said. "Patrick wouldn't expect you to pay for something you're not happy with. He'll shoot you again, I'm sure."

"No, it's all right," she said. "I'm not going to make a fuss. There are some that are lovely."

Seeing her pay up without a murmur struck me as supremely ironic. Her notorious husband had gone down in folklore for - among other things - demanding with menaces, and here was his wife, too timid to ask for what she had every right to.

Chapter Eight

DESPITE his fears over the movie, Charlie loved black-tie First Nights and was looking forward to taking his son, Gary and Judy to the premiere at the Leicester Square Odeon, on 26 April 1990. What should have been a memorable occasion, however, was a huge, and embarrassing, disappointment, for Charlie was told he had to pay for all three tickets, which he felt was "a right liberty." With his earnings from the film not quite gone, he could easily have stumped up the money, but, on a point of principle, boycotted the screening and reception afterwards – hosting, instead, a party in his honour at Browns, a fashionable Mayfair nightclub.

He didn't get around to seeing the film until it was released and then wished he hadn't. It was everything he dreaded. Sadly, it wasn't only his mother the film got wrong, he told me; his father was portrayed as an idiotic drunk, when in fact he was a decent man who worked hard all his life for an honest living. In the film, Charlie Snr was so frightened of going to war he went on the run from the Army, but, in reality, he didn't enlist because he hated authority and could not tolerate being told what to do.

Charlie was embarrassed even more by a scene which showed the twins – as young men – fighting each other in a fairground boxing booth, and Charlie running away crying, because he was so worried they might hurt themselves that he wanted his mum to go to the booth and tear them apart. In reality, the twins were only ten when they boxed each other in Victoria Park, Hackney – and Charlie wasn't even there at the time. Moreover, if he had been, being seven years older, he would have stopped the fight himself. He thought *The Krays* was a load of sensationalist rubbish and he was ashamed he played any part in the production. God knows what the twins would think when they heard about it.

The twins reacted as badly as Charlie feared. And, predictably, they blamed him, as the film's paid "adviser," for the "diabolical" inaccuracies they had been told about. Ronnie was so incensed, he couldn't bring himself to talk to Charlie, leaving it to Wilf to tell Charlie he wasn't welcome at Broadmoor. Reg was typically vitriolic, bombarding Charlie with abusive letters, reminding him, yet again, that as far as he and Ronnie were concerned, he was nothing more than a waste of space – a lazy playboy, living off their name. Charlie tried to make light of their reactions, but he was deeply hurt; Sue and I and other close friends, such as John Corbett and Flanagan could see that. He did say, more than once, how he wished he hadn't signed the film contract, but that wasn't really the point: having done so, and accepted five thousand pounds to be "adviser", he perhaps should have stood up to the producers over those scenes that were so fundamentally, and embarrassingly, wrong and said: "You can't possibly portray our mother like that...I won't have you embarrassing me in that fairground scene...how can you have the two murders happening on the same night when there were 20 months between them?" But that could have ruffled a few feathers, maybe made people think he was getting a bit above himself, or, worse, a troublemaker. Sadly, Charlie had such a low opinion of himself he found it impossible to do, or say, anything that might make people think badly of him. After the turmoil he'd been through since his arrest, all he wanted was a quiet life, to get on with people, and have a "nice few quid" to enjoy himself. So, in his role as the film's "adviser," he'd kept schtum, took the money, and hoped everything would turn out all right.

I didn't hear from either of the twins for quite a while after that and, busy with my own projects, I didn't have time or inclination to chase them. But in mid-August, I received a letter from Reg – the first communication since he'd let me know he didn't think much of me as a ghost-writer, one week short of a year before. Seeing the familiar scrawl on the envelope, I was mildly excited: who knows, I thought, Reg might want to renew contact and had an idea that could make some money for us both. It was a brief letter, even by his standards – just seventeen words, on a single sheet of yellow paper – and designed only to wind me up. Clearly dissatisfied with Fred Dinenage's work on *Our Story*, Reg had now collaborated with a music magazine writer, Carol Clerk, on a new book. He didn't say what it was about, only that it was being published the following month. He gave me her phone number, should I want "more details," but neglected to say why he thought I'd be interested enough to want more details. What an odd, impertinent letter, after such a long silence. The only reason I could think of for Reg writing it was that he had the hump with me, and was trying to boost himself in my eyes, make me aware he didn't need me. But why? I was the one who seemed to have been dumped, but perhaps he'd heard I'd been in the States researching one book and was now busy on another one and was miffed that my world did not begin and end with Reginald Kray.

I didn't have time to dwell on it, however, because I had been working virtually non-stop on ghostwriting biographies of the New Kids on the Block and Paul 'Gazza' Gascoigne, and as soon as they were finished, another project came up. "Mad" Frank Fraser had always fascinated me and, after reading a revelatory newspaper article about him, I felt I had to approach him about writing his autobiography. Frank loved the idea of doing the book so much that he turned up half an hour early for our first meeting, but brought his friend, Charlie Richardson, for support. I wasn't in, having popped to the post office, and Sue had the unexpected pleasure of finding South London's most notorious villains on her doorstep.

Over the next couple of months, Frank came to the house, twice a week, to relive his memories on tape. I was thrilled: Frank, an engaging, amusing man with a wicked sense of humour, had a great story to tell, and, like Charlie Kray, was a joy to work with. Neither he, nor I, had felt the need for a written agreement: we'd struck a verbal deal that suited us both, and we trusted each other. The signs were good; he ate with us and even slept over sometimes.

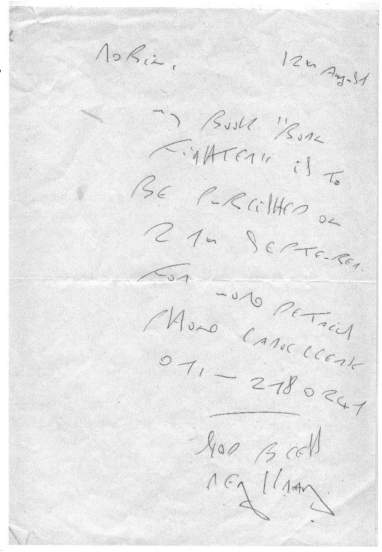

12th August
Robin,
My book
"Born Fighter"
is to be
published on
27th
September
for more
details phone
Carol Clerk
071 278 0241
God Bless
Reg Kray

*

That November, the DVD of *The Krays* was released, and the twins were able to see for themselves what a ridiculous piece of fantasy it was. They reacted differently: Reg was so disgusted, he didn't want to talk about it. In keeping with his positive mental attitude, he felt it was negative rubbish that was best forgotten. Ronnie was angry that, apart from portraying their mother as a foul-mouthed harridan, the script was weak and made the twins lightweight, compared to how they really were. He watched the film in a small room at Broadmoor with Wilf, and spent much of the time shaking his head in disbelief. At the end, Wilf asked what he thought. "A load of shit," Ronnie said. "What we done, we done. If you're going to do the story, do it the way it fucking happened." Something the twins did agree on, however, was Charlie. He'd sold them down the river, they felt. And they wanted nothing more to do with him. Ever.

Then, to add to Charlie's misery, Diana didn't either: she caught him and Judy having sex, and told him to leave her home. Charlie moved in with Judy and her children.

*

In February 1991, Wilf Pine's youngest son, Scott, just twenty-three, hanged himself at the house, in Chertsey, Surrey, where he lived with his wife, Julia. Wilf finds it hard to talk about the death even today, but admits that Reg wrote him "the most wonderful" letter and showed a surprisingly compassionate side to his nature. That meant a lot to Wilf and, while he and Reg would never be buddies, their meetings did – for a while – become less hostile.

Ronnie, on the other hand, was a revelation, and pulled Wilf out of a pit of despair that was threatening to destroy him and his family. Wilf told me: "I was a terrible mess and being extra violent with all the bastards I'd put on the back burner. Joey Pyle did his best to control me, but even he couldn't. Eventually, I went to see Ronnie and was feeling even worse because I'd just learned that Scott had tried to kill himself once before."

"Let me tell you something, Wilf," Ronnie said. "Scott trying once, then doing it again, means it was meant to be. He didn't want to be here. He *chose* to end his life, unlike Teddy Smith. He didn't have a choice."

Wilf looked at Ronnie, not understanding. He'd heard of 'Mad' Teddy Smith, of course: he was a young guy, who'd been involved in the disappearance of Frank Mitchell, the 'Axeman' the twins had sprung from Dartmoor, but he didn't know what Ronnie meant about not having a choice.

"I killed him," Ronnie said. "I strangled the life out of him. He didn't have a choice of living or dying. But Scott did."

Wilf told me he never asked Ronnie *why* he killed Teddy, and Ronnie never volunteered anything. But the conversation made Wilf think, and he started to calm down. Like most of us he felt sorry for Charlie; the twins were his family, after all. Visiting Broadmoor one afternoon that March, Wilf suddenly came out with it: "Ronnie, it's time to forgive and forget. Charlie's your flesh and blood. I want to bring him next time I come."

"Don't," Ronnie snapped.

Wilf let the silence hang in the air for a few moments, then hit Ronnie where he knew he was vulnerable. "Be honest, Ronnie, do you think your dear old mum would like the way you're treating Charlie?"

Ronnie thought for a few seconds, then said; "Okay, bring him down next time. If you must."

Wilf did and the reunion went so well, he was sure that Ronnie would write to Reg that evening, urging him to make it up with Charlie. I don't know what was said, but certainly something happened because a few days later *The Star* newspaper carried an interview with Reg, saying how happy he was that all three brothers had reconciled their differences.

As always with him, however, all was not how it appeared, as I discovered when he wrote to me a few days later. Surprise! Surprise! He was upset with Charlie again, accusing him of setting him up to be used by *The Star* reporter. I had no idea what he was talking about and, when I asked Charlie, he had no idea either. As far as he was concerned, everything was fine now between him and the twins.

That letter from Reg was odd. He started off, putting me in my place for supposedly trying to arrange a meeting with him for someone. "*With respect to all concerned,*" he wrote, "*you are not my visiting agent. So if anyone should wish to visit me they can contact me direct.*"

Then, after whingeing about Charlie, he got to what I felt was the prime purpose for writing: he wanted my help. He'd written a book of his "*Thoughts,*" and thirty poems, and was full of the fact that he was going to publish them himself. This, he considered a challenge, and a story that might interest the papers – was I interested in handling it? If I was, I should let him know – "*by return of post!*" – and he would make the next move. "*But please be positive,*" he added. "*I do not wish to waste time on negative response.*" In case I hadn't appreciated the enormity of the task he was undertaking, he added a pompous postscript: "*I'm sure you'll be able to imagine the hard task to publish from with in beyond the walls. Apart from finance I look for a sense of achievement in all I do. This can be explained in detail should you be in a position to negotiate the story of this challenge.*" Then, to hammer the point that he didn't want me to waste his time, he said that if I was interested, he'd see me on my own. I wrote back, saying I had no time to publicise "Thoughts," but wondered if he could get me a copy of Billy Hill's autobiography. Since Reg also asked for my new phone number, I found it bizarrely comforting to know that I was back in favour – though I was to discover that poor Charlie wasn't. Wilf had seen him getting on so well with Ronnie that he took a chance and went with him to Gartree, where Reg had been transferred. He admits now he should have known better. No sooner had they sat down than Reg started laying into Charlie as usual, venting the fury he'd been bottling up since hearing about his lack of control on the film. Charlie took an abusive, foul-mouthed rant for fifteen minutes, then glared at his brother. "Fuck you," he said, a bitter edge to his normal mild tone. "I don't need this. I'm out of here." And he was, leaving Wilf to do his best to pick up the pieces.

*

Gartree Prison   Near Leicester   20th March Lunch time
Robin, Thanks for letter. With respect to all concerned you are not my visiting agent
etc so if anyone should wish to visit me they can contact me direct. Glad you
enjoyed "Born Fighter". Did Charlie tell you that I went out of my way to get Star
reporter to Lewes to report reconciliation between Ron, Charlie and I – Charlie was
present for a story and has not been in touch since so I was used for benefit of the
media in my opinion by Charlie In 8 hours I wrote basic book on phyllosphy and
(cannot decipher) which all came by inspiration and is called Thoughts   Have also
got about 30 poems which I did over a period of time that I am going to add to
Thoughts to complete it as a book. I intend to publish myself! As you know
publishers are not too keen on poetry. To publish myself I consider a challenge which
I intend to achieve from in Gaol.   I figure this could be a good story plus use of some
of "Thoughts" and poetry.   Let me know if you could handle it at a price by return of
post then Ill make next move but please be positive I do not wish to waste time on
negative response.
God Bless   Reg Kray

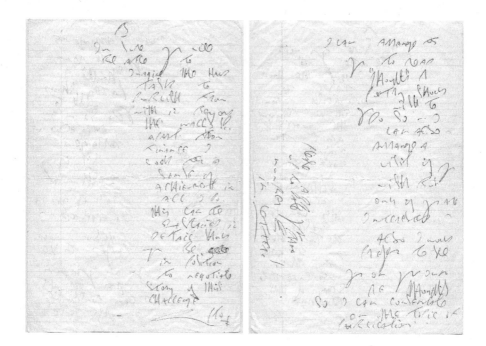

PS   Im sure you will be able to imagine the hard task to publish from with in beyond the walls!?   Apart from finance I look for a sense of achievement in all I do.   This can be explained in details should you be in position to negotiate story of this challenge. PTO   I can arrange for you to read "Thoughts" and poetry should you wish to do so and I can also arrange a visit if you wish but only if you are interested.   Also I would prefer to see you on your own re Thoughts so I can consentate on the topic of publication.   Please add up to date phone number in letter!

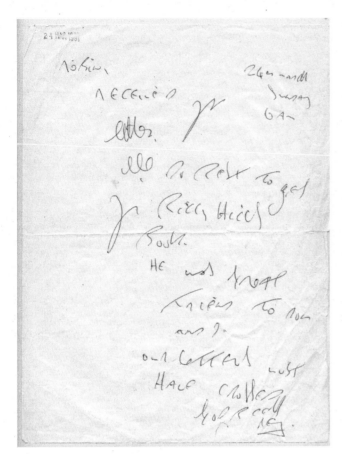

24th March
Sunday 6 AM
Robin, Received
your letter. Ill do
best to get you Billy
Hills book.
He was great friend
to Ron and I. Our
letters must have
crossed.
God Bless Reg

One of the many thousands fascinated by *The Krays* movie was a teenager in the North East, named Steve Wraith: he'd been interested in the Krays since reading *The Profession of Violence* and writing about them for his GCE English Literature exam. Now, having learned from the end-of-film credits where the twins were held, he wrote to each, hoping to strike up a postal relationship. They replied quickly, thanking him politely for writing, but made it clear they could not keep up a correspondence. Steve was disappointed and thought that was the end of it, but, the following February, his mother showed him a magazine article about an eleven-year-old schoolboy named Brad Lane, who was hoping to become Reg's legally adopted son. Steve was intrigued and decided to write to the boy at an address in Doncaster, East Yorkshire, where he lived with his mother, Kim.

In the first week of April, Kim invited Steve to the house to see Brad's bedroom shrine to the Krays. She'd obviously told Reg about Steve because he rang while Steve was there. After asking a few basic questions, Reg told Kim he'd arranged a VO for Steve to visit – with her and Brad – the next day. For the nineteen-year-old, it was the most exciting moment of his life. For Reg, it was the start of a plan he'd been mulling over since Kim had sung Steve's praises. He sensed the enterprising young Geordie could be useful. And he was right.

Several times during their visit, Kim left Brad chatting away on his adoptive "father's" knee, while she went to buy cartons of orange squash from the canteen. Brad would then add whisky from a small bottle hidden in his pocket. Within half an hour, Reg's face was flushed and he was slurring and repeating himself. But he was interested in Steve and when the teenager told him he ran a post office and football magazine, Reg said: "That's it. I knew I had something to ask you. I'll write to you about it," leaving Steve fearing that Reg's interest in him was to rob his post office!

As visiting time closed, Reg gripped Steve's hand in the customary Kray manner, then hugged him. "Thanks for a smashing visit, Steve," he said. "I'll sort out for you to visit my brother, Ron." Then he swigged down the last of his "squash" and walked, unsteadily, towards the cells' areas.

Over the next few weeks, Steve was clearly flavour of the month, because Reg wrote regularly, asking him to keep an eye on Brad, to look for a mansion, with land, where Reg could live on his release – and to visit Ronnie and tell him that Reg disliked Kate and didn't trust her. Steve was excited that he was being given the chance to meet the other twin, but not looking forward to the nine-hour trip to Berkshire.

That visit – with Kim and Brad – was arranged for 19 April. And after pouring them all cups of tea, Ronnie leaned forward, put his hand on Steve's knee, and said: "You don't mind that I'm bisexual, do you, Steve?" Shocked, Steve swallowed a mouthful of tea and told him he wasn't bothered, as long as Ronnie didn't fancy *him*. Much to Steve's relief, Ronnie found that amusing and smiled. "Good, good," he said, softly.

Ronnie spent most of the visit, chain-smoking his JPS and talking to Kim, who passed on messages from friends and associates. But, always the considerate host, he would frequently look at Brad and Steve, asking if they were "all right," before turning back to Kim, and to what was going on in the outside world. Ronnie told them all he was reading a book about world cruises and said he'd like to go on one when he was released. Looking at Brad and Steve he added that it would be lovely to take them, too. He'd send them a brochure.

After an hour or so, Ronnie started asking Steve about his personal life and was interested that he was a keen sportsman who worked out in a gym. He was interested that Steve did a lot of weight-training, and asked him to send some photos. Then, with half an hour of the visit still left, Ronnie decided he'd had enough and was going back to his room, "to beat the crush." A few days later, Steve received a letter from Ronnie, promising him £200 "to cover his expenses." Also included was a travel brochure – something, Steve later learned, that Ronnie sent every new young visitor who took his fancy.

After visiting Ronnie several more times with Brad and his mother, Steve was invited to go on his own, and he found Ronnie very distressed: he had been shown a newspaper cutting about a nineteen-year-old boy, Colin Budd, who had been shot dead by the owner of a gunsmith's he was trying to rob. The story told how the kid idolised the Kray twins – he even had a tattoo of them on his body – and how he wanted to emulate them.

Deeply affected by the story, Ronnie told Steve: "If I have any regrets, it's that we're looked on as heroes by some kids today. There's nothing clever winding up being locked away. Kids have a lot more choices than me and Reg had. You make sure you keep on the right side of the law, hear me?"

*

That summer of 1991, Wilf, still in deep grief, had to go to Gartree to see Reg on a business deal he was putting together. When Reg was agitated, he ripped things into little pieces, and Wilf arrived to find Reg's notes in a pile in front of him. As soon as he sat down, Reg threw a postcard on the table.

"What have you got to say about that?"

Wilf told me he looked at a photograph of Reg with Ronnie, sitting on the settee, smoking, at Vallance Road, and said: "That's a good photo, Reg."

"Look on the back," Reg snapped.

Wilf looked. It said: *Copyright, Charlie Kray.*

"So?" said Wilf.

"*Charlie fucking Kray!*" Reg yelled. "It's not his to give away. It's a picture of me and Ron. We should be having that."

Wilf glared at him. "Who the fuck are you shouting at?"

"You. You're responsible for him."

"Oh, I'm now responsible for your older brother, am I? You fucking…"

That was it, Wilf told me. Suddenly he and Reg were on their feet, eyeball to eyeball, ready to slug it out.

Within seconds, two prison officers were there. "What's going on?" one wanted to know.

"It's okay, we're all right – we're just showing off some moves," Wilf said, quietly.

"Well, sit down again."

They did. But then Reg started again and looked as if he was going to lash out. "Don't even fucking think about it, Reg," Wilf said. "You're flesh and blood like any other cunt. You bleed as well as anybody, you fucker."

And, with that, Wilf got up and went to the toilet. In less than a minute he was surrounded by half a dozen riot squad officers, in helmets, carrying shields.

"What's the problem with Kray?" one asked.

"Fuck all," Wilf said. "We were just having a ..."

"Well, don't," the other man interrupted. "One, you'll be out the door. Two, we'll intervene and you two fuckers won't like it. Understand?"

"Yes," said Wilf.

When Wilf got back to the table, Reg had calmed down.

"You prick," Wilf said.

Most of their meetings were tense, he said. But that was the nearest they had come to blows.

*

Throughout the spring and summer, I was immersed in Frank Fraser's autobiography. Normally, I would not have started writing without a publishing contract and advance, based on a synopsis, but I believed in Frank's story – and him – so much that I made an exception, feeling that, with a completed manuscript we'd get a better deal. We'd shaken hands on a 50-50 split, with me acting as ghost-writer and agent, and got down to work, me interviewing Frank, and Sue transcribing the many thousands of words of his memories.

Despite the severe beatings Frank had taken during forty years in various prisons, his memory was excellent and, equally important, he was aware that he needed to give me emotion and poignancy to make the book more than the usual blood-and-guts gangster's tale. He was thrilled to see his story on paper: he'd sit on his own in the study, reading the latest segment, then come out, happy. Once, it was clear he'd been crying. "It's lovely, Robin," he said. "It's as though you were there."

Sue's mother, Betty, was living with us, after the death of Sue's father – sadly, as we knew, with only months to live herself – and Frank would play up to her, making her laugh. One lunchtime, eating fish and chips in the garden, Betty bit on a crispy chip and lost part of a tooth. The Richardsons' so-called enforcer, who supposedly extracted teeth from villains who'd upset the brothers, patted her consolingly on the shoulder. "Don't worry, Bet," he said, smiling wickedly. "I've got me pliers to get the rest of it out."

Unfortunately Frank had a new girlfriend, Marilyn Wisbey, daughter of Great Train Robber Tommy Wisbey, and when he brought her to Bickley to meet Sue and I, she quickly made it clear she didn't think much of the deal Frank and I had agreed verbally.

"He should be on sixty per cent," she said. "And you should both have a contract drawn up by a lawyer."

I pointed out that the 300,000 words Sue had transcribed, and the 50,000 I'd written, on the basis of a handshake, was proof enough of our good faith.

Why was there any need for a legal contract when Frank and I had proved, over many months, that we trusted each other? But Frank was under Marilyn's thumb and he now insisted we *should* have a legal document, changing the 50-50 deal we'd agreed.

I was furious: I didn't think Frank should be trying to move the goalposts so far down the line. I knew I was cutting my nose off to spite my face, but I told Frank he was out of order, and walked away from the deal. Frank wasn't happy; I'd called his bluff and he didn't like it. But I was less concerned with his feelings than those of Kelvin MacKenzie, who had shelled out £5,000, on the basis of my synopsis, to secure first serialisation rights of Frank's book. I now had to break it to Kelvin that I'd have no say in the serialisation. Kelvin would have had every right to ask me to repay the money, but what chance would I have of getting Frank's half share, which I'd given him in cash, in April. Happily, Kelvin was as understanding as he always was with me and, as they say, wiped his mouth over the debt. That made me feel even worse because I'd persuaded him to pay Frank £1,000 in cash for information that would expose corrupt police – which Frank had not done. So much for the "my word is my bond" code of London's self-righteous, but self-serving, underworld.

In the fourth week of August, after Frank and I had terminated our friendship with a heated phone conversation, he was shot by a motorbike pillion passenger outside a nightclub in Clerkenwell. When I rang St. Bartholomew's Hospital, asking how he was getting on, Frank was quick to praise his deal-breaking girlfriend. "Marilyn was marvellous, Robin - she didn't tell the police my real name," he said. "She coped brilliantly – better than Sue would have done."

Who said the age of charming old-world courtesy and gratitude was dead?

Chapter Nine

EIGHT days after Frank was shot, Reg wrote to me, about Brad Lane. At that time, I hadn't met Steve Wraith and knew nothing about Brad, apart from what I'd read in the papers. I'd written to Reg, asking if it was true that the boy had changed his name to Kray by deed poll. On 31 August, he replied, confirming it was – adding that only narrow-minded people would view the relationship negatively. I didn't know what to think, but I certainly wasn't going to dwell on the implications of Reg's interest in such a young boy. Having wasted so much time on Frank Fraser, I now needed another project to generate some money – so I decided to approach Ronnie about an idea I'd been mulling over since sitting through that dreadful movie.

Eager to see him as soon as possible, I rang the one person I knew spoke to him every day – a sweet-natured, very efficient woman, who acted as the twins' secretary. Stephanie King was around forty-five and lived on a modest housing estate in Nottingham. Earlier that year, she had written to Reg, asking his help with a charity event, and, although she never met either of the twins, she became their Miss Fixit – a willing and reliable secretary, who, for the next few years, would write letters and make phone calls and generally act as a go-between for what passed as a social life for Ronnie and Reg.

Like everyone else close to the twins, I never met her but she was always friendly and helpful on the phone, just as she was that day in September 1991, when I called asking to see Ronnie as soon as possible. She confirmed a visit the following week.

Over the customary Barbicans and pots of tea, I told Ronnie what I had in mind. Like he and his brothers, I said, I was shocked and disappointed that *The Krays* movie had ignored many of the more dramatic incidents in their lives – the time Reg walked into the Epsom mental hospital and Ronnie walked out, for example, and the tragic circumstances in which poor Frances killed herself. These emotionally-charged episodes could make riveting viewing in a TV documentary, I said, particularly with key people speaking about them at authentic locations. To my delight, Ronnie loved the idea as much as me, but shook his head when I suggested taping him for his own memories. "I don't like hearing my voice," he said.

Obviously, a TV documentary could be made without any of the Krays speaking, but what a coup it would be if even one of them was heard describing real events. So, knowing Ronnie's love of the countryside, I said: "Think of the impact you'd have, explaining to viewers how happy you were in Suffolk during the war. That's a side of Ronnie Kray few people know. We could even film the house you lived in and fields where you played."

That did the trick. "Okay, Robin," he said. "When do you want to start?"

"I can't start before next week," I said, smiling.

"You're keen," Ronnie said, returning the smile.

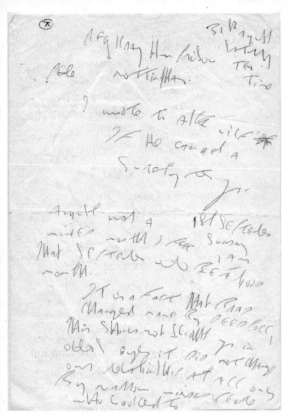

Reg Kray HM Prison   Pele Nottingham   31 August Saturday Tea Time
I wrote to ask Wilf if he can get a surety for you.
1st September   Sunday   1 AM
August was a mixed month I feel that September will be a good month. It is a fact that Brad changed name by deed poll. This should not slight you in others eyes it did not change our relationship at all only by narrow minded people who looked to slight you.

I could say a lot more on the subject but to do so would encourage the narrow minded. I personally do not feel they merit interest to make topic if whats your mortgage position etc. Financing these days?! I (cannot decipher) write to Lee Hollister each week Don't even know him My mail gets more daily and it even more so now Born Fighter is out in Paper back it has just had order of 17,000 copies Sorry to learn of your ankle strain.

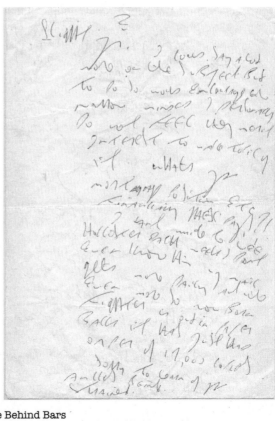

One afternoon the following week, I walked into Broadmoor's visiting hall, thankful that security was so lax that no one had detected the cassette tape recorder in my inside jacket pocket. I handed Ronnie a packet of JPS and chatted about this and that until his can of Barbican and my pot of tea arrived. Then, I placed the recorder unobtrusively among them and switched on. As usual, the din was hardly ideal for such a serious taping session, and I feared that transcribing our conversation would be difficult. But I had no choice.

Unlikely to endear myself to Ronnie by starting off with the murders, I decided to warm him up by asking him about that wartime evacuation. By reliving happy childhood memories, I felt he would be relaxed, articulate and, hopefully, amusing, but he was irritatingly stilted – almost monosyllabic - and, frustratingly, I was forced to prompt him more than I wanted to. Not only did he hate being recorded, he clearly didn't like talking about himself.

I knew from *Me and My Brothers* that Charlie had gone to Suffolk, with the eight-year-old twins, and their mother, and had worked in a fish and chip shop, and later, as a mattress factory teaboy, so I was surprised when Ronnie said he couldn't remember him. "It was just me and Reg and my mother," he said. "We stayed with Mrs Styles in a mansion. We liked the countryside. The quietness. Peacefulness. Fresh air. Nice scenery. Totally different to London. In the winter, we used to go sledging on a big hill, Constitution Hill."

And in the summer? "We used to go apple scrumping. Very nice. Very nice there." Cowboys and Indians? I ventured. "Yes, we used to play Cowboys and Indians," he said, prompting me to remember that their friend Jeff Allen, who hid them from the police, at his house in Stowmarket, had told me Ronnie had accidentally shot a friend in the eye with a slug gun. "I know about the gun," I said. "I'll come on to that later."

Ronnie wanted to tell me about it now, though. "Yeah, the slug gun – I shot someone called Dickie, in the eye. Nice fella he was, a friend of mine. We were messing about. I accidentally shot him in the eye."

Although Mrs Kray took her boys back to the East End after about a year, the country life had made such an impression, I wondered how long it had taken for them to return. "We were nineteen," Ronnie told me. "We used to go there every weekend. We used to go cycling along country lanes. We'd go to antique shops." Surprised, I asked what they bought. "Clocks, ornaments, different things," Ronnie said. "We'd go to local inns and have a drink there. And a sandwich. I was drinking brown ale at the time, and gin and tonic. Reg would have a gin and tonic, too, and a light ale."

It wasn't until I asked whether they took their mates with them that I realised Ronnie wasn't talking about Suffolk, but Steeple Bay, 20 miles from Southend, in Essex, where the family owned a caravan. "We went there every weekend," Ronnie said, "to get away from the hurly burly of London life." The twins paid for everything, he said, but wouldn't say why. I was keen to know whether he regretted being so generous to guys who later betrayed him and Reg, and whether he ever heard from them, but Ronnie just answered Yes and No. I complained, gently, that he was making it hard for me, but he didn't react, making it clear our "interview" was more of an ordeal than a joy and he'd be glad when it was over.

The locals were very nice to him and Reg, he said. Some knew who they were, from photographs they'd seen in the papers, but it didn't make any difference. "They liked us," Ronnie said. "We got on well."

"You weren't looking for trouble."

"No," Ronnie said. "We never looked for trouble. It came to us."

That was interesting, I said, and asked him to expand on it, but he just said: "It used to find us. I don't know why." He did agree, though, that they had a reputation for being tough and were a target for other villains, who wanted to enhance their own reputations. I found it interesting that Ronnie quickly pointed out that no one had overpowered them, but he made it clear he didn't.

"You don't want to talk about your violent past, do you?" I said.

"No," he said. So, frustrated and disappointed, I dropped it and ordered another cup of tea while thinking of ways to encourage Ronnie to relax, worry less about the tape, and open up.

I asked him to tell me about the good life he and his brothers enjoyed in the sixties, when they were reportedly making a thousand a week.

"Yes," Ronnie said. "At Esmeralda's Barn [a Belgravia casino they had taken over]. We had nice cars. Nice clothes. Jewellery. Went to pubs and clubs and parties, enjoying ourselves. We mixed with the rich, poor, famous, infamous."

"Can you name some?" I asked.

"Lord Effingham. Tom Driberg, the MP, Joe Louis, Henry Cooper, Sonny Liston…"

I asked what places he went to. "Whites Club, I went there with Boothby and met a judge there, name of Cohen…"

I chuckled. "Pity he couldn't have been in Melford Stevenson's place," I said, referring to the Old Bailey judge who'd jailed the twins for 30 years. It was a poor joke and Ronnie didn't react.

Hoping for something new about Ronnie's much-publicised relationship with Lord Boothby, I asked why the peer had taken him to Whites. "No special reason," Ronnie said. "We just met there for a drink, same as other people."

I had to press him. "What did you think about Lord Boothby?"

"Nice man," Ronnie said. "Just a nice man."

Fighting to hide my exasperation, I said: "Can you say a bit more than that, Ronnie? I'm sure there are many nice men around. What attracted you to him?"

"I wasn't *attracted* to him," Ronnie said, showing some emotion for the first time. "He just became a friend of mine. Just a friend. That's all there is to it. Nothing *attracted* me."

I did believe that. But, like most Fleet Street journalists, I knew that

Charlie Kray, with Maureen Flanagan, the "sister" he wished he had had.

Charlie and me, in light suit, at the launch of Me and My Brothers, in 1975. Far right, next to my then secretary, Rita Fenn, is Ken Follett. Far left is my publicity manager Burnett Rigg, next to Charlie's ghostwriter Jonathan Sykes.

Steve Tully, aged twenty-seven,
in Parkhurst, in 1985.

Iris Burton, Editor of
Woman's Own from 1980-86.

Charlie, with the Harris twins, Mike, left, and Chris.

Flanagan and Suzanne Mizzi, with George Best, in Blonde's night club.

Tragically, Suzanne died on 22 May, after a year-long fight against cancer. She was a warm, very genuine, human being, who is much missed. As husband Frank Camilleri - father of their two children, George, six, and Sienna, seven - says: "She was beautiful, inside and out."

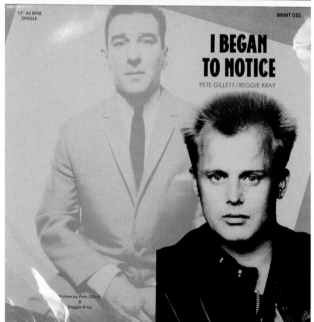

The cover of the record Reg and his Parkhurst pal made, in 1986.

The author's wife, Sue, in the garden of their Kent home, where Charlie worked on the re-write of *Me and My Brothers*, in 1987.

Charlie with the author, after a signing session for *Me and My Brothers*.

Kate Kray, dressed up as a Russian for Ronnie's enjoyment, shortly after their wedding, in 1989.

Tom Petrie, far right, with Sun Editor Kelvin MacKenzie, centre,
and fellow executive Martin Dunn.

The mansion, in Hadleigh, Suffolk, where the twins and Charlie were evacuated,
early in the Second World War. It is now on the market for £1million. Photograph by
Richard Barber, a friend of the author.

Bobby Ramsey, left, at an East End charity function, with Billy Webb, who attacked
Ronnie in Broadmoor to avenge the death of his brother, who never recovered from
being beaten up by Ronnie, and died prematurely.

Charlie and Steve
Tully, with Brad
Lane, after visiting
Reg, in Lewes
Prison, in 1989.

Steve Wraith, with Brad Lane, outside Broadmoor.

Steve Wraith, with Brad's mother, Kim Lane, outside Broadmoor.

Reg, with Lady Alice Douglas and Simon Melia, after the performance of Macbeth, in Blundeston Prison, in 1993. Photo: Reuters.

Cherri Gilham, the model Reg wanted to get engaged to, in 1993.

Dave Courtney, his wife, Jenny, left, her twin sister, Julia, and one of their friends, Ian Tucker, outside *The Blind Beggar* pub, while promoting the *Release the Krays* rap recording, in 1993.

Charlie, with Dave Courtney, after visiting Reg, in Maidstone Prison, in 1994.

Reg, in reflective mood, at Ronnie's funeral, in March 1995.

Inside St. Matthew's Church, in Bethnal Green, for Ronnie's funeral: the author and wife, Sue, are far right.

Charlie and Reg, sharing their grief, approaching Ronnie's graveside, at Chingford Cemetery.
Photo: Tony Furby.

Reg, at the grave of his first wife, Frances Shea, after Ronnie was laid to rest.
Picture by Cherri Gilham

Dave Courtney, with some of his "Firm," on holiday, in Tenerife.

Charlie, with the author's son, Rob, and, from left, daughters Jayne, Katrina and Ali, at a party at the author's home, in October 1995.

Judy Stanley, with John Corbett, left, and another of Charlie's friends, Mick Morris, on their way to Redbridge Magistrates' Court, after the arrest.
Photo: Press Association

Charlie's girlfriend, Judy Stanley, and the author, leaving Ilford police station, after Charlie's arrest on drugs' charges, in 1996. Photo: Press Association

Steve Wraith, at a charity function with Chris Lambrianou, whose autobiography, *Escape from the Kray Madness*, the author ghosted.

The author with Barbara Windsor. The picture was taken by celebrated showbusiness photographer Terry O'Neill, who was hired to photograph the cover of Barbara's autobiography, *All of Me*, which the author ghosted.

Wilf Pine and his wife Ros, with Joe Pyle, centre.

The author's wife, Sue.

One of Reg's Parkhurst paintings.

Ronnie's painting of the stream that flowed through Jeff Allen's Suffolk home. When Flanagan asked Reg why his brother painted the swans black, he said: "Because they're elegant, vicious bastards – just like us!"

Boothby's interest in Ronnie was more than just business, which was what both had always implied. Referring to the 1964 scandal when the *Sunday Mirror* published a photo of him and Boothby together, insinuating they were having a homosexual relationship, I asked: "How did you react to all that business? Were you bothered by it?"

"We *were* bothered by it," Ronnie said. "But it wasn't true, was it?"

I was aware that I was on dangerous ground that could irritate him and, perhaps, scupper the interview. But having Ronnie in front of me, with a tape running, I had to press him. "So you went to Whites," I said. "Did Boothby take you to any other places?"

"I had dinner in the House of Lords," he said.

"What did you think about the House of Lords?"

"It was all right," he said. "Interesting."

"Was it just the one trip?"

"No, I went a couple of times."

"Did Reg go?" I asked.

"No."

I groaned inwardly. What should have been an enlightening and revelatory interview was bland and boring. And spectacularly uninteresting. Apart from having a Kray twins' thin, reedy voice on tape, I had nothing of any consequence, and was relieved when the first side of the tape ran out. I made an excuse to go to the loo, determined to come back and try to force something useful out of Ronnie. But, frustratingly, he seemed to have decided to clam up even more.

Having ordered another Barbican and pot of tea, I turned the tape over and switched on. Brightly, I asked Ronnie to tell me some amusing stories of their good life in the sixties.

"I can't think of any amusing stories," Ronnie said.

"I'll tell you one I like," I said. "The one about the donkey."

At the twins' nightclub, The Kentucky, in 1962, a midget singer, named Little Hank, was about to perform when Ronnie emerged from the wings, leading a donkey on a leash. As Little Hank sang his opening number, Ronnie stood alongside, straight-faced. Afterwards, he led the donkey to the bar and it stood next to him, patiently, while he had a few drinks. Later, he gave the donkey to a club member for one of his children. At around 3 a.m., Ron was woken by the grateful recipient, who wanted to know what to do to stop the donkey's hee-haws. "Put a sack over its head," a sleepy Ronnie said, and went back to bed.

I found the episode hilarious, but Ronnie clearly didn't. "No, I don't want to talk about that," he said.

"Why?" I wanted to know.

"There's nothing to tell," he said. "I took a donkey into a club, that's all. I put a sack over its head, so it wouldn't bray. In The Kentucky. I took it in there for a laugh."

"You must admit it's a bit unusual, Ronnie."

"Yes, it was," he said. "But sometimes we did unusual things."

"Can you remember why you did it?"

"Just for a laugh. That's all."

"And did it produce a laugh?"

"It did, yeah."

For some obscure reason he didn't explain, the episode triggered a memory that interested Ronnie. "Billy Hill came into our club."

I had heard of Billy Hill. But, to get Ronnie talking about him, I asked who he was.

"He was the old gang boss," he said. "He's dead now. He left a million pound. He was a very nice man. He had a place in Tangier. We stayed there... he invited me and Reg over there. An interesting place, Tangier."

I was aware of Ronnie's love of the Moroccan city. Several months after the Cornell murder, Charlie had suggested the twins leave the country for a while, and they'd stayed at Billy Hill's home. Taking Charlie's advice for once, they had told no one outside the family, and kept in touch with him by calling a phone box in Bethnal Green Road, every Tuesday and Thursday night at 8 p.m. It always amused Charlie; he said he felt like a spy on a top-secret mission!

Unfortunately for him, one piece of advice the twins didn't heed was given by Billy Hill himself. In 1961, when the money was rolling in from *Esmeralda's Barn*, they got the first warning that the police were keeping an eye on all three of them. First, Ronnie and Charlie were charged with loitering with intent to steal from a parked car; then Reg was accused of stealing jewellery from an old lady's house. Both cases were thrown out, which gave the police the hump. When they retaliated by closing *The Kentucky* and another of their clubs, *The Double R*, Billy Hill summoned the twins to his West London home. They were fortunate to have an older brother who was not involved in villainy in any way, he told them, and it was vital to keep it that way. Charlie would always be an ally – a weapon they could use to set legal wheels in motion, should things go badly with the law again. "*Never* involve Charlie in anything crooked," Hill urged them.

As the police trusted Charlie, the twins asked him to speak with someone influential to find out why they were marked men. Charlie met secretly with two high-ranking CID officers who – for a cash payment – showed him telexes to Scotland Yard, from forces in and around Britain and other countries, giving details of where the twins had travelled, and who they had met. There was a lot of communication on Tangier and their visit to Billy Hill's home.

"So what did you find interesting about Tangier?" I asked, aware of Ronnie's penchant for good-looking young boys; which he'd admitted to me on a previous visit.

"The Kasbah. Clubs. Bars. People," he said.

"Yes." Then, taking a deep breath, I said. "You did say to me that you found the boys very attractive. Do you remember talking about that?"

"No," Ronnie said, rather sharply.

"I didn't think you would," I said, forcing a chuckle. "How many times did you go there?"

For the first time, Ronnie brightened. He told me he'd been to West Africa four times, to explore a building project with the son of a Labour MP, and was thrilled to have been shown the federal prison. He was eager, too, to tell me that he'd seen a tribal dance – "very interesting" – and had eaten monkey meat and drunk palm white wine. Suddenly he seemed keen to talk and quickly went on: "I saw a bullfight in Spain… Barcelona, I think. Xavier Cugat, the bandleader, was there at the same time, just in front of me." Ronnie said he enjoyed the bullfight, but felt it a cruel sport. Now that Ronnie was more chatty, I asked him if he'd done anything else that was unusual – not that a bullfight was unusual.

"I went to a brothel in Turkey," he said, with the hint of a smile. "Istanbul."

"Why did you go there?" I asked, stupidly.

"To have a bird – a girl," Ronnie said. He grinned. "What do you think I went there for? Me supper?"

We both laughed, and I seized the moment to ask what I'd been building up to.

"What do you say to those people who believe what they read in the papers? That you're totally gay?"

"I'm bisexual," he said. "Not gay."

"Have you always been bisexual?"

"Yes," he replied, with a loud, impatient sigh.

Sensing Ronnie was as near as he'd get to enjoying talking about sex, I asked him, whether, as a late teenager, he went out with girls, or was he attracted to boys?

"Both," he said.

"Even at that early age – seventeen to twenty?" I wanted to know.

"Yeah. Both."

"Was Reg aware of this?" I asked. "Or was it a secret that you wanted to keep to yourself?"

"Up to that time, it was a secret."

"Up to what time?" I asked, excited at the prospect of getting something revelatory.

"Up to when I was about twenty-five," Ronnie said. "Something like that."

"How can you keep something like that secret for so long?"

"You can if you want to."

"From a twin brother!"

"Yes," Ronnie said, emphatically.

That was a hugely interesting point and I seized on it. "I don't know if you can remember, Ronnie, but why did you want to keep it secret from Reg. I mean, it's…"

"I don't know," he interrupted. "But, then, I thought I'd let everyone know. And I did."

Ronnie clearly wanted to drop the subject, but I couldn't let it go. I asked if he had been worried, or even ashamed, that he was attracted to the same sex.

"I was not worried *or* ashamed," he said. "It was just a private thing I preferred to keep to myself."

"You *are* a private person, aren't you, Ronnie?"

"Yes," he replied. "Even though everyone seems to think they know everything about me."

I feared I might be taking a step too far, but had to try to get more about Ronnie's sexuality. So I asked what Reg said when his secret came out.

"Nothing," he said. "Nothing at all. He said it was up to me."

What about Charlie?

"He said it was up to me, as well."

"And your parents?"

"They didn't know about it until later."

"Can you remember when it came out?"

"*No*," Ronnie said, showing the first signs of impatience. "I can't remember."

"I know; I appreciate that. I'm just thinking that it's interesting what your mum said when it came out."

"I can't remember."

I said it must have been a traumatic moment for him, but, again, he said he could remember nothing about it. And this time there was a stronger hint of impatience which, I felt, would be foolish to ignore. I asked if he had any stories he could think of and when he said, without hesitation, "I can't think of any off-hand," I thought that might just be about it; that Ronnie had had enough and wanted me to switch off the tape recorder. But he just sat there, smoking one of his JPS, waiting for my next question.

"Let me ask you this, then," I said, taking a new tack. "When the good life is going on, and the money's rolling in, when did it start to go wrong?"

"When we were arrested!" Ronnie replied, deadpan, demonstrating, in one moment, everything I'd heard about him being unintentionally funny. "They was watching us all the time. We just lived with it…got used to it… became a way of life."

"Was there a time when you were really worried that someone very high up had decided the Krays had to…"

"No, we weren't worried about nothing," Ronnie broke in. "We knew they were after us, so we just accepted it. That's all there is to it."

"Did you get a warning that they really meant business?"

"We knew all along they meant business. It kept coming back to us that they were out to nick us."

"Why do you think they didn't?" was my obvious question.

"They didn't have much on us," Ronnie said. "It was only when we were in Brixton they got people who gave evidence against us."

"Do you think you could have gone on forever if the Cornell incident hadn't come along?"

"No," Ronnie said, emphatically. "They probably would have done us for tax evasion."

"Could they have done you for tax?"

"I don't know if they could have done us for tax," Ronnie said. "But they would have tried to."

"Were you evading tax?" I wanted to know.

"Well, we never paid no tax - so you could put it that way."

I cracked up at that. And when Ronnie realised what he'd said, so did he. We sat there, looking at each other, laughing; it was one of those magical moments when you had to be there.

"Yeah," I said, still laughing. "I think you could put it that way. Have you *ever* paid tax?"

"No," he said. "I've never paid tax in my life."

"Has Reg?"

"No."

"I won't ask you about Charlie," I said.

After we'd had our little chuckle, I said: "The tax thing wouldn't have been a long stretch, though, would it?"

"I think it would – for us," Ronnie said. "We'd have got ten years each, I reckon."

We'd been talking for nearly an hour and I was conscious that, for someone who was supposed to be getting together material for a TV series, I'd seemed interested only in revelatory confessions, not dramatic scenes. But Ronnie had not seemed to notice, or, wasn't bothered, so I decided to move on to a subject that had interested me on my last visit. Ronnie wasn't the type to slag off anyone without reason – particularly another criminal – so I was surprised that he had spoken badly of John McVicar, an armed robber, labelled "Public Enemy No. 1" by Scotland Yard in 1970, after escaping from Durham Prison's top-security wing. He was on the run for two years before being recaptured, in Blackheath, South East London, and jailed for twenty-six years. While in prison, he gained a first-class Open University degree in Sociology.

To jog Ron's memory now, I said: "There's been a lot of lies and untruths printed about the Cornell killing, but wasn't there someone who said something that particularly upset you?"

"Yes," Ronnie said, immediately. "John McVicar. He seems to think he knows everything, and he knows nothing. He's just a petty criminal. And he never had no money. He said that when I walked into The Beggar to shoot Cornell, that George said, 'You haven't got the bottle to use it.' Well, he never said nothing. He never said one word to me. I don't know how McVicar thinks he knows, because he wasn't there. He knows nothing about what he's talking about. So, I don't know where he got that rubbish from. He seems to think he's an expert on crime, and he knows nothing. He was a failure at crime anyway. He never had no money. He's just a mug, who thinks he knows everything."

It was the longest I'd heard Ronnie speak in all the time I'd been visiting him. If only I could get him talking like this about other topics.

I asked Ronnie what he thought about McVicar making a living from writing, and he said: "He thinks he's a genius. But he knows nothing. I think he's ignorant. He said bad things about Charlie Richardson which wasn't true. Charlie is a much better person than he'll ever be."

Now that he was opening up, I was eager to know what Ronnie thought of the guys in the Firm, who betrayed him and Reg.

"I despise them," Ronnie said. "They're rats, that's all. No one likes a traitor, do they?"

"Is there *anything* forgiving in you?"

"No," he said. "They're supposed to be villains, aren't they?"

"Do you regard yourself as an out and out villain?"

"No, I don't," Ronnie started, but then stopped himself. "I don't want to talk about that."

A shame, I thought; that would have been interesting. But I pressed on, quickly. "Looking back, do you wish you hadn't done Cornell?"

"It was part of my life," Ronnie said. "I *did* do it. That's all there is to it. Too late to change anything."

I'd always had my suspicions about the motive for the killing – that, some months before, Ronnie had heard that Cornell had threatened "to blow that fat poof away." But, from what I knew of Ronnie, I doubted he would have waited so long to take revenge over such an insult.

So, I asked if it were true that he killed Cornell because of what he was supposed to have said.

To my delight, Ronnie reacted immediately. "He never called me a fat poof in his life. If he had, I'd have killed him then and there. He never called me a fat poof. It's lies and rubbish."

"So, why did you go there that night?"

"Because he issued threats against me. Said he was going to kill me. So, I thought I'd do him first. Best way, innit?"

"So that line about fat poof…"

"Is all lies and rubbish," Ronnie said. He trod on my toes too much. That's why I got him."

"Was it threats to other people, or threats to you?"

"Threats to other people…he just said he was going to kill me, that's all.

He didn't say why. He didn't like me."

"I don't know why," I said, smiling. "You seem a nice enough bloke."

Ronnie laughed, then got up. "I've got to go to the toilet, Robin."

I watched him walk through the hall, head high, looking straight ahead. When he came back, his expression had changed and I could tell he thought the session was over. I had some tape left, however, and had to make the most of it. As soon as he sat down, I said: "We've got about ten minutes of the visit left, Ronnie. What do you want to talk about? What interests Ronnie Kray?"

"Nothing much," he said. "I don't like talking." Then he giggled. "You've already had me talking too long."

Fearing he might think I wouldn't need to tape him again, I asked: "Are you happy with me coming here and talking with you like this?"

He smiled. "Yes, I'm happy with you coming, Robin," he said. Then he glanced at the cassette recorder and sighed: "Is it off now?" The past hour had clearly been an ordeal for him and he hoped it was over. I shook my head.

"No, Ronnie. I'd like to use these last few minutes."

The exchange that followed might not seem to add up to much, but I feel it shows two interesting sides of Ronnie's character: one, his politeness and courtesy; he could easily have turned on me, rudely telling me he'd had enough, but, instead, he answered my questions, albeit briefly; and two, his refusal to boast about his reputation.

I started by asking: "Has there ever been anyone you were frightened of?"

"I wasn't frightened of anyone," Ronnie replied, without a hint of bravado.

"Was fear an emotion you ever felt?"

"I suppose we've all felt fear at times."

"What sort of things made you feel fear?"

"I can't think off-hand."

"There can't be many things."

"I can't really talk about that."

"I think that would be one of the most interesting things to talk about. People think the Kray twins terrorised the East End, putting fear into other people. I think people would assume you've never felt fear yourself."

Ronnie shook his head. "I don't know. I really wouldn't want to talk about it, Robin."

"From what I hear, you never really wanted to be violent."

"We didn't want to be violent," he said, shaking his head again. "We had to be. We lived in a violent world…pubs and clubs, violent times…"

A story that Charlie had told me came into my mind. It was in the Spring of 1965, shortly after the twins had taken over the Hideaway Club, in Soho, and renamed it El Morocco. Ronnie was sitting, chatting to a friend, when he became agitated by two tall, hugely-muscled bodybuilders, shouting and swearing at the bar. Ronnie went up to them. "Excuse me," he said, quietly. "There are ladies present. They don't like your language. Nor do I."

Ronnie never gave anyone the chance to argue with him so, having made his point, he returned to his table. No sooner had he sat down, the guys started mouthing off again. Ronnie put up with it for a couple of minutes, but then his face went white and he went over to them. Grabbing each by the arm, he said: "You're leaving. Don't come back. You're not welcome here." Then bundled them out the door.

Now, in Broadmoor, I said: "What happened when those bodybuilders were swearing at the bar."

Unsurprisingly Ronnie didn't want to talk about it.

"Why?" I asked. "Because it would be boasting?"

"Well, it would be, wouldn't it?" he said.

And, with that, the tape ran out and the visit was over.

*

Playing the tape in the car on the way home, I was disappointed, but, at the same time, quietly optimistic. There was far too much of me on the tape, particularly in the first twenty minutes when Ronnie was self-conscious and inhibited. For some reason – probably paranoia, due to his condition – he seemed wary of giving too much away, as though it were some sort of police interview that might be used against him. And although I hadn't let on, I already knew most of what he was telling me. A couple of years before, Ronnie had given me a typewritten document with brief details about himself and eating monkey meat and drinking palm wine, on the West African trip, was on it. On the positive side, however, I did have some revelatory copy, such as the visit to the Turkish brothel and Ronnie's admission that neither he, nor Reg, ever paid tax. And, of course, I had *him* talking about his bisexuality, and admitting for the first time, on tape, the real reason he'd murdered George Cornell. So, I arrived home that evening, confident that my next taping session would be less like pulling teeth and I'd get the information necessary for a TV proposal.

Chapter Ten

DISAPPOINTINGLY, my next session with Ronnie was not much better; nor the next. Like Reg, he did not enjoy talking about the past, which was obviously a major problem. Part of me felt a TV documentary *was* a goer, but, to be honest, I'd lost heart and, having spent so much time on Frank Fraser, Sue and I now needed a project guaranteed to make money. We'd got the taste for self-publishing with the success of our *New Kids on the Block* book, which had sold more than 800,000 copies around the world. So, when we read that Phillip Schofield was to star in *Joseph and the Amazing Technicolour Dreamcoat*, at the Palladium, we decided to bring out an unauthorised biography of him, to go on sale during his run in the Spring of 1992.

I still found time to go to Broadmoor and, during one visit, in November, Ronnie was, strangely, in the mood to stroll down memory lane. He told me about Bobby Ramsey, a former East End boxer, who the twins knew in their early twenties when they had The Regal billiard hall. One summer night, in 1956, Ramsey, a bodyguard for Jack 'Spot' Comer, so-called King of London's underworld, walked into the Regal, with a pal, and persuaded Ronnie to join them in a revenge attack on a rival East End gang who had beaten him with an iron bar a few weeks before. They drove to a local pub and attacked the brother of one of the gang's leaders with a bayonet, which was found – heavily bloodstained, next to an axe and a crowbar – in Ramsey's car when he was stopped for speeding.

Ronnie got three years for grievous bodily harm, and Ramsey seven, but Ronnie bore no signs of a grudge when he mentioned Ramsey during our visit. Indeed, all he wanted to talk about was Ramsey's boxing prowess and how he could have made a good living from the fight game if he had not become a criminal. He gave me a photograph – with a message on the back – which he wanted me to give to Ramsey. That driving to his old mate's home in Essex meant a two-hour round trip for me would not have crossed Ronnie's mind, and I didn't enlighten him. He clearly wanted me to meet Ramsey, so, the day after I received the photograph, I set off for Waltham Abbey. I'm glad I went. Ramsey, a shortish, stocky man, in his sixties, was somewhat punch-drunk from all his years of violence – in and out of the ring – but he and his wife were a charming, cheerful couple, who made me welcome. I spent a couple of hours there and, when I left, Bobby went into the boxer's crouch, weaved in front of me, fists clenched, and smiled: "Keep punching, son," – a friendly, positive signing-off phrase he never forgot to use whenever I rang. Despite what had happened, he and Ronnie clearly liked each other, and the photo Ronnie sent reflected that friendship.

During that visit to Broadmoor, Ronnie told me he was unhappy with *Our Story*, but was working on another book with Fred Dinenage. Four weeks later, however, he wrote saying he was not, but, if he did another book, he'd like *me*

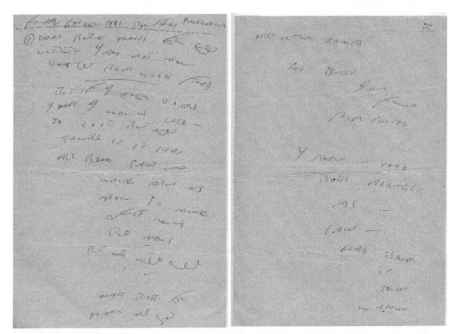

Friday 6th Dec 1991   Ron Kray   Broadmoor (1) Dear Robin   Thanks for the letter. I am not now doing the book with Fred   But if I ever do one I know I would like you to do it. But the trouble is it has all been said and wrote about us now so none of it would be news but we will see   Thank Bob for thanking me   PTO   xxxx with enclosed   God Bless   Your friend   Ron Kray   I knew you had Bobs address as you said you had been in touch with him

to write it: the trouble was, he said, it had all been written. I had to laugh at that: in my opinion, *Our Story* should have been far, far more of what the twins had done throughout their lives, and how they felt.

*

I saw little point in writing to Reg, and the feeling was mutual, but there was still money to be made out of the Kray name, no doubt about it, and Reg, more than Ronnie, seemed to think he was blessed with the business acumen to do so. But a lively, streetwise mind, and endless energy, is not enough, and nearly everything he tried, failed spectacularly. And not only because of his ineptness and lack of attention to detail; his choice of personnel was questionable, too – until Steve Wraith came into his life. Reg sensed a hunger in the young man and put him in touch with former Parkhurst cellmate Peter Gillett, who wasn't making the twins as much from a merchandising operation as they wanted.

All Reg had in mind was for Steve to advertise and sell the merchandise in and around the North East, but Gillett was happy for him to take over the whole operation. Thankful for someone else to have the pressure, he sent Steve six enormous boxes – containing hundreds of copies of *Our Story*, T-shirts with a photo of Reg above the slogan, *Enough Is Enough*, and copies of an artist's impression of the twins, priced at £250. Gillett was happy for Steve to get on with it – and he did. Using his Newcastle post office as his base, he gave a professional touch to what had been an amateurish shambles: he sent sticky labels to the twins to sign, then stuck them on copies of *Our Story*. Soon, the 'personalised' limited-editions were selling for £20 – £7 more than the retail price in 1988. He improved the design of the T-shirts, put the image on shopping bags, tea towels, calendars and mirrors, then, using post office envelopes, advertised them in a mail-shot to more than 800 Kray sympathisers who had written to the twins for over twenty years. Steve admits he was up for most ideas, but drew the line at personalised Kray condoms – even though the idea was ironically unique in that it was the ultimate in protection!

Today, Steve is reluctant to tell me how much he made the twins from that merchandising, but doing well for the twins came at a price. Reg now saw Steve as the ideal contact to meet an assortment of wheelers and dealers who'd written with various money-making ideas – and nearly all were con men, crooks or cranks, eager to cash in on the Kray name. One guy from Birmingham wanted to use Reg's name to publicise a charity function in aid of a young boy with brittle bones disease. After Reg sent him signed artwork, the guy wanted £25,000 to give Reg a 50 per cent share in a used car business, but Steve discovered he was a known con man, whose "office" was merely a brick wall with a door, leading on to a pile of rubble. Another approach was from a guy in Essex, who was such a Kray admirer, he offered Reg 25 per cent of the profits from his scaffolding business; all he wanted in return was to be able to say Reg was a partner. Confident he was genuinely kind-hearted, Reg agreed and whatever doubts he might have had vanished when he was sent headed notepaper and business cards, bearing his name, alongside his "partner's". Steve wasn't so convinced, however, and, after some enquiries, discovered the scaffolder had called on Reg simply because he was in debt to a lot of "heavy" people and felt that being associated with a Kray twin would get them off his back.

Then there was a Scotsman who wanted a five-figure sum to launch a gentleman's club, where sexy girls in school uniform would offer more than meals on a plate. Reg was prepared to find the money for that, but bailed out when Steve found out that the Scot was a dubious character who even claimed to have found Lord Lucan. By no means was Reg naïve or gullible, but he was a soft target, and, had it not been for Steve Wraith, I'm sure he would have been embarrassed, if not rooked, by unscrupulous con-artists, looking for a quick and easy killing.

*

Once more I left any Kray projects on hold and spent the first half of 1992 working flat out on biographies of *Phillip Schofield* and the *Simply Red* singer, Mick Hucknall, but one summer evening, on my way up North, to where Hucknall grew up, I went to Brad Lane's home in Doncaster. I'd heard that *The Sun* were trying to put together a story on him and felt I might be able to get a story for the *Express*. Brad's mother was not home, and I spoke briefly to a young man. A message passed on to Reg about my visit clearly upset him, because, shortly after I arrived home a few days later, he phoned, from Blundeston Prison, in Suffolk. Angry. I switched on the answerphone tape, as I sometimes did when he called.

"You've been asking questions about my tax affairs," he said, curtly.

Tax affairs?

"Sorry," I said, puzzled. "Who said this?"

"Kim Lane," he said. "Doncaster."

"No, no, I went up there to see…" I said, rattled, quickly trying to remember who I'd spoken to. "I thought there was a good story in this for the *Express*."

"She said you said that Ron had sent you. Either Ron or I had sent you. Which wasn't the case. And it caused me a very bad argument, which, even now, is still going on, you know."

Exhausted from the long drive home, and in no mood for an unwarranted interrogation, I responded, equally sharply. "I didn't even see her. I don't tell *lies*. I went up there, I was on my way to Manchester to…"

"Yes, yes," Reg broke in, irritably, probably angry that he hadn't nailed me, bang to rights, for doing something behind his back.

"…to write a book."

"I understand, yes," he said.

"I called in there because Pete Gillett had given me the address. I thought there could be a story, because *The Sun* was sniffing around."

"Yes, but I…" Reg tried to interrupt.

"But, anyway, I didn't speak with her. I didn't speak with Brad. I had about ten minutes with the guy there and just said…"

For some reason that seemed to satisfy Reg. "I accept that," he said. "Anyway, how are you? All right?"

But I didn't want to let it go. "I left a note saying can you call me in Manchester, I'll explain. She rang, or someone rang, Charlie about one o'clock in the morning…"

"Yes."

"So, anyway, there was no way I would ever tell…"

"Let's forget it," Reg said. "How are you keeping. All right?"

"Not bad at all," I said. "But bad news about Pete. I spoke to Steve yesterday."

"Who's this? Steve Tully?"

"Yeah. I'm going to try to do something for him with a heavyweight paper.

He's having a rough time at the moment…they keep picking him up."

"Yes, so I understand. Yes."

"Anyway, can I just say one thing as you're on the phone, Reg?"

"Certainly," he said.

I took a deep breath: what I was about to say had been playing on my mind since being told about it by Gillett, and I was tired and angry enough to say my piece.

"It came back to me that you said I was not a very good friend – and had warned Peter off talking to me…"

"No," Reg said. "What I warned him against is seeing any – and I mean, *any*, newspaper reporters, because they have never done me any favours in the past. And I still maintain that most reporters are not worth seeing, you know."

"But I have always done good for you and your brothers."

"Yes. Well, I won't say otherwise."

"I chased around trying to get some royalties for you, and writing to people. *And* the Prime Minister for Charlie."

"Okay, yes," Reg said, not relishing being pulled. "How are you anyway?"

"I'm okay, thanks."

"How are you?" he repeated, for some reason.

"Well, it would be nice to strike a happier relationship with you – because I'm sure there's a few quid to be earned, one way and another."

"Well, perhaps we can do that as from now, eh?"

"Well, I'd like to because I've never…when that came back to me that you'd said don't speak to him because he's not a friend of yours…"

"I said, *all* reporters," Reg repeated. "I warned him against *all* reporters. Steve and Pete and anyone else. I warn them against all reporters."

Not wanting to let him off the hook, I said: "Pete showed me a letter you wrote him. It mentioned me by name. I just felt … I couldn't believe it … I thought that's a bit daft…So just to put your mind at rest, I would never say that you sent me or Ronnie sent me."

"That's the message I got, you see…So how's your family, Okay?"

"Not bad," I said. "We are doing a book on… do you know the band, Simply Red?"

"The what?"

"There's a pop band called Simply Red."

"Is there? And you're doing a book on them?"

"Yeah, Mick Hucknall is the singer."

"That should be okay, then, eh?"

"How did your *Thoughts* go?"

"Well, it was made a mess of in the promotion," Reg said. "But it is going to be re-promoted, anyway. In a different way... So it will be okay."

"How's Ronnie and…."

"He's okay," Reg broke in, quickly.

"He had a hernia didn't he?"

"Yes, he's okay."

"Is it true you went down to see him?"

"Yes. I did go to see him, yes."

"What's he looking like?"

"He's okay. He's looking well."

"Has he put on weight?"

"He seemed well. Just the same. Doing well. Yes."

I told Reg I hadn't seen Charlie for about a month, but he wasn't interested.

"Well, he's never in touch with me and Ron," he said. "So I wouldn't know, you know. He doesn't get in touch with us, does he? It has to stop somewhere, doesn't it? Eh?"

I told him that Charlie always says he has a lot of admiration for the way he and Ronnie were handling their sentence. But Reg was very dismissive: "Yeah, yeah."

"I'm sorry to hear that you haven't been in touch with him," I said, but just got "yeah, yeah," again.

"Anything I can do on that front?" I asked.

"No, no," Reg said, brusquely. "It's his choice. He either wishes to get in touch, or he doesn't, that's entirely up to him. I couldn't care less myself, one way or the other. And that's it. I reached out to him on more than one occasion and he just snubs me and doesn't get in touch so I won't be reaching out to him anymore. That's it. That's it."

To change the subject, I told him I'd found his book, *Born Fighter*, interesting, but felt he could have written more. He seemed to agree, but excused himself. "Prison is not exactly a good place to be sitting writing books, you know. You must appreciate that. Most people can't get their heads together to write a letter in prison. I don't think a lot of people appreciate this."

"I suppose, in theory it's all right," I said. "Because you've got all the time in the world. But, then, your mind plays tricks, I would think."

"Well, it's not exactly a good place to be for anything, really, is it?"

I brought up his friend, Joey Pyle, who was currently on trial with Gillett on drugs charges, but Reg did not want to discuss anything about Joe, or the case. He thanked me for my offer to help then said he had to go, signing off with a positive: "I'm glad I leave you at a happier level."

However, less than a minute later, having inserted a fresh phone card, he was on the line again, keen to capitalise on our comfortable exchange.

"That's very good of you to ring back like that," I said.

"If you get any ideas how we could get a few quid together I'm prepared to chuck them around with you, eh? But the only thing is, what you must appreciate, I only get two visits a month, so unless there is something really positive, I can't afford the visits, you see. It's very bad – two visits a month is terrible, you know."

"I can't believe that," I said.

"Personal things I have to see about, and business, and this is really ridiculous."

"Can I just say this? I would like to do what you just said. I was going to drop you a line anyway. But can you just have a bit of faith and trust in me?"

"Yes. I can," he said. "I can only chuck things around with you, you know."

"If we do get off to a fresh start, I just want you to trust me."

"Well, I would, otherwise I wouldn't be getting off to a fresh start. Okay. Let's forget the past, eh?"

"Okay."

"And if you get any ideas - it would have to be something positive though… so if you can get any ideas, I'm always in for them – you see that's the way I keep occupied, really. I don't kind of live in prison, I live outside the walls, you know…in my own way."

"I have got a couple of ideas," I said. "But I wouldn't want to put them in writing."

"It's okay," Reg said. "Because they are not read anyway."

"Aren't they?"

"The rules have been changed."

"Really?"

"The phones are tapped periodically, whenever they feel like it, but the letters are not read because censorship has been stopped for some time. Recently anyway."

"Okay."

*

The following month, Charlie phoned: he didn't say why, but he wanted all the personal photos he'd brought to the house. Perhaps I should have been curious, if not suspicious, and asked what had prompted him to ask for them back after all this time. Surely he wasn't going to sell them? But with the Mick Hucknall biography more on my mind, I *didn't* ask. And Charlie didn't tell me. He didn't look his normal self, though. And when he came to collect the photos, he didn't stay long, not even for a cup of Sue's coffee that he loved so much. He did look embarrassed, however, and, as he left, I wondered why.

*

With Christmas approaching, the 'lifers' in Blundeston were allowed what the Governor called a "Family Day" – a relaxed occasion when they could enjoy six hours, and two meals, with a loved one of their choice. It says much about Reg that he chose not Charlie, nephew Gary, his cousins in Kent, his "adopted" son Brad and his mother or, indeed any of the close friends, but Steve Wraith.

For the likeable, but impressionable teenager, it was an honour to be invited – a day he'd remember the rest of his life because it meant Reg viewed him as part of his family. For Reg, however, I'm sure it was more about nurturing the young man's usefulness for the future.

With typical arrogance and rudeness, Reg quickly rebuked Steve for being half an hour late, making no allowance for the near-400-mile journey the kid had made by public transport, in treacherous conditions. But, having made his point, he calmed down and, from midday to 6p.m., did his best to entertain Steve amid the laughter of other inmates' children. Steve had been worried that, with Reg not keen to talk about the past, or repeat himself, they'd run out of conversation, but he'd worried unnecessarily: the first two hours flew by and, after a three-course lunch of soup, turkey, with all the trimmings, and jam roly-poly, Reg was so relaxed he did, for once, open up about the "old days" – admitting that, despite everything, he would not have changed his life in any way, and that he had no regrets about killing Jack McVitie, because "he got what he deserved." The only regret he did have was not having made it as a boxer.

As that December afternoon progressed, Steve saw a side of Reg he hadn't witnessed in the twenty months he'd been visiting him. In the happy, relaxed atmosphere, surrounded by colourful Christmas decorations, the intimidating intensity that was Reg's trademark was gone, replaced by a friendliness and almost joyous bonhomie, as he took Steve round other tables, introducing him to fellow 'lifers.' Watching him greeting his friends' families, laughing and joking, and hugging their children, Steve got a brief glimpse of the gregarious, sociable young man Reg had been, and was surprised by the sadness the feeling brought on.

An hour or so before the end of the visit, a prison officer handed Reg a huge brown box, which he gave to Steve. "I got you a few things for Christmas as a thank you for all you've done," Reg said. And he watched, with undisguised pleasure, as Steve looked inside at countless socks and shirts, pens and pencils, and various books, featuring the twins. Later, it dawned on Steve that everything in the box had been given to Reg by various admirers. But it didn't matter: Reg was grateful for what Steve had done, and clearly took pleasure rewarding him.

As I hadn't generated a penny that year, I didn't rate even a Christmas card. But the next year would be far, far different.

Chapter Eleven

THE twins had a reputation for "demanding money with menaces," but Charlie found it hard to ask for money – even if it was rightfully due to him. Take the royalties for *Me and My Brothers*, for example. We received them twice a year, in March and September, and, Charlie would always ask me to ring the publishers, a month or two before, to find out how much we were due. "Why don't you give them a call yourself, Charlie?" I'd say, not wanting the publishers to think I was desperate.

"No, no, you do it, mate," Charlie would say. "I don't want them thinking I'm pushy."

So, I'd swallow my pride and ring. But not this time. Looking through *Publishing News*, I was shocked to see that Charlie had written a book with another author, and it was coming out in April. So that's why he wanted his photographs and had made such a swift exit. Charlie was aware that if I'd known he was planning to write another book, I'd do my best to stop it: for not only would it be unfair on Sue and I, who'd treated him royally over the years, but he'd also be breaching his contract with the publishers of *Me and My Brothers*, who had an option on a second book.

I was steaming at Charlie's betrayal, but decided to wait until the eventual phone call about the royalties. Either Charlie had some cash for once, or he was too embarrassed to ring, because I didn't hear from him until March when he knew I'd have received the cheque.

"Can I meet you some place, Rob, to get my money?" he said.

"Pop over to the house, Charlie," I said. "There's something we need to talk about."

Whether he suspected, from the sharpness of my tone, that he'd been caught out, I don't know, but he brought his son Gary with him, probably for moral support. Charlie was his usual amiable, smiley self, but I was stony-faced, and when he sat down in the kitchen, I put *Publishing News* in front of him, open at the relevant page.

"Nice one, Charlie," I said, staring at him.

He looked at the book cover, then the words below. Whether he read them I don't know, but when he finally looked at me, his face was a picture of embarrassment.

"Why, Charlie?" I said. "Why didn't you tell me?"

"It's nothing, mate," he said. "Nothing. It's all a load of rubbish. I only did it for a few quid."

"But why didn't you tell me?" I persisted.

"I don't know, Rob," he said, quietly, shaking his head. "Maybe I should have."

Obviously, I was angry enough to lay into him, but, to be truthful, I can't remember what I said: certainly I would have told him he'd treated me like an idiot – *his* expression – and I was disappointed in him. But I'm sure I let him off lightly because of Gary: he was such a fragile, sensitive soul I didn't want to distress him. For his part, Charlie did his best to shrug off the matter and there was little I could do apart from accept that, when there was a few quid to be had, Charlie, lovely and charming as he was, had no scruples. It was a character fault I didn't like, no matter how hard I tried to make allowances.

Doing the Business his book was called.

Doing the dirty was more appropriate.

*

Having been immersed in my own work, I hadn't written to the twins for a while. However, I was less concerned about Reg than Ronnie, and my feelings of guilt were made worse in June, when I got a call from Charlie telling me Ronnie was in a terrible state. For some reason, his medication level had been reduced and he'd attacked another patient, Lee Kiernender. Apparently, the man had irritated him by whistling too much, so Ronnie had grabbed him by the throat and held him until he went limp. Convinced he'd killed him, Ronnie poured out his feelings of remorse to his pal, Charlie Smith, vowing that he'd never be violent again: all he wanted was peace and quiet.

All *was* calm the rest of the summer. But then, in September, not one, but two, books were published that sent Ronnie over the edge. Wilf Pine was the first to know. He went to Broadmoor, not suspecting anything was wrong, and was told that one of the psychiatrists wanted to speak with him before the visit. "He told me Ronnie had not been his normal self," Wilf told me. "He'd become very paranoid and they weren't sure how he'd be on the visit. We talked for a few minutes and then I was taken down to a room where all the inmates waited before being allowed into the visiting hall. Ronnie was sitting in a chair, his back to me, staring at a window, waiting to be told I was there. When I went over, he got up quickly and looked around, clearly shocked. 'What are you doing here?' he said, confused. In his paranoia, he obviously thought I'd become part of the system."

The first I knew something was wrong was on Tuesday 7 September when Ronnie wrote to me for the first time in nearly two years. Ronnie's barely legible scrawl had never been anything to write home about, but this latest communication indicated he was unhappy or under stress, particularly the second sheet, which contained just nine words – his signature and a message of best wishes to Sue. He said he wanted to see me once he had the all-clear from Doctor Gordon, who supervised his medication and general well-being. Four days later, my fears were confirmed when I received the first of sixteen very distressing letters, all written in just fourteen days. The first letter asked me *"to put it in the papers that Our Story has a lot of lies in it that I never said."* Worried the letter wouldn't reach me, Ronnie had written again, the same

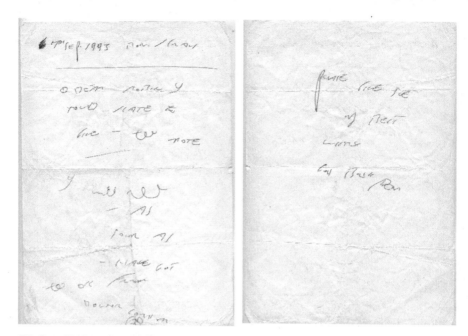

7th Sep 1993   *Ron Kray*   (1) Dear Robin I told Kate to give you the note
I will see you as soon as you have got the ok from Doctor Gordon
PTOPlease give Sue my best wishes   God Bless   Ron

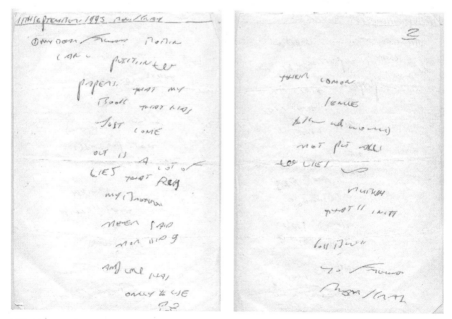

11th September 1993 *Ron Kray*   (1) My dear friend Robin   Can you put it in the
papers that my book that has just come out is a lot of lies that Reg my brother never
said nor did I   Any one has onlly to use   PTO   their comon sencce to know we
would not put all the lies and rubish that is initt   God Bless   Your Friend Ron Kray

14th Sep 1993   Ron Kray (1)   Dear Robin   Can you put it in the press that my book is all lies that is in it   I trust and rely on you   God Bless   Ron Kray Your friend   PTO Please send all your letters to me register mail as I am not getting a lot of my mail.

Tuesday 14th Sep 1993 Ron Kray
(1) My dear freind Robin I trust you   Can you get in the press that the book of mine   My Story by Ron Kray Fred Dinage   has a lot of lies in it that me and Reg never wrote
God Bless   Ron Kray
(Send all your letters to me registered post)

day, saying the same thing only stronger: "*My book that has just come out is a lot of lies that Reg my brother never said nor did I. One has only to use comon sence (sic) to know we would not put all the lies and rubbish that is in it.*"

Three days later, I was still wondering if Fred Dinenage knew how unhappy Ronnie was with his work when I got another letter, with the same request, and a poignant message: "*I trust and rely on you.*" Worryingly, a postscript – "*Please send all your letters to me registered mail as I am not getting a lot of my mail.*" – suggested the return of his paranoia.

The following week, Ronnie wrote a longer letter – four pages – which made it clear that Dinenage wasn't the only one who had upset him: his wife, Kate, had, too. She'd told him, the previous year, that she'd been commissioned to write a book, *Murder, Madness and Marriage,* but he had no idea what she was going to say. Now, he had seen a pre-publication serialisation in a Sunday tabloid, and was beside himself. He told me that what she'd written was "diabolical" and, unless she stopped the book, he was going to divorce her. He was anxious to see me, and said Doctor Gordon was putting me on the visiting list: when I came, would I take a packet of John Player Special cigarettes and some change for the coffee machines. The paranoia, however, was still evident: he said that if anyone phoned, cancelling the visit, I should believe it only if the caller was Stephanie King. His next letter was even more poignant: "*My dear freind (sic) Robin. Take no notice of anyone, only me. Try to come to see me as soon as you can. I must see you Robin, believe me, I am not mad. I must see you. It is ergnt (sic) don't take any notice of no one only me. I must see you. God Bless Ron Kray.*" The paranoia and the dramatic decline in Ronnie's handwriting added up to one thing in my mind: he was suffering the most terrible emotional turmoil. I wondered: Should I let Doctor Gordon know how worried I was?

What was bothering Ronnie about Kate so much was that he felt that she had embarrassed and humiliated him by what she'd written in her book. He also felt she'd betrayed his trust. He'd told her that he didn't expect her to live like a nun; that she should enjoy whatever sexual relationships she had, provided she never embarrassed him by flaunting them. Unfortunately for Ronnie, she *had* flaunted one of her encounters. Ronnie knew she was seeing the guy, but had no idea she viewed their relationship more deeply than merely a sexual fling. Then, to make matters worse, she allowed graphic descriptions of their passion to be serialised in a Sunday newspaper. That was enough to embarrass Ronnie, but what sent him off the dial was Kate's admission of her appalling behaviour while driving with her lover – nicknamed "Pa" – in a busy street. After Pa broke her sunglasses and threw them out the window, Kate said she stopped, opened the passenger door and kicked him in the face. When he got out and forced her against a parked van, she stabbed him with her car keys. She drove off, but was so angry she turned round, drove into him as he walked up a hill, then got out and started beating him with a lump of wood she'd found

22nd Sep 1993   Ron Kray   (1)   Dear Robbin   I have seen Doctor Gordon and he is going to put you on my list of visitors   Can you ring him and let me know when you find out when you have been cleared   Unless Kate stops her book   PTO   That is diabolical I am going to devorce her   I will check this end about our visit and write to you as soon as I find out OK   PTO   If any one rings you to say I have cancelled the visit only belive it if it is Steph King   God Bless   Ron   PTO   Can you bring 20 JPS sigarets and some change for the coffie maker   Thanks   Best to Sue

by the roadside.

By now the police had arrived, but Kate gave a false name because, she said, she didn't want Ronnie to know about the incident. "He would have been livid at me for making such an exhibition of myself," she wrote. She was spot on there. When Charlie went to Broadmoor, Ronnie was incandescent. He told him he was going to divorce Kate. "She's taken a right liberty," he said. "I told her to enjoy herself, but she's showed me up and made me a laughing stock." I'm not sure that was true: only naïve idiots believed in the bizarre union anyway – and, even if they did, I didn't think many people would see Ronnie as a laughing stock; if anything, they would feel sympathy for him being betrayed by someone he had trusted. But it wasn't only Kate's betrayal in her book that concerned him; he feared that, if there was money to be made, she would tell lies that would further embarrass him.

*

While all this was happening, an enterprising young bodyguard, named Dave Courtney, was invited to Broadmoor to discuss a business deal involving his partner, Jennifer Bean, and her twin sister, Julia. The girls had recorded a song, *They Took the Rap*, which they planned to release to publicise a *Free the Krays* march on Downing Street the following month – and, although they didn't need the twins' approval, they felt it only courteous to ask them, as the song was about them.

Dave, who organised security for most London nightclubs, admits that meeting Ronnie was the most unnerving experience of his life because, for more than an hour and a half, Ronnie stared into his eyes, without blinking. "As a club doorman, I've spent my life eyeing people up, and to be looking at someone who did that better than me was a shock," Dave told me. "Ronnie stared at me so hard I didn't know whether he liked me or hated me on sight. Jen and Julia were with me, but he didn't look at them, just me. I could almost see his wheels turning, thinking: 'What can I get out of him? Is he a threat? Do I trust him? Who does he know? Where can I fit him in the big jigsaw of my life?'"

In view of what happened on a subsequent visit a week later, it's clear that Ronnie was eager to talk to Dave on his own. For after telling Dave he would write to Reg about the record deal, he said: "Shall we send the girls to the shop? Have they got money?"

But Dave didn't pick up the signal.

"I've got money," he said. "I'll go to the shop."

Ronnie shook his head. "No, send the girls."

"They haven't any money," Dave said. "I'll go. What do you want?"

Disappointed, Ronnie handed Dave a list. When he got to the shop, Dave looked at it and, as he put it, "nearly fell over." Top of the list was 200 JPS cigarettes, two mugs, packs of cards, a red quilt cover, tea bags and various other items, clearly not all for Ronnie. The total cost was £75 and Dave remembers worrying that, if he paid for it all, he might not have enough for petrol to get home to Plumstead, in South London.

Surprisingly, perhaps, Dave did not think Ronnie was, as they say, taking a liberty. "He must have done it to everyone. And everyone expected it. If he said, 'Get me that, it was got.' At that time, I was no different to everyone else. I was easily impressed and eager to please."

The following week, Dave went to Broadmoor again, with a pal, Ray Bridges, for company. Ronnie quickly got the business out of the way, saying that he and Reg would okay the rap record, in return for £500, then turned to Ray, a muscular six-footer. "Would you do me a favour?" he said, quietly. "Would you pretend to be a kissogram for me?"

"Pardon," Ray said, not sure he'd heard right.

"My wife's a kissogram girl," Ronnie said. "I'm not happy with her at the moment. I want to find out what she's up to. I don't trust her."

Ray stared into Ronnie's piercing eyes, not knowing what to say. What *was* there to say? Ray looked at Dave, who thought of asking why Ronnie didn't trust his wife, but thought better of it. Silence hung in the air. Then Ronnie said: "Ray, would you go to the canteen and get me a drink and some cigarettes."

Grateful to be off the hook, Ray got up and walked towards the refreshment area. Once he was out of earshot, Ronnie leaned towards Dave and whispered: "Do you do girls?"

"Of course, I do," Dave said, adding quickly, "not that I'm anti-gay or anything."

"No, no," Ronnie said. "Do you murder women?"

"Not as a rule, "Dave said, thinking Ronnie was joking.

"Could you, though? Would you? There's someone in my life, who I want taken out."

"Ok…ay," Dave said, wondering where Ronnie was going with this.

"You're going to meet her," Ronnie said. "You're going to give her the five hundred pound. My wife. Kate."

Puzzled, Dave was about to ask why Ronnie wanted to give five hundred quid to someone he wanted dead when Ronnie said there was something else he wanted Dave to do.

"I want you to murder Frankie Fraser, as well."

"Why?" Dave said. "What's he done?"

Ronnie tapped the side of his nose slyly. "Politics," he whispered.

Once outside, Ray couldn't wait to say that he – like Dave the week before – had got stung for more than £70 to help clear Ronnie's canteen bill.

"Consider yourself lucky, mate," Dave said. "Ronnie's asked me to murder his wife. And Frankie Fraser!"

One is tempted to laugh off Ronnie's requests, but the reality is that, during those distressing weeks, he was clearly losing his mind because Dave wasn't the only one he asked to bump Kate off. Steve Wraith remembers visiting in the last week in September and finding Ronnie in the worst state he'd ever seen him in. "To say he was in a bad mood comes nowhere near it," Wraith told me. "His first and only topic of conversation was Kate and her book. He kept clenching his fists, calling her a slag over and over again. He was more wound up than I'd ever seen and asked me if I'd take care of her. I thought he meant look after her, but he said, 'No, no, I mean kill her.' He looked and sounded deadly serious and I believed him. After all, I'd been here with Peter Gillett and Kim Lane – Ronnie wanted me to get rid of them for upsetting Reg. Film producer Dominic Anciano was another one on the death list. Ronnie wanted me to take him out for giving him and Reg such a lousy film deal – even though it was nothing to do with him. At the time, I was *sure* Ronnie wanted those people dead, but having thought about it, I feel that saying he wanted someone killed was his way of eliminating a person, and the upset they'd caused, from his mind. Once he'd 'killed' them, his anger went, and he would relax." Knowing that Ronnie compiled death lists in the sixties, I'm sure Steve has a point.

Ronnie had sounded so convincing when he told me, on tape, why he killed George Cornell that it came as a surprise to hear that he told Steve Wraith something different. Ronnie told him he shot George because he'd murdered an idol of his – the boxer, Freddie Mills. I do find that hard to believe, but, then, there are so many unanswered questions surrounding the former world light heavyweight champion's death. He was found shot dead, in his car, near his Soho nightclub, in 1965 – eight months before the Blind Beggar killing – but to this day no one knows whether it was suicide or murder.

Personally, I believe what Wilf Pine told me while I was researching this book: that Ronnie murdered Cornell in revenge for a severe beating Cornell had given him only a few months before. It has gone down in criminal folklore that Ronnie was invincible, but, as Frank Fraser told me in the early nineties, Ronnie came off worst in many rows with Cornell. "The twins grew up with George and he knocked them about many times," Frank told me. "They were frightened of him, no doubt about it. If Ronnie did want revenge, shooting George was the only way he was going to get it."

Most people believe that Ronnie's motive was to avenge the killing of a friend of the Krays by members of the so-called Richardson gang, at Mr Smith's Club, in South London, but, as Fraser said at Ronnie's trial, the Krays and the Richardsons were friends, not enemies. More likely, in my opinion, is that, if Ronnie had been beaten up by Cornell, his pride would have been seriously hurt, and it was in his nature to deal with it if the opportunity presented itself. And, that March night in 1966, it did.

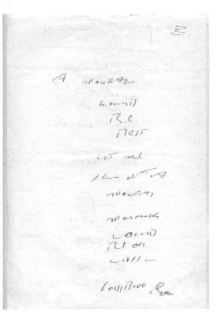

27th Sep 1993   Ron Kray   (1) Dear Robin   You have been cleared to see me by Doctor Gordon   Give it one week and I will arainge a date for you to come to see me PTO   A Monday would be best let me know if a Monday morning would be ok with you   God Bless   Ron

27th Sep 1993   Ron Kray (1)   Dear Robin   This is my latest letter to you   you can come to see me, not next Monday but next Tusday in the moring at 10 ocock OK   I am on Abingdon Ward OK   God Bless   Ron   (Please bring cash so I can have a drink and a packet of sigarets)

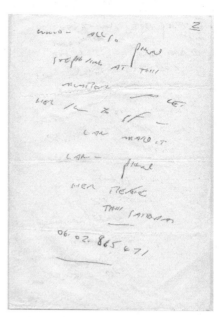

27th Sep 1993   Ron Kray   Monday   Abingdon Ward   (1)   Dear Robin   Can you come to see me next Tusday morning   Would you write and let me know if this is OK with you   Visits start at 10 till 12 in the morning that when I would like you to see me PTO Would you allso phone Steph King at this number and let her know to if you can make it   Can you phone her before this saterday

29th Sep 1993   Ron Kray   (1)   Dear Robin   I am in hospital can you come to see me next wensday morning its the only time I can see you   Next wensday morning   Let me know if this is OK   They think I may have angina   PTO   God Bless Ron   Write to me and phone Steph King   and phone the ward to

29th Sep   Ron Kray   (1) Dear Robin   Please phone Steph King and tell her if you can see me on Wensday next week in the morning 10 till 12   Don't phone no one else   God Bless   Ron Kray   Only Steph   Phone Steph as soon as you get this letter OK

Ron Kray 29th Sep Robin I wont now be able to see you next Wensday I will write to you again next week OK God Bless Ron

2nd Oct 1993 Ron Kray Infermary (1) Dear Robin Can you come to see me on any day any time right away   Don't let any one cancell it God Bless Ron Kray

During the last week of September, my concern for Ronnie grew. He wrote, saying I'd been cleared to visit – was Monday morning okay ? – but then, after I said it was, two letters arrived in the same post, one asking me to visit at 10 a.m. on Tuesday, the other changing the time to 11 a.m.. Ronnie's mind, like his handwriting was all over the place. Doctor Gordon was supervising his visiting list, but was he monitoring his mental state, too?

Two days later, Ronnie wrote *three* letters on the same day. In the first, he said he'd been taken to hospital - possibly suffering from angina - and asked if I'd visit him the following Wednesday morning, the only time he could see me. In the second, he was anxious for me to call Stephanie King to tell her if I was going or not. And, again, he was paranoid, insisting: "*Don't phone no one else, only Steph.*" The third letter, scrawled hurriedly across just the top half of a page, said he could *not* now see me, but would write the next week.

Three days later, a Saturday, he wrote, from the "*infermary*," asking me to visit him - "*any day, any time*" – and, if I could, "*don't let anyone cancel it.*"

He must have been so desperate, because Stephanie phoned me that Saturday – obviously before I'd received the letter – saying that Ronnie had told her to call me to ask if I could visit him as soon as possible. I went the next afternoon, and was shocked to see him looking nothing like the Ronnie Kray I'd got used to. No smart suit and shiny shoes this time: the dishevelled ashen-faced man who greeted me in the infirmary was wearing a crumpled, faded mauve rugby shirt, heavily creased, baggy casual trousers and canvas slipper-like shoes. And, for once, his usually neatly groomed hair was uncombed and standing on end. He looked awful and sounded worse.

He apologised for being scruffy, saying his best clothes hadn't been sent over from the special care unit where he'd been sent after attacking Kiernender. For the next hour or so, Ronnie poured his heart out to me, not only about the untruths in the books, and remorse over Kiernender, but death too, and a rumour that he was so depressed he'd lost the will to live. He told me he'd thought about dying when he collapsed, but wasn't frightened because he believed in reincarnation and often dreamed of who he was going to be in future lives. He was at pains to stress that he wasn't going "all nutty and religious," but was convinced God had saved his life in hospital.

"How come?" I asked.

"God performs miracles, like a baby coming out of the womb, and a caterpillar changing into a butterfly, so who is to say God didn't perform a miracle so that I'd recover?" was Ronnie's simple reply.

I had to smile: that was a side of Ronnie the public didn't know. All the tabloids wanted to write about was the evil gangland killer with a thirst for violence. As if reading my mind, Ronnie asked me to put it in the papers that

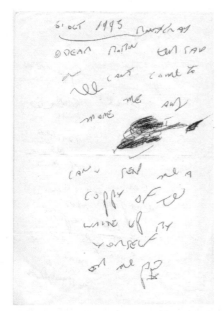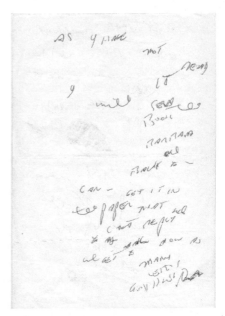

6 Oct 1993   Ron Kray   (1) Dear Robin   They said you cant come to see me any more   Can you send me a coppy of the write up by yorself on me   PTO   As I have not read it   I will send the book Barbara one back to you   Can you get in the paper that we cant reply to any mail now as we get to many letters   God Bless   Ron

he was divorcing Kate and to say that he was "a humble man, with principles, not the flash, rude, arrogant and ignorant idiot she's made me out to be." He also wanted me to make it clear that he was sorry about Kiernender.

Immediately the visit was over, I went to the phone box, opposite Broadmoor's main entrance, and told *The Sun* what Ronnie had said. On reflection, this wasn't the brightest move: although acting editor Stuart Higgins put the name of a staff reporter, Ian Hepburn, on the next day's story, the hospital's powers-that-be knew it could only have come from me and, two days later, Ronnie wrote, saying he'd been told I must not visit him any more. He'd obviously been told about the story, because he asked me to send him a copy of *The Sun*.

In the same letter, Ronnie asked me to "get it in the papers" that he and Reg were receiving so many letters that they were unable to reply to everyone. He also promised to send me back a copy of Barbara Windsor's first autobiography, *Laughter and Tears of a Cockney Sparrow,* which I'd foolishly sent him. I say "foolishly" because I never did get it back. It was precious because I'd bought the copy in the foyer of the Churchill Theatre, in Bromley, in 1990, before watching Barbara in the Joe Orton play, *Entertaining Mr Sloane* and, over a drink afterwards, she'd written a long message inside the cover. Barbara and I had known each other many years and she knew how disappointed I'd been not to have ghost-written that book. So, that night, she

For the attention of Dr. Gordon

From Robin McGibbon

6 October 93

Dear Dr. Gordon,

As promised, I'm writing (a) to apologise for the embarrassment I caused you by my visit to Ronnie Kray on Sunday; and (b) to confirm that, should the ban on my visits be lifted, I will disclose nothing at all to the media without your consent.

I would like to make it clear that I am an author of books, not a national newspaper journalist, and have no intention or need to exploit Ron to newspapers and/or magazines for his financial gain or mine.

It is true that, in some of his letter, Ron did say he wanted to set the record straight about alleged lies in his current book. But I can say, quite honestly, that I did not visit him on Sunday solely to discuss ways of doing that. I had been moved by the emotional tone of his letters – two of which I'm faxing to you – and I am not the sort of person to turn a cold shoulder to that sort of SOS. I was anxious to see him, because he was anxious to see me; it is as simple as that.

When we met, Ron quickly told me about his planned divorce, and his remorse over the recent assault, and asked me to try to publicise his feelings. I was happy to comply with his wishes; after all, other visitors have done so over the years. Certainly I did not think for a moment that I was breaking any hospital rules or betraying your trust by speaking to newspapers.

Ron has made it clear to you, and the hospital authorities in general, I believe, that I am someone he trusts and wishes to see, and I wonder if it would help matters if I made an appointment to see you, so that you can judge for yourself whether I am suitable to visit on a regular basis. Perhaps you would let me know your views on this soon, because I got a message today that Ron enjoyed chatting to me and wants to see me again.

Thank you very sincerely for your kindness and co-operation whenever I have called. I know you are busy.

7th Oct Ron Kray
(1)   Robin   Can you
get my brother Charlie
to viset me with Gary
God Bless   Ron

8th Oct 1993 Ron Kray (1) Dear Robin   Thanks for the letter   Can you send me
a coppy of the write up on me that you put in the paper about me as I have not seen
it PTO Please give Sue my best wishes God Bless Your friend Ron
Hope to see you soon, but if I go back to Abingdon Ward I wont see you their if I get
out of their I will see you

10th Oct 1993 *Ron Kray*
(1)   Dear Robin Please give
Sue my best wishes Robin
did you give my cash to
Heatherwood Hospital
And the cab drivers fund?
Let me know I hope to see
you soon God Bless Ron
Your friend

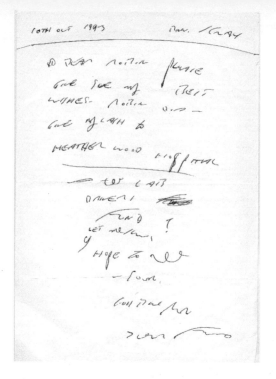

wrote: *"This would have been a far better book if you'd written it. Don't worry, you'll write the next one."* I'd like to have my copy of that book, because, in 1999, Barbara was asked to write another autobiography – and she *did* ask me to write it. The book, *All of Me,* reached Number 2 in both hardcover and paperback bestsellers' lists.

That the Broadmoor authorities thought *I* was *Sun* reporter Ian Hepburn and had signed in as Robin McGibbon was unimportant. They had seen fit to ban me from visiting Ronnie and that was an embarrassment, as well as a nuisance. To try to make amends, I wrote to Doctor Gordon, explaining that Ronnie had asked me to publicise my conversation: he desperately wanted the public to know that he was getting divorced, and was sorry about assaulting a fellow patient. I told Doctor Gordon I didn't think I was breaking any hospital rules or betraying trust, and offered to meet him, so that he could judge for himself whether I was suitable to continue visiting Ronnie. I hoped the letter would get me back on the visiting list, but wouldn't hold my breath: seeing details of a patient's Sunday afternoon visit in the country's biggest-selling tabloid the next day was embarrassing, and the hospital wouldn't forgive easily.

The following Saturday, none of the celebrities who had pledged support for the *"Free The Krays"* campaign turned up for the march to Downing Street, headed by Jennifer and Julia. But more than two hundred Kray sympathisers did, and a petition bearing 100,000 signatures was duly delivered to No. 10. A heavy police presence attracted much media attention which delighted the twins – and Stephanie King, who organised the march – although none thought it would not make the slightest difference.

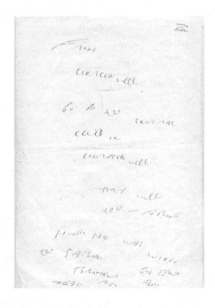

17th Oct   Ron Kray
(1)   Dear Robin   Can you
seen Reg and me some
stamps if you don't mind   I
hope you and Sue are both
well   You should do a book
on Bert Marsh the old
Italian   PTO   From
Clerkenwell   Go to the
Central Club in Clerkenwell
they will tell you about him.
He was with the Sabini
brothers years ago   God
Bless   Ron

Wensday 20th Oct 1993 Ron Kray (1) Dear Robin I see Kate today and told her I am finished with her I am going to get a divorce over her book what was all lies God Bless to you and Sue Ron Your friend

5th Nov Ron Kray Robin I will write to night Let me know if you get this note God Bless Your friend Ron Kray Best wishes to Sue

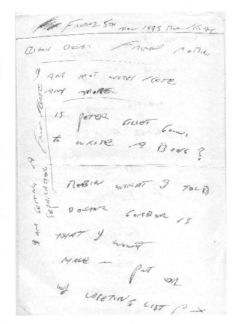

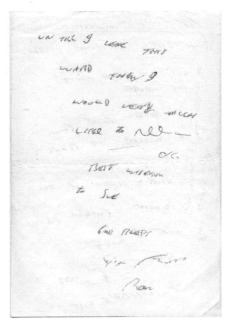

Friday 5th Nov 1993 Ron Kray (1) My dear freind Robin I am not with Kate any more Is Peter Gillet going to write a book? Robin what I told Doctor Gordon is that I wont have you put on my visiting list (I am getting a separation from Kate) PTO Un till I leave this ward then I would very much like to see you OK Best wishes to Sue God Bless Your friend Ron

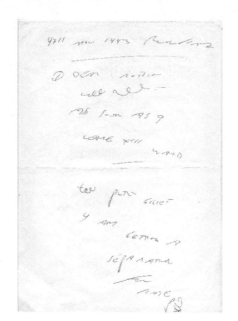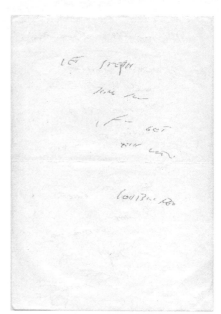

9th Nov 1993   Ron Kray   (1)   Dear Robin   Will see you as soon as I leave this ward Tell Peter Gillet I am getting a separation from Kate   PTO   Let Steph King know if you get this letter   God Bless   Ron

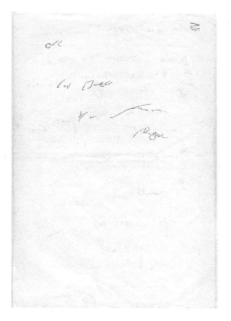

24th Nov 1993   Ron Kray   (1)   Dear Robin   Am keen to do the business with you but will leave all to Reg.   Please give my best wishes to Sue   I will now get you put on my visiting list I will see Doctor Gordon next Monday   PTO   OK   God Bless Your friend   Ron

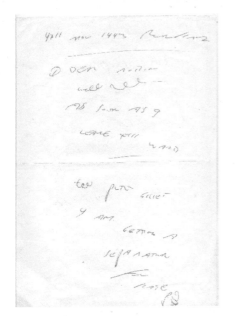
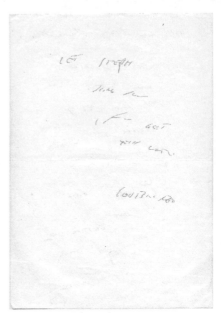

Wensday 15th Dec 1993 (1) Dear Robin   I am divorcing Kate as soon as I can
I hope to see you in the new year   She took a liberty what she said
PTO   About our brother Charlie   Would you tell him I never told her to put in what
she did about Charlie in her book   God Bless   Ron

Ronnie continued to write to me, stressing again and again how hurt and angry he was with Kate, and I knew that when he told her he was divorcing her, there would be no going back. So, it was no surprise to receive a letter two weeks later, confirming he was no longer with her. That letter – written from a ward he clearly hated – was startling, in that Ronnie seemed so unbalanced he'd gone over everything he'd written, as though he was tracing it. It seemed to me that he was going through some form of breakdown and I wondered, again, if Broadmoor's psychiatrists were aware of his mental state.

Thankfully, as 1993 drew to a close, he came out of it. He wasn't one hundred per cent, but was clearly feeling better because he wrote, saying he was "*keen to do business*" and hoped to see me in the New Year. In his final letter that year, he said he was divorcing Kate as soon as he could, and he urged me to tell Charlie that he didn't make any of the nasty comments she attributed to him in her book. "*She took a liberty,*" Ronnie wrote.

*

Ronnie had made it clear to Dave Courtney that he didn't want to see him any more and wouldn't be writing; he'd prefer that Dave struck up a relationship with Reg. That was fine by Dave and when he drove to the Suffolk prison the following month, he was relieved to find Reg far friendlier than his twin.

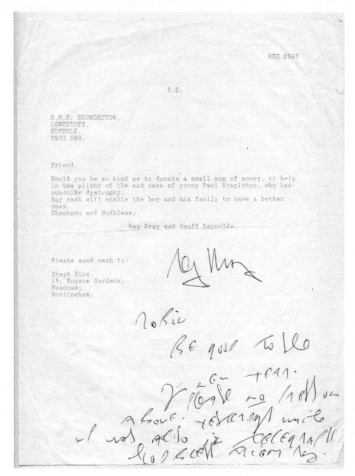

REG KRAY

R.K.

H.M.P. BLUNDESTON,
LOWESTOFT,
SUFFOLK.
NR32 5BG.

Friend,

Would you be so kind as to donate a small sum of money, to help
in the plight of the sad case of young Paul Stapleton, who has
muscular dystrophy.
Any cash will enable the boy and his family to have a better
xmas.
Thankyou and Godbless.

                    Reg Kray and Geoff Reynolds.

Please send cash to:

Steph King.
14, Eugene Gardens,
Meadows,
Nottingham.

UNDATED
Robin Be good to see you New Year Please no Press on above Yesterdays write up was also in Telegraph God Bless Friend Reg

He seemed interested in Dave and what he was doing and, unlike Ronnie, liked to laugh and have a chat. He was the sort of person, Dave thought, he wouldn't mind visiting again. The feeling was mutual. And as Dave shook his hand to leave, Reg said: "Next time you come would you mind bringing a pair of trainers, size eleven."

Later in their relationship, Dave would discover that Reg was always trying to ponce a pair of trainers for the latest love of his life. But, at that moment, and driving home to London, the only thought Dave had was that, in the months to come, Reg would be wanting far more from him than just a pair of trainers.

I'd heard nothing from Reg since he wrote to me at the end of 1991, telling me Brad Lane had changed his name. But then, coming up to Christmas, he made contact with a round-robin letter – signed by him and someone named

26th Dec Sunday 6 - 40 AM Robbin,   Bet you said to yourself on receipt of this letter "Ive seen that handwriting before" !   See the way I spelt "Robbin" !   Hope your family and self had good Xmas and I wish you all a happy new year   As I said "no rest for the wicked" as for me being wicked "it's a falacy" !   Being serious I want your advise should I publish those letters or not?!   I think they should be published in part not in there entirety and you are mentioned in one letter as negotiator.   Ill get Steph to send you a copy of one letter   Ill send you copy of one I have here   The crux of the matter is she gets payed as neccessary   I must have received over 500 Xmas cards total increase each year   You should invest any cash with me then you no need to worry as you wont see it again instead of in the car game!   Im going to start to do Yoga exercises again so as to keep subtle   Ive been doing dinamicc tension in my cell regular   Ill have a cold shower once the door clicks unlock at 5 minutes to 8 am to start the day   I guess my hand-writing suggested Im Chinese but I come from the East End   Take it easy   God Bless   Friend   Reg Kray X

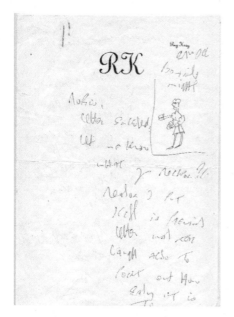

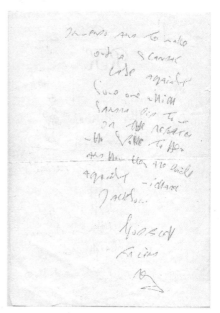

27th Dec   Boxing Night   Robin,   Letter enclosed, let me know what you reckon?!
Reason I put kiss in previous letter was for laugh also to point out how easy it is to
innuendo and to make out a scandal case against some one which Sandra did to me
on the reporter who spoke to her and how they are quick against Michael Jackson
God Bless   Friend   Reg

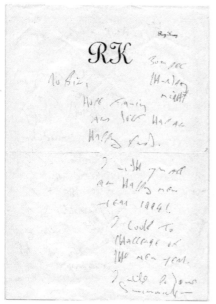

30th Dec   Thursday night   Robin,   Hope family and self had a happy Xmas.   I wish
you all a happy new Year 1994!   I look to challenge of the new year   I will do some
swimming – they have a pool at Maidstone   I will rely on you to put things right re
weight lift write up in February as you are the journalist so I pass the buck to you
God Bless   Friend   Reg

Geoff Reynolds – aimed at raising money for a little boy, Paul Stapleton, who had muscular dystrophy. The undated, typewritten letter asked the recipient to donate "a small sum of money" – via Stephanie King – so that Paul and his family could have "a better Christmas." Strangely, though, Reg stressed, in a handwritten note at the bottom of the page, that he didn't want me to tell the media about the appeal. I wondered why. What he didn't mention was his pompous book of "*Thoughts*," which he'd asked me to promote. After I said No, he'd turned to Steve Wraith, who spent six months sorting out the various legal issues from the first publication, and deciphering Reg's barely legible handwriting, before being told that the book was being abandoned and, er, would Steve mind helping him on another one. I was pleased to learn that Steve politely declined the offer.

Although he never mentioned it, I felt sure Reg knew I'd been in contact with Ronnie, because that note also said "*it would be good*" to see me in the New Year. And, surprise, surprise, I received not one, but two, letters - dated Boxing Day - that were more light-hearted, and friendly than any he'd sent before. As a way of introducing himself again, he began the first, six-page, letter: "*Bet you said to yourself on receipt of this letter, 'I've seen that handwriting before.*'" And then, for some reason I never fathomed, he was keen to point out that he'd spelt my name '*Robbin*.' He clearly had the Christmas spirit because he made a rare attempt at humour, joking that "*there's no rest for the wicked*," and, as far as him being wicked, "*it's a fallacy*." Also, that if I had any spare cash, I should invest it with him, and not worry, "*as I won't see it again*." Then, to complete an uncharacteristically chatty note, intended to encourage me, perhaps, to resume our friendship, he laughed off his barely legible scrawl, saying "*it suggests I'm Chinese*."

Reg had lost none of his self-obsession, however: deciding that his letterhead needed to be more striking, he'd arranged for *Reg Kray* to be printed in italics, with the initials *RK* centred, in big, bold type, below. And he boasted that he'd received more than 500 Christmas cards – "*the number increases every year*" – and that he was strengthening his muscles with dynamic tension. Oh yes, he was planning to take up yoga again, "*to keep subtle*" (sic). Bizarrely, Reg signed off the letter with an X against his name – something I didn't notice until Reg pointed it out, in his next letter. The X was a kiss, he said, and he'd put it in, not for a laugh, but to demonstrate how easy it was to create a scandal out of an innocent, but suggestive, innuendo – a reference to a slur on him in a newspaper by a woman, named Sandra Wrightson, who had named Reg as "the other man" in her divorce case. Clearly, Reg was buttering me up for a reason – and early in the New Year, I found out why.

He'd fallen in love with a young weightlifter and desperately wanted my help in making him famous.

Chapter Twelve

THE weightlifter was Kevin Bourner. He was tall, with dark, good looks and aged just twenty-one. And when Reg heard Kevin was on his way from Wandsworth, early in the summer of 1993, he was so excited that he used his considerable clout to have an unpopular prisoner removed from a cell close to him, so that he could be near the newcomer.

An unworldly youngster from the Home Counties, Kevin was flattered that a gangland legend was impressed with his weightlifting prowess and, over the next six months, they became as inseparable as one can be in prison. Not surprisingly, a rumour went round that they were having a homosexual relationship, which upset Kevin, who was not that way inclined. He was so distraught that Reg went to see the prisoner behind the gossip – a blond guy, six feet four, eighteen stone, like a massive Viking. Reg marched into his cell and told him to repeat what had upset Kevin. The bloke was terrified and denied he'd said anything, so Reg head-butted him. Having made his point, he then walked out and that should have been that. But another prisoner, who'd gone to the cell as well, felt the big guy was out of order for not going down after the butt, so he gave him a severe beating. Such was the respect that Reg commanded.

Reg was besotted and obsessed with Kevin. He convinced him he had the looks and physique to make it big in films and that Reg had the contacts to make him famous after his release. That's where I came in: Reg wrote to me in the first week of January, wanting me to get Kevin's photo and story in the national press. Had it not been for a big story I'd done with Barbara Windsor that week, however, I doubt whether he would have got in touch. Barbara and I had broken the news of her marriage break-up with Yorkshire-born chef, Stephen Hollings, on the front page of the *News of the World*, and seeing my by-line had clearly brought me back into Reg's mind. In a letter designed to flatter me, he said I'd "done well to get so much out of very little." His snide comment showed how naïve Reg was about tabloid newspapers. What he considered "very little" was Barbara's confession that she hadn't had sex for six years and was leaving her husband for a former school pal's son – sensational revelations, for which the paper paid many thousands.

The story had clearly given Reg an idea which he believed I could develop. He said he had a "big story" himself, which he hoped to discuss with me when he saw me. He promised that I'd be interested in the story – and other projects he was working on – then said he was going off "*to polish my shoes like my old man taught me.*"

I found it hard not to be pleased that Reg had written: he seemed to have forgiven me for what shortcomings he felt I had, and was keen to be mates again. Who knows, I thought, we might actually make some money this time.

It turned out that the "big story" was not Reg's weightlifting buddy; it was

4th Jan   Tuesday   7 AM   Robin – Good to talk to you.   Happy New Year 1994 to your family and yourself.   I read your Babs article   You did well to get so much story out of very little   I think Ive a big story for you for News of World and I hope to discuss it with you when I see you   This year I hope to see some of my projects Ive been working on bare fruit .   You will be interested when you know what they are   The next time Pete phones tell him Ive a new name for him "Clog Face"!   Going to polish my shoes now just as my old man always taught me   God Bless   Friend   Reg

4th Jan Robin, Photos to follow
Try to make it front page! God
Bless Friend Reg Kray

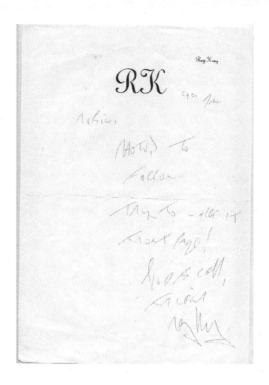

an impending engagement - his. Reg had read a story in *The Sun* about one of Flanagan's ex-modelling mates being one of Lord Weymouth's so-called "wifelets," and wanted to know if I thought it would be financially worthwhile, newspaper-wise, if he got engaged to her. The lady in question was Cherri Gilham, and, although she had made something of a name for herself in minor TV roles, I remembered her more from the early days of my *Experience* magazine. Whether Ms Gilham was aware that one of Britain's most notorious killers was sizing her up to co-operate in a cynical scam I didn't know. I suspect she didn't because, when Reg outlined his idea, he stressed that her name be kept "*strictly confidential.*" However, he clearly wasn't totally sold on Cherri – now coming up to fifty - as the candidate. "*Do you think a young model would be better?*" he asked. "*I can get a young model, if necessary.*" Either way, he didn't want any publicity until he had been transferred to Maidstone later that year. But when I did do the story, he wanted me to go for "*top money.*" In case I didn't get the message that revenue was his priority, Reg illustrated the point with two ludicrously childish drawings – one a gangster, demanding: "*We want cash,*" the other, a matchstick man, carrying what might be a case, marked: "*CASH.*"

The next day it became clear that getting money for an "engagement" was

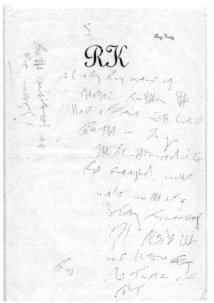

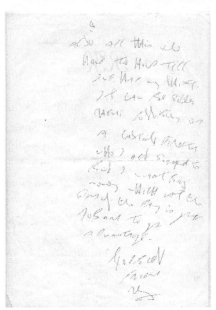

PART OF LETTER *(must be first of letter of 5 January)*   A lady by name of Cherie Bingham   She had affair with Lord Bath – do you think her and I to be engaged would make much of a story financially?! Please let me know by return of post
Also all this will have to hold till Ive had my shift   It can be either Cherie possibly or a casting director who I get engaged to but I want big money which at the end of the day is your job and to your advantage   God Bless   Friend   Reg Both candidates are ex models!

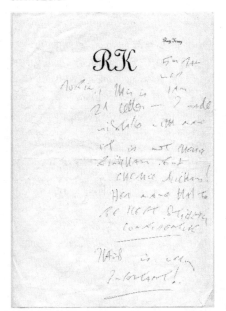

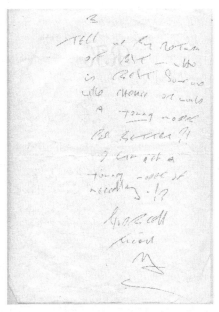

5th Jan   Wed   1 AM   Robin,   This is 2nd letter – I made a mistake with name it is not Cherie Bingham but Cherie Gilham!   Her name has to be kept strictly confidential   This is very important!   Tell me by return of post – who is best some one like Cherie or would a young model be better?!   I can get a young model if neccessary!?   God Bless   Friend Reg

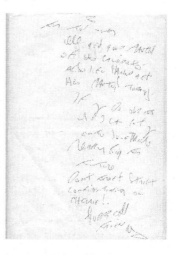

5th Jan   Wed   5 – 30 AM   Robin,
Please no publicity on Kev or
engagement till I have left here – Kev
is due home leave soon and I don't
want his chances spoilt.
Lets do the engagement in style and
go for top money.   Ill get good photos
of the candidate   Also Kev should get
his photos today   If you do OK on it I
can put you on to something really big
for future,   Don't forget strict
confidentiality on Cherie!
God Bless   Friend   Reg

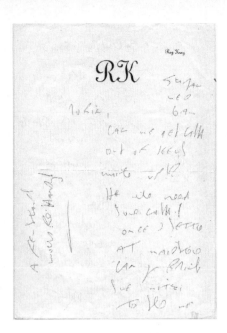

5th Jan Wed 6 AM Robin, Can we get cash out of Kevs write up!? He will need some cash! Once I settle at Maidstone can you bring Sue Mitzi to see me   (A few stamps would be handy!) Ive always been a fan of hers. If you need finance for possible TV series Im sure I can help   Send me a long letter on all topics when you have God Bless   Friend Reg

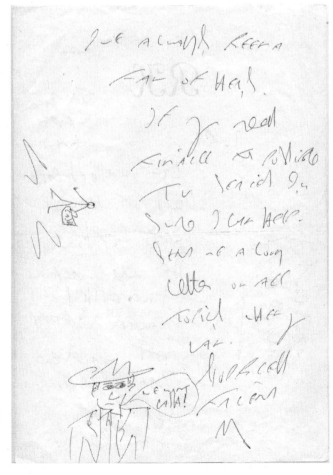

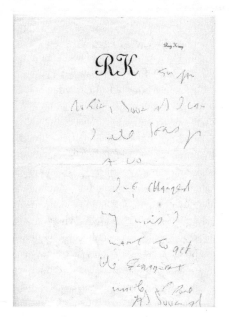
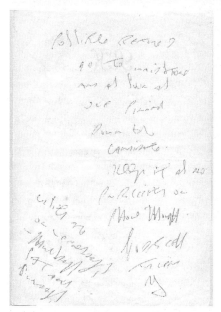

5th Jan   Robin,   Soon as I can I will send you a VO   Ive changed my mind I want to get the engagement write up done as soon as possible before I go to Maidstone and as soon as Ive pinned down the candidate   Keep it as no publicity on phone though God Bless   Friend   Reg   Visits are on Wednesday Thursday Sat and Sundays

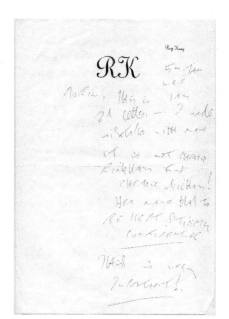
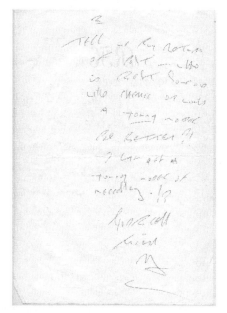

5th Jan   Wed   9 – 15 AM   Robin,   You will get fed up with my letters at this rate Who do you think is best candidate to raise finance?!   Cherie, Flanagan Helen Keating or a young model   Let me know who you think the lucky girl should be! God Bless   Friend   Reg

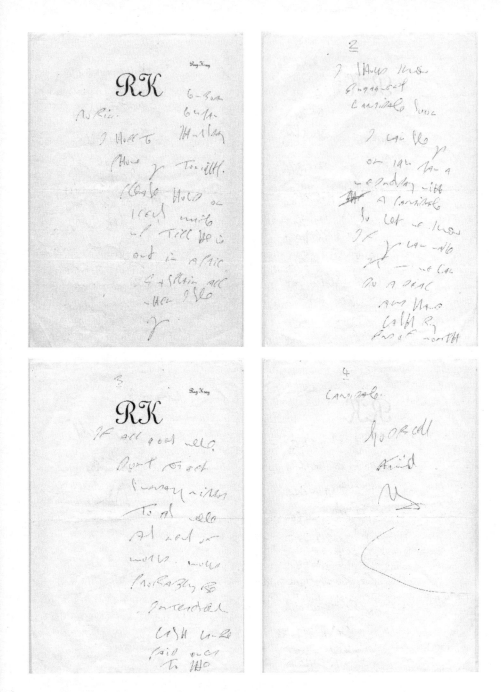

6 – 30AM   6th Jan   Thursday   Robin,   I hope to phone you tonight   Please hold on Kevs write up till he is out in April   Explain all when I see you   I should know engagement candidate soon   I can see you on 19th Jan a Wednesday with a candidate so let me know if you can make it – we can do a deal and have cash by end of month if all goes well   Don't forget Sunday Mirror to as well as News of World would probably be interested   Cash can be paid over to the candidate   God Bless Friend   Reg

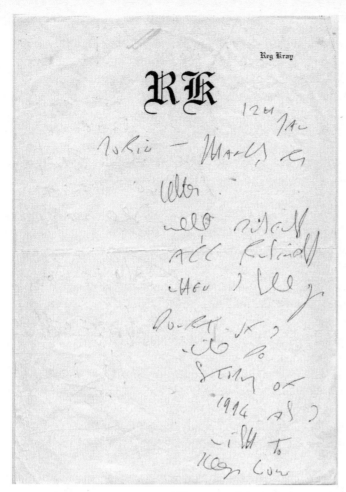

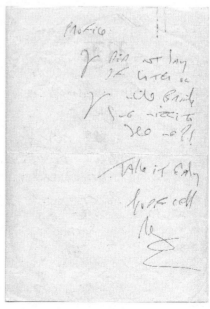

12th Jan   Robin   Thanks for letter
Will discuss all business when I see
you
Doubt if I will do story of 1994 as I
wish to keep low profile   You did
not say if later on you will bring Sue
Mizzi to see me me?!   Take it easy
God Bless   Reg

not Reg's only motive for contacting me: he phoned, wanting publicity for *"this young prisoner, Kevin"* – a weightlifter who had, apparently, won all sorts of competitions. I couldn't see much in it for me, because, traditionally, sports' stories don't pay well, but Reg quickly made clear that he saw Kevin's future as far more than a weightlifting champion. *"I've got his career in films mapped out,"* he said. *"I've already got him a part in the Lenny McLean film. I've done this because Lenny's a friend of mine, if you want to quote that. He's been to see Kevin and me and he's a friend of Kevin as well."* Then, for some reason that puzzled me, he told me to do the story without any gay innuendoes. *"Newspapers usually try them things, don't they?"* he said.

I didn't know what he was talking about. Was he suggesting that the Guv'nor was gay? I felt sure Lenny wasn't: I'd been to his home, in Bow, and met his wife, Val, and their lovely son and daughter, and had seen no signs whatever of homosexuality in Lenny. Quite the opposite.

Was Reg referring to himself and Kevin? It honestly didn't cross my mind: all Reg wanted, it seemed, was for me to do for Kevin what I'd done for Gillett and, at the time, I was sure that Gillett wasn't gay. And whatever Reg hoped the story might achieve, I did believe he wanted it more for Kevin than himself. For when I reminded him that I could get hold of photos of himself lifting weights, Reg quickly said: *"Keep me out of the weights part. I had nothing to do with it. That was down to his coaches. You've got the coaches' names, haven't you?"*

I didn't see much mileage in the story, if any, but that wasn't what Reg wanted to hear, so I ended the conversation positively, saying I'd do my best. In the end, I didn't bother writing anything, which was just as well, because two weeks later, after several letters on the subject, Reg wrote, telling me Kevin didn't want any publicity. No explanation was given for the change of heart; I could only assume that it had suddenly dawned on Kevin that, while the Kray connection helped him in prison, it would not bless him outside.

I've often wondered whether Reg created his ludicrous "engagement" stories to conceal his real sexual desires. Certainly it seems coincidental that while openly courting the company of young prisoners, he was asking me to publicise nationally, his heterosexuality and supposed wish to be married. First, he'd proposed to Linda Calvey, a murderess from East London – dubbed "The Black Widow" – who was serving life in Holloway, for shooting dead her husband. Calvey having declined his offer, Reg had moved on.

I could see the tabloids going for a Reg-to-wed story, no matter which "candidate" he picked to wear the ring, but, typically, Reg chose to complicate matters. First, he said he wanted me to hold the story until his move to Maidstone – then wrote, the same day, saying he wanted it to appear while he was in Blundeston.

Choosing the "candidate" was bothering Reg: should "the lucky girl" be Cherri Gilham or Helen Keating, an actress in the TV series, *London's Burning*?

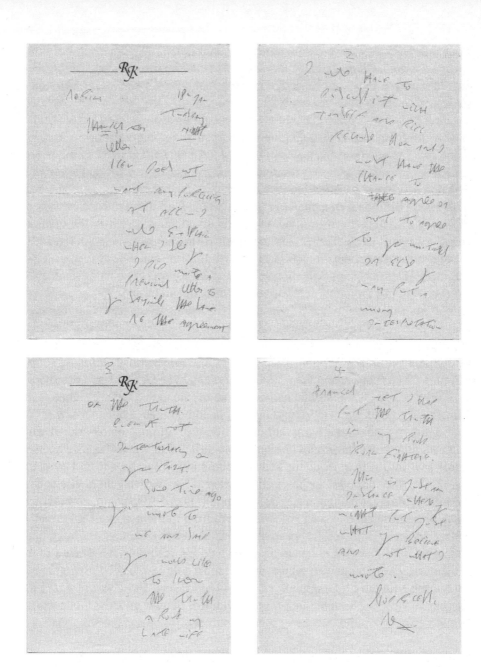

18th Jan   Tuesday night   Robin,   Thanks for letter.   Kev does not want any publicity at all - I will explain when I see you.   I did write a previous letter to you saying the same   So the agreement I will have to discuss it with yourself and Bill because Ron and I must have the chance to agree or not to agree to your writings or else you may put a wrong interpretation on the truth even if not intentionally on your part.   Some time ago you wrote to me and said you would like to know the truth about my late wife Frances yet I had put the truth in my book "Born Fighter".   This is just an instance where you might put just what you believe and not what I wrote.
God Bless Reg

The following day, Reg wrote, saying he'd know the "*candidate's*" identity within the next two weeks: she was going to visit him and he wanted me to go to the prison to meet her. Ever the optimist, he added: "*We can do a deal and have cash by the end of the month.*"

The story never happened, of course. Although I never checked with the women Reg mentioned, I doubt they knew anything about his scheming. And, if they did, they would not have wanted to know. But that was Reg: he was so caught up in believing he could achieve anything that he was blinded to reality. Whatever I thought of him, though, I had to marvel at his chutzpah. Having given Suzanne Mizzi the elbow on the Isle of Wight because he didn't want a mere Page Three Girl stealing his boy's "thunder," he now had the gall to ask me to take her to visit him in Maidstone, once he'd he settled in. "*I've always been a fan of hers,*" he wrote.

Yeah, right.

Chapter Thirteen

REG did not get engaged, much less married. And our own honeymoon period, where I was flavour of the month, was about to end. The first sign came in a letter, Reg wrote on 18 January, about a TV drama series I wanted to write on the Krays: I'd put the idea on the back burner while I wrote the Hucknall and Lambrianou books, but, clearly, Reg had been thinking about the project. He was concerned that neither he, nor Ronnie, would have control over what I wrote, and reminded me that I'd questioned why Frances had killed herself – even though he'd told me he'd written the truth in his recently-published book, *Born Fighter*. "*This is just an instance where you might put just what you believe and not want I wrote,*" he said. What was, or was not, the truth was bothering him because, three days, later he accused me of having "*the same attitude*" as Fred Dinenage to what I thought was the truth. Incensed, he wrote: "*It's the second time you have made reference to others telling you what is the truth. Who are these cloak and dagger people you refer to as authority on the truth?*"

Also, he was upset that I wanted to know why he was photographed with so many celebrities. "*There is no real fascination to be seen or photographed with celebrities – that's reporter shit talk,*" he fumed, adding icily: "*I don't think you and I will get on to (sic) well re project with your present attitude, Tell me where you were born?! I doubt I would understand your way of life no more than you do ours. I've never met a reporter yet who understood an East End villain. I did not like joint book by you and Charlie. I'm sure you won't like Born Fighter because it is the truth...*"

No matter how insulting he was, Reg had no shame asking for my help. With his move to Maidstone imminent, he was keen for me to tell the papers that, after so many years in top-security Category A prisons, he was being moved to a Category C one. And, to enhance the story, he told me – with bizarre pride – that his seventeen years on Category A was longer than anyone in the country, except police killer Harry Roberts, and the eighteen years at Parkhurst was longer than anyone had served there in one stretch.

He was keen, too, for me to place a story, praising his Blundeston inmates as "*the best crowd I could have been with,*" a sentiment in contrast to what I was to learn later. In that February letter, Reg promised to send me a VO once he was settled at Maidstone, and, interestingly sent his "*respect,*" as well as his love, to Sue – something he'd never done before. What had brought *that* on? I wondered.

I knew that Peter Gillett had been jailed in a much-publicised drugs' trial, but was unaware, until Reg told me, that he was now in Maidstone. Reg was pleased he would be reunited with his old pal, but didn't want me to tell the Press that Gillett was there – which was a pity because *The Sun*, particularly, would have been interested in the reunion.

Robin,   Thanks for letter   I did get the card   You seem to have same attitude as Fred Dineage as to what you think is the truth.   You also do not understand East End people same as he didn't.   Hence his spoiling Our Story to distort my version   How can you let a lousy few quid to buy Born Fighter get in the way of a deal   I don't see why I should have asked you to ghost write Our Story   Im as difficult as anyone else when rubbish is written about us – Im in here on principle.   Its 2nd time you have made reference to others telling you that is the truth – who are these cloak and dagger people you refer to as authority on the truth!?   Also there is no real fascination to be seen or photographed with celebrities that's reporter shit talk   I don't think you and I will get on to well re project with your present attitude   Tell me where were you born?!   I doubt I would understand your way of life no more than you do ours   Ive never met a reporter yet who understood an East End villian   I did not like joint book by you and Charlie   Im sure you will not like Born Fighter because it is the truth   I have yet to be given a date of leaving here   All the best   Reg

Now busy ghosting the autobiography of Chris Lambrianou - who'd been jailed for his part in the McVitie murder - I had little time to spend on newspaper stories, but then, in the last week of February, Reg wrote with a suggestion which I felt could be profitable. He and another prisoner had had their photo taken with Lady Alice Douglas – former wife of the 12th Marquis of Queensberry - who ran a drama workshop at the prison, and Reg wondered whether there was any money in it. "The Lady and the Gang Boss" sounded good to me, and I was hardly surprised when he said the *News of the World* were interested. Lady Alice was offered £5,000 – presumably to reveal what he was like behind bars – but had turned it down because she didn't like the reporter assigned to interview her. Now, Reg wanted me to interview her and negotiate a fresh deal. He gave me a London phone number, but no one ever answered and, after a few weeks, I forgot her – and the photograph.

Then, sixteen years later, while researching this book, I decided to try again to contact Lady Alice. And found out more about Reg and his weightlifting mate than he had ever wanted me to know.

Lady Alice was now living in a converted chapel, in Snowdonia. She wasn't there when I called, shortly after Christmas 2010: tragically, her young nephew had just died, and she was comforting the family. But the courteous gentleman who answered the phone was more than a little interested to hear why I was calling because, hard though it was for me to take in, he was the other prisoner in the photo: Simon Melia. And, to shock me even further, he said he was Lady Alice's former husband, and father of her two children.

Simon told me the photograph had been taken after a prison production of Shakespeare's *Macbeth*. He'd played the title role and Lady Alice his wife, and they had fallen in love during rehearsals. They had married while Simon was on home leave later, but, sadly, were now divorced. They had an eleven-year-old daughter who seemed destined for a spectacular career as a harpist, and a ten-year-old son, who had just been voted Young Genius Inventor of the Year. Simon, a highly intelligent, but clearly troubled man, was very open, and what he told me about Reg's fondness for the weightlifter explained why he'd been so eager for me to get the young man publicity, so keen to *"map out his film career."*

"When he was not queueing to use the phone, he'd spend all his time talking to Kevin," Simon said. "He told him he had a great future in acting, and was going to guide his career. But Reg was too intense, and was following Kevin around all the time, crowding him, making him feel uncomfortable."

The beginning of the end came when Reg had an idea for a film, based on Kevin's real-life relationship with his girlfriend, Kelly, and his struggle to make a success of his life after being jailed. Predominantly a heterosexual love story, it was also about an ageing prisoner besotted with a younger man. Reg was obsessed with the idea and wrote more than thirty pages of what he called a "film treatment," in which he likened Kevin to the finely-muscled, stripped-

9th Feb   Tuesday   6 AM   Robin,   Ill let you know date of my departure a few days before   These pieces may help you in write up on it   I was on Cat A 17 years longest in the country other than Harry Roberts who killed 3 law men   I was at Parkhurst for a total of 18 years longest period ever served there in one stretch by an inmate   It will have taken me 26 years to get to such a gaol – I will have served 26 years by May 8th which included 13 months on remand at Brixton   Pete Gillett has just gone to Maidstone I was on phone to him. He is OK   I will be pleased to see him but I don't want fact he is there mentioned in any write up   If you wish to know anything else which will help me then let me know by letter as phone is tapped as I told you before   I still wish to know who gave out information of my shift!
My love to Sue and your son   God Bless   Friend   Reg

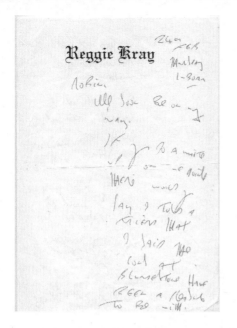
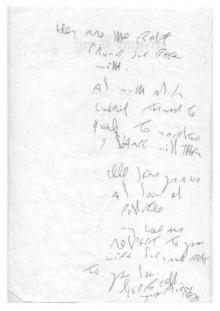

24th Feb   Thursday   1 – 30AM   Robin,   Ill soon be on my way.   If you do a write up on me going there would you say I told a friend that I said the cons at Blundestone have been a pleasure to be with they are the best crowd Ive been with.   As much as Im looking forward to going to Maidstone I shall miss them   Ill send you a VO as soon as possible   My love and respect to your wife Sue and best to your son God Bless   Friend   Reg

to-the-waist model in the *Joe Bloggs Jeans* TV commercial. The movie character should have a calm, quiet disposition, Reg said, adding that he once saw these qualities in Kevin, watching him place a note in an envelope and drop it out of a window. Reg's admiration for Kevin's youth and vitality – and the way he was handling his sentence – was very evident, Simon said. That was one way of putting it. Another was that Reg fancied the jeans off him!

All started to go wrong with the relationship when Reg showed Kevin this "treatment" and asked him to type it out. Kevin refused and told Reg he'd had enough of him following him around "like a dog." This prompted Reg to bare his soul, in an impassioned letter – which he asked Simon to type – in which he promised to cool it. He admitted following Kevin around and apologised, saying it was his own fault, not Kevin's. He would now meet only if Kevin wanted to, but would continue to plan his career, regardless. He would arrange

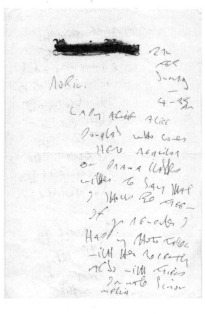

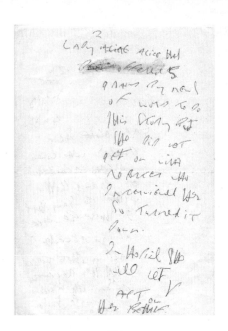

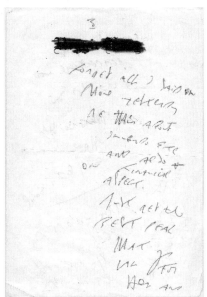

27th Feb   Sunday   4 – 35 AM   Robin,   Lady Alice Douglas who comes here regular on drama classes wishes to say that I should be free – if you remember I had my photo taken with her recently also with friend inmate Simon Melia   Lady Alice has been offered 5 grand by News of World to do this story but she did not get on with reporter who interviewed her so turned it down   Im hoping she will let you act on her behalf   Forget all I said on phone yesterday re this about innuendo etc and also on financial aspect   Just get the best deal that you can for her and negotiate your percentage with the lady.   This is her phone number   Try make it big deal   God Bless   Friend   Reg   Don't mention her name over phone

for Kevin to play himself in the film, and they would get publicity by saying he'd been in *The Krays* movie. When Kevin pointed out the movie had already been released, Reg said he'd arrange for the film to be edited, to contain images showing Kevin; he would also fix it for him to be in the credits. Reg was clearly besotted and saying, and doing, anything to keep the relationship alive. But it was already too late. Kevin, now very worried at what he was getting himself into, was eager to find a way out. The final straw, Simon says, came when Reg invited Kevin into his cell and insisted on holding hands. That was taking the friendship too far, Kevin decided. After that, he kept his distance.

This is Reg's bizarre "film treatment," based on his obsession with 21-year-old weight-lifter Kevin Bourner, in Blundeston. Reg felt that actress Sadie Frost was ideal for the part of Kelly. I know that Ronnie listened to Puccini, but had no idea that Reg liked opera, although Charlie did tell me he once went to La Scala, with Frances.

1.   Kevin had stayed away from crime almost since he had met Kelly, she was a good influence on him and Kevin had given his word he would not commit another crime, but Kelly had accused Kevin wrongly of committing a crime and this,   [(side note) Lindsey As you know everyone loves a success story and romance]

2.   Had hurt his feelings very badly. Kevin thought a lot of Kelly. He liked the musical sound of her name and felt he was in love. A kind of first young love to his way of reckoning, but she said wrong to accuse him, she had also said to

3.   Kevin that he would never make the grade in life and this had left him with a desperation to prove her wrong and he so wanted to be different to others who led a dull routine existence, hence his second spree into crime when on home leave, as he felt

4.   If he had been wrongly accused then it should become a fact that he did commit another crime.

Lindsey: I suggest a scene be taken outside Baker Street. Here the tables are on the sidewalk.

5.   And this is where Kelly accuses Kevin and he gets up from the table and walks away and another scene where Kelly is watching the screen showing The Kray film and Kevin's' name is shown on the film credits as the list

6.   Of names unfold.

I strongly suggest the screen to depict a young love story and success story. Young love story Kevin and Kelly which breaks up and shows the ultimate success of Kevin as a somebody.

(Side note)   Sadie Frost could play Kelly!

7.   Kev
Squat   175
Bench   105
Deadlift 210
   Place this in Kevs' history.

8.   Lindsey, Mannerisms.   Kev has a way of nodding his head in agreement at times. Take note.

9.   Mannerisms of Kev.

Best mannerisms to capture on camera of Kev are when he is standing up and looking down at the floor this shows his profile and long lashes and you can see him in a thoughtful frame of mind.

Another is when he is sitting on a sofa with someone sitting to his right and Kev looks toward this person, it is as if he cocks his head and is in a quizzical manner of curiosity.

He also has a way of looking up from half closed eyes if he feels someone is looking at him. At all times he comes across as the strong silent type, a man of few words.

One time I watched him place a press cutting in an envelope and fold the flap of the envelope inside the letter to drop out of the window to someone beneath the window and it was the actions of a precise and calm disposition of personality, I feel these should be watched on screen.

The Joe Bloggs (advert/ image?) In jeans stripped to the waist should show Kevin in a good light. Also when Kev listens intently his eyes seem to cloud over when he is in deep thought or conversation.

      Please note these mannerisms for the future.

10.   Lindsey. Sometimes during the early night I would press the button on my cell wall to be allowed out of my cell to go to the toilet but instead of going to the toilet I would walk round to Kevs' spur and go to his cell door to talk to him or pass him a

11.   note of advice written on paper which I would pass beneath his door and we would talk through the cell door- it would be either advice or a chat in general or to congratulate Kev on how well he copes.

12.   Visits for Kev and I how it all came together for Kev. We had a visit off of Lennie (Maclean) – Dave Lea which the Bodybuilder Dave offered to help Kev all he can.   We had a visit from Lennie – Dave and Penny who agreed to be Kevs' casting agent. We had visit from Lennie – Penny – Lindsey and Sadie, all offered to help Kev and

Lindsey agreed to Film idea Reg Krays' protégé. Razor Kev and I.

13.   Helen Keating agreed over the phone to be Kevs landlady and friend for home leave appeal! Helen visited us with Willie Reid? And Willie said he would help Kev with his lines when Kev is in Eastenders-   The Sun newspaper showed photos of Willie visiting Kev and I at Blundestone.

14.   Kev. The competition night went well for Kev he was star of the show. We all shouted his name. We got together a banner which read "Ice cool Kev" this was placed on the front row of the spectators seats for all to see and each time Kev walked on the he got a great applause.

(Side note) Kev was next due home leave on the same day as his weights competition the 9th of Sep.

15.   Kev made the weight easy (after?) he got us both scared before the competition, Kev only failed one lift, a deadlift- the next he did easy without trouble- he is now a Bronze grading, when he was going for his black grading. The banner was placed above his cell door for when he got back to the wing and I got him two steak suppers and sandwiches. (side note) Kev weighed in at 12 stone 7 lbs

16.   18th Sep. We had contingency plans ready to put into effect Saturday if Kev got a knockback on his home leave which would prevent his recall in 2 films the Lennie Maclean film "The Governor" and the Jack Palance film which Kev had been offered parts in. The contingency plan was for Kev to still be able to still get a big part despite being kept inside. (Side note) Billy sell Kevs story to a national.

17.   The plan was to get him in the Kray sequel film and this was achieved when at my suggestion our friend Wilf Pine approached those in charge Kev has been promised this particular part.

The film is to be made in the spring that is when Kev shall be released. I had a visit with Wilf but Kev was not present as we had a fall

18.   out, so Kev never knew of the news 'til 24 hours later when I gave it to him and he was as delighted and we shook hands and forgot our differences.

The difference was mainly due to prison pressures, anyway all Kevs and our friends were happy for him getting the part as Kev showed them the note.

19.   His ....? To the part.

Night exercise is finishing here on the field so the time I exercise has been let down as the winter months draw closer. Kev goes in for his black grading on October the 5th, which he should be able to get. We need to rig past so as to put something solid in Kevs film as success story.

20. Bill, Lynsey- I feel we must make the most out of the fact that they refused Kev home leave despite they had letters from film producers re: Lennies film part for Kev, which he could have appeared in on his home leave and despite fact I personally spoke to number one Governor Robinson for ½ an hour.

21. As I have always said there is no rehabilitation in prisons and it shows plainly in the clear disappointment of Kev. Though he remains strong physically and mentally they are just delaying the inevitable, (side note) 10th sep. Today Kev got put on a charge for wiring up his radio to the light instead of using batteries.

22. BOOKS
Mapsheet by Blackie Aldett
I Willie Sutton by Willie Sutton
War book by Captain Ron Famel
All 3 are in the library
(side note) The Mighty Atom

23. SHOWS
West Side Story
OPERA
Madame Butterfly at La Scala
Joan Sutherland at Covent Garden

24. FILMS
Lawrence of Arabia   Peter O'Toole
Gordon of Khartoum
The four feathers

SHOWS
Oh what a lovely war.
Things ain't what they used to be.
Oliver

This is the letter to Kevin that Reg asked fellow inmate Simon Melia to type for him

Kevin please read this carefully and weigh up.

I ask you to forget the misunderstandings so we can remain friends, most friends argue in these places – Pat and Tony did but they remain friends.

Also I will make some changes to suit you. Instead of me following you round like a dog?

I'll go back to being a basic loner I will only come round to your spur to see you if really necessary, as of late I have only been mixing a lot to please you. I don't like a lot of company, also it will be up to you if you want to get your own meals or not its not a big issue.

I will cut out the Friday nights if you wish and only consult you if I feel it's really important. We will not discuss the things you do not wish to hear. You can rely on me to get on with your career the best way I can.

The only things I need your cooperation on is for you to type up the treatment in your own time as I prefer you to do it rather than anyone else. Billy and Lynsey need it.

I am also happy for you on the weights and on all visits I'll mark your card so you can agree to see whoever will visit. Wilf and Lyall will be here on Wednesday. And I wish for you to be present, if you agree. I ask you to weigh up one bad fault Re; typing which has spoken against all my good intent. So we can both get on with our lives in here and be reasonably happy.

Billy Lynsey and Lenny are our friends. We owe them for their faith in us- what more can I say other than

 (side note) we need to speak to Wilf and Lyall about your past as time is important.

The fact I wish for us to remain friends. I'll come round when I have given you time to decide.

God Bless affection Reg.

(side note) Just so as there are no misunderstandings it is not your fault I followed you round but mine. I've ordered zinc tablets for you!

There was another young prisoner, however, who Reg became close to – too close, in Wilf Pine's view. The young man's name was Paul and when Wilf arrived at Blundeston to discuss some confidential business with Reg, he was in the visiting room, too.

"This is my friend," Reg said, as Wilf sat down.

"Hello, mate," Wilf said. Then, as Reg started speaking, Wilf leaned towards him and said: "I need to talk to you, Reg."

"You can talk to me," Reg said.

Wilf glanced at the young man. "Reg," he said. "I need to talk to *you*."

"Anything you have to say to me, you can say in front of Paul," Reg said.

"Reg," Wilf said, impatiently. "I've come a long fucking way. It's important I talk to you. It is in the interests of my business, your business and Ronnie's business."

"Anything you need to say, you can say in front…"

Furious, Wilf got up, stuck his face close to Reg and glared at him. "See ya," he said. And walked out.

The journey from Dorset had taken him over four hours. The visit had lasted less than two minutes. But, such was Wilf's disgust at Reg, he didn't care.

*

If I was surprised to hear that Simon Melia had set out to become a top-class criminal after leaving the Army at twenty, I was shocked at what he told me about Reg's life behind Blundeston's bars: "If you were around Reg, you could be out of your face with drugs 24/7," he told me. "As long as one was prepared to graft for it, he had stuff that needed selling, people he wanted beaten up. We had parties with big bowls of cocaine, then went to bed with five or six valium. I never saw Reg take coke or even have a puff of cannabis, although he said he used to. He did valium, though.

"He was always on the phone. We were allowed only a couple of phone cards each, but Reg would buy loads, in return for all kinds of drugs. The deals were done, openly – on camera – in the main drag between the two Wings, nicknamed "Bond Street." I sold drugs for Reg and, basically, he looked after me. Once, somebody short-changed me by £2, and Reg expected me to do something about it. The next time we heard the guy was on "Bond Street," I went up to him – Reg behind me – and smacked him. I'm six-feet and boxed in the Army and was able to take care of myself, but the guy pulled out a big knife, and Reg being there was the only reason he didn't use it. I never saw Reg get into physical violence with other prisoners. He didn't do anything to warrant it and, anyway, he had so much respect from people around him, it wouldn't have been allowed.

"He always dressed smartly – cufflinks and pressed jeans – and wore lots of jewellery, but was not overtly bigheaded about his reputation. He never wanted to discuss what was going on inside. He found prison politics boring and negative, a waste of time, and if anyone started banging on, he'd change the subject as quickly as he could. He told me he'd always tried to live his life outside the prison walls, not inside. That's why he had an insatiable appetite for phone cards. They were his lifeblood, and he'd think nothing of queueing for hours to make his calls."

*

On 1 March, I rang Charlie after reading in the *Daily Mail* that he'd been questioned for more than six hours the previous day by police investigating the murder of a London financier, named Donald Urquhart. The story was below a headline, *KRAY BROTHER QUIZZED IN MURDER PROBE*, and I knew that Charlie would be upset that, once again, the Kray name was causing him grief.

"What's that all about?" I asked.

"You tell me, Rob," Charlie said. "What is it with these people? I'm sixty eight years old. What would I know about the murder of someone I haven't met?"

"We've got to do something about it, Charlie," I said.

"What can we do?" he said. "I was arrested and now it's in the papers. People will think, no smoke without fire."

"I'll come up with something," I said. "Can you shoot over?"

"Of course, I can. Anything you can do, I'll be grateful, you know that."

"Yeah, yeah," I said, smiling to myself; Charlie never expected anything and when he got something he was *always* grateful. "Just get here ASAP."

"I'll have Gary with me. Is that okay?"

"Of course."

Less than an hour later, Charlie arrived from Croydon and Sue put the coffee on.

"Charlie are you prepared to go on television?" I asked.

"Of course," he said. "Why?"

"To let people see you're a lovely bloke who happens to have a name that's making your life hell."

"Do you think anyone will want to have me talking about that?"

"I think so," I said. "An exclusive interview with you on the back of a murder inquiry should be perfect. Would you be prepared to go on this evening?"

"Of course," he said.

"Well, let's see if they want you."

So I rang *London Tonight*, put the idea to someone on the News Desk and, later that afternoon, Charlie was on his way up the Old Kent Road to tell the programme's viewers what it meant being a Kray. He was interviewed live by the programme's very professional and likeable presenter Alastair Stewart and came over brilliantly, very focussed on the sole reason for him being there.

That was one side of Charlie Kray. Unfortunately, and frustratingly, I saw a different side the next day when I set up another interview on the same basis, with the producers of the *Richard and Judy Show*, which was screened live from Liverpool, and had a national audience. Charlie and I were flown up in a six-seater plane, that, very conveniently, took off from Biggin Hill – 15 minutes from my home – and all the way there, and in the hospitality room at the studios, I coached Charlie on how to handle the interview. I didn't think that Richard Madeley or Judy Finnigan would have their own agenda, but one can never be sure. I told Charlie there was one reason why he was going on the show, and that was to talk about the curse of the Kray name; to describe how it was affecting his life, to the extent that he'd been arrested and questioned about a murder he knew nothing about.

I pleaded with him to boss the interview, to stick to the point and not be side-tracked into talking about all the usual rubbish everyone had heard before. I could have saved my breath. The first question Madeley asked him was: "What was it like with the twins in the sixties?" – and Charlie was off, reliving the oft-told nonsense. I'd be less than truthful if I said I couldn't believe he'd blown a heaven-sent opportunity to get his feelings across to millions of people. I could! That was Charlie. He didn't have the confidence to say he wasn't there to talk about the old days, couldn't steer the conversation his way. It was this lack of arrogance that made him so different from the twins. Unlike them, he never forced himself on anyone – even when he had every right to. It could be irritating at times, as it was that day, and, frankly, I did give Charlie a hard time on the bumpy flight back to Kent.

*

The following month, after he'd arrived at Maidstone, Reg wrote to me, saying he didn't want to go ahead with my TV drama series idea. He'd given a lot of thought to the idea, he said, but felt he would not be able to put "*the necessary visit time into it*." That didn't add up to me and, two weeks later, he admitted that wasn't why he'd kicked the idea into touch. The real reason, he said, was the percentage: he didn't want to give away a third to me. Reg pointed out that the next day was the 26th "anniversary" of the day he and his brothers were arrested – an ideal peg, I thought, on which to hang an in-depth, revealing interview. But, since Reg hated revisiting the past, I felt it a waste of time to suggest it.

A week later I heard from Ronnie for the first time in five months, when he wrote, replying to a letter from me. Ronnie thanked me for my "*nice letter,*" and said, again, that he wanted to collaborate on a book with me. He was being monitored by a different doctor – a woman named Jones - and was going to

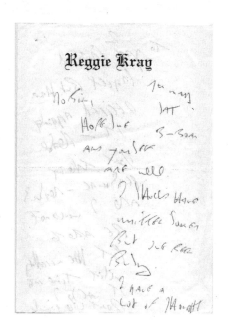

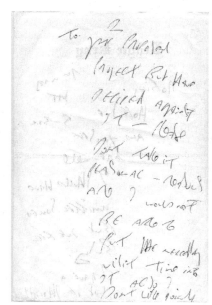

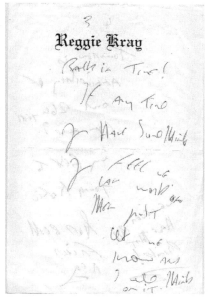

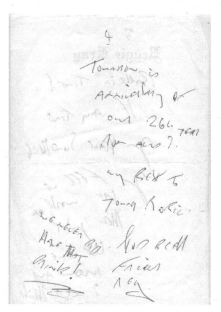

7th May   Sat 3 – 30AM   Robin,   Hope Sue and yourself are well.   I should have written sooner but Ive been busy.   I have a lot of thought to your proposed project but have decided against it – please don't take it personal reasons and I would not be able to put the necessary visit time into it also I don't like going back in time!   If any time you have something you feel we can work on then just let me know and I will think on it.   Tomorrow is anniversary of our 26th year Ron and I.   My best to young Robin   God Bless   Friend   Reg   We never did have that drink!

Sat 14th May 1994 Ron Kray (1) My dear Freind Robin Thank you for the nice letter I am now back on Henley Ward so will see you as soon as PTO Doctor Jones clears you   I have told Doctor Jones that I want to do a book with you   She is going to let me know if it is OK or not   If Doctor Jones can clear you next Tusday when I see her I will see you the following Monday morning if that is OK I will let PTO you know God Bless Love to Sue Your friend Ron

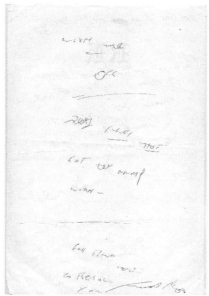

Sat 11th June 1994   Ron Kray   (1) Dear Robin   Let me know as soon as you have been cleared to see me and I will see you OK   I want you to do a book with me OK   Reg has not got the hump with you   (xxxxxxxxxxxxxxxxxxxx – cannot decipher) Your friend   Ron

ask her permission to work with me; if he got the go-ahead, he wanted to see me the following Monday morning. He never said what happened when he saw Doctor Jones, but a few weeks later, Ronnie wrote again, repeating that he wanted to do a book with me.

I must have told Ronnie I'd had a disagreement with Reg, for he went on to say that his brother "*had not got the hump*" with me. I'm not sure that was right, because, ten days later, Ronnie wrote again, telling me he was now *not* going to do a book with me, but I could handle his business affairs if he was released; indeed, he didn't want me to visit any more unless we had business to discuss. Ronnie knew I wouldn't be happy about this because he signed off, telling me not to be upset, "*as I do hold you in high regard.*"

I didn't have long to be upset! The next day, a letter arrived, telling me to take no notice of what he'd written, and that he would see me "*as soon as I can.*" Two weeks later, I received another letter, saying I'd been cleared; could I visit in August? I was delighted: I'd missed speaking with Ronnie and would make sure I was free to go to Broadmoor. Sadly, the visit never happened: nine days before our scheduled meeting, he wrote, saying he couldn't see me because his face had come up in lumps.

I never saw Ronnie again.

Tusday 21st June 1994 Ron Kray Broadmoor (1) My dear freind Robin Thank you for the letter I am not now going to do a book with you Robin but if I get out you can PTO Handle all my business OK Please give Sue my best wishes as allways I have not read the Sabini book Robin PTO I wont see you now on a visit as I don't like visets only if I have business to do PTO Please don't be upset by this as I do hold you in high reguard God Bless Your friend Ron

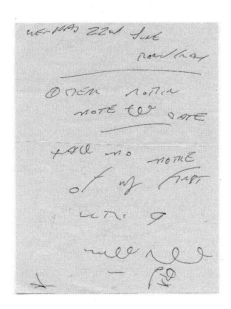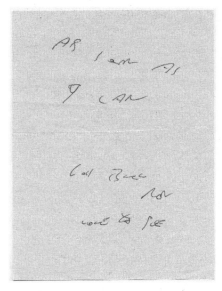

Wensday 22nd June   Ron Kray   (1)   Dear Robin   Note the date   Take no notice of my first letter I will see you   PTO   As soon as I can   God Bless   Ron Love to Sue

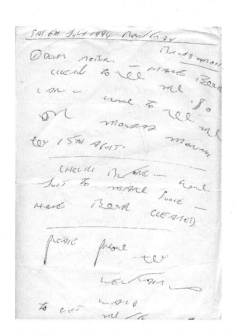

Sat 6th July 1994   Ron Kray   Broadmoor   (1) Dear Robin   You have been cleared to see me so can you come to see me on Monday morning the 15th Agust   Check before you come just to make sure you have been cleared   Please phone the Welfair and ward to let me know   PTO If you can make it   Please give your dear wife my best wishes   God Bless   Ron

6th Agust 1994   Ron Kray   (1) Dear Robin   Cant see you now next Monday as all my face has come up in lumps   Will get in touch soon   Best to Sue   God Bless   Ron Sorry

Chapter Fourteen

KELVIN MacKenzie's News Editor, Tom Petrie, had left *The Sun* and was now News Editor at *The People.* Every Tuesday morning, he'd ring me, asking: "Have you got anything up your sleeve for us this week?" – and, on the first Tuesday that August, I had.

The previous Sunday, the paper had run a double-page spread on Lord Longford wanting Myra Hindley to be given extra privileges, now that she had, supposedly, found God. And it had given me an idea I was sure Tom would find irresistible. Knowing how Reg felt about the evil bitch, I was sure he'd love a platform to air his feelings. I was equally sure the paper would give him space: indeed, depending on how controversial Reg was, and how much he said, the article could even make another double-page spread. A gangland legend attacking the country's most despised child killer was vintage Sunday newspaper copy and, unsurprisingly, Tom – and his editor, Bridget Rowe – went for it.

The only way I could see the story working was for me to get some key questions to Reg, via Stephanie King, and interview him on the phone. Then I'd write a piece on his behalf, which the paper would run as a long "To the Editor" letter, with Reg's signature at the end.

"Sounds great, Rob," Tom said. "Obviously, we'll need it for this week."

Stephanie confirmed that Reg liked the idea and I faxed her some questions, which, if he did his part, would give me the ammunition for a potent 2,000-word letter. It was straightforward and should have been easy, but, as usual, Reg made it complicated and, for a while, worryingly difficult. When he rang, as arranged, the following afternoon, I was ready to record an interview. But Reg said: "I've written the letter and posted it today."

"What do you mean, you've written the letter?" I said, curtly. "Didn't Stephanie give you my questions?"

No, she hadn't, Reg said. But he'd decided to write the letter himself anyway. I wanted to scream: "You idiot – you're killing a five grand deal here!" Instead, hoping to hide my irritation, I said: "I need to ask you some questions, Reg."

"Yeah, yeah," he said.

"Do you feel Myra Hindley should stay in jail for the rest of her life?" I asked.

"I've put all this in the letter," Reg said. "I've put it all in the letter."

Not sure that Reg had read the previous Sunday's article, I told him that Lord Longford felt that Hindley would make a super secretary and should be let out immediately. "Well, I have also made a mention about him and her in my letter," Reg said.

"So, what do you think about Hindley being allowed all sorts of privileges?"

"I haven't mentioned that because my letter takes care of every aspect,"

Reg said.

Good grief! Then, just as I was thinking I wouldn't get the piece Tom was expecting, Reg hit me with another worry.

"There's only one thing you might find a problem – which I don't," he said. "I want it printed in its entirety, or not at all. Because, if it doesn't get printed in there, I'm putting it in my book anyway."

"Right, okay," I said, thinking the conversation was anything but right and okay.

"What I've done," Reg went on, "is I've written a letter, ad-libbed to my friend, dictated it to my friend…he's written it in his own longhand and I signed it. It covers every aspect of the whole thing."

"All right," I said, doubting that. "Can I ask you this, then? Do you think, if *you'd* said that you had found God, you would be allowed out for shopping trips?"

It was a simple enough question, and Reg's answer, whatever it was, would make usable copy. But he said: "I'd rather discuss nothing about myself. I'm not seeking publicity for myself. Okay, forget that. But I think you'll be pleased with whole letter. But it must be in its entirety, and not changed. Otherwise, I'm not bothered about it."

I ignored him. "How do you feel about child molesters, Reg?"

"Well, that's a different aspect, innit? I won't get involved in that one."

"It's *not* different," I said. "It's the whole *point*."

"No, no, no. Sometimes some of these women are mixed up, ain't they?" I felt he hadn't grasped the point, and I was right, because he then said: "You're talking about child *what*?"

"Molesters."

"Oh, I don't like child molesters. But just forget me on that one. I've done what I have had to do, you know, about Hindley, and that is all I'm going to do, okay? So, I don't want to be drawn into anything else, eh?"

"Okay," I said, fearful that I was losing the battle, and wouldn't give the paper the spread they expected.

But Reg was rattling on, convinced he'd done what was asked. "You decide when you get the letter, and let your editor decide, and if he accepts it as it is, in its entirety…I can't just change things, just with questions."

"You can't expect an editor to say that they'll use something in its entirety," I snapped. "Not even Jeffrey Archer can do that."

That clearly rankled with Reg, because he said, with ill-disguised pomposity: "They have asked for a letter. They asked for a letter on my views on Hindley. And that is what I have given. And if they don't like it, I'm not bothered, because I'm putting it in one of my books anyway." Then, realising he might be pushing me too far, he added: "I'm not being awkward about this, but I can't be asked to write a letter and when I do so, they change it."

Resisting the temptation to tell him he hadn't been asked to *write* anything,

I said: "I asked you to speak to me on the phone…and to…"

"In my opinion," Reg interrupted, "I have done better than the questions you asked me. I have answered every aspect…"

"Reg, you've got a platform here – *mate*!"

But even that didn't cut any ice. "I'm not looking for publicity myself on the strength of little children who died, you know," he said.

"I know."

"I'm not interested in myself. I am not interested in myself. You understand?"

Now seriously worried I was going to be embarrassed with Tom Petrie, I was unable to hide my irritation: "We can't really speak, can we?"

"We *can* speak," Reg said. "But you think I'm going to get fucking publicity down to deaths of little children? I'm not a fucking slag, you know."

"It's not about them," I snapped. "It's about Hindley."

"I know it's about Hindley… I'm doing this because you asked me a question and I have answered it. I've done what you asked me to do and I can't do no more. So, I don't see why we're arguing."

"Did Stephanie give you the questions?"

"No," Reg said.

"Right. Well, I'm trying to ask you them. Do you think Hindley is lying about her remorse merely to get parole?"

Again, it was a simple enough question that might provide a headline. But, frustratingly, Reg stonewalled it. "Every aspect, I have covered in my letter. Otherwise we could continue for ever more. I have done a letter, which has covered every angle, in my opinion."

"Okay."

"And it condemns the woman, and that is all I have set out to do."

"Right. Have you said you feel she should stay in prison for the rest of her life?"

"Yes. Words to that effect, yes. So, you be the judge when you see it. I've sent it today, so you should have it first thing tomorrow, I would imagine. What time do you get post?"

"Well, it's just come," I said. "I've just got a letter from Ron. He can't see me Monday because he's got lumps all over his face. Did you know?"

Reg was not interested in the slightest. "Yeah, yeah. I don't see why he keeps publicising his afflictions. Anyway, what's the best time to phone you tomorrow morning, after you've read the letter?"

"Any time," I said.

"I don't see why we're arguing…I'm not in for arguing."

"It's just that you always seem to say you know best. I'm the journalist. I'm trying to get something in the paper that matters a lot to you, Reg."

"Yeah," he said. "And I've done what you asked me to. You asked me to do something on Hindley, and that's what I've done. To the best of my abilities.

You can't tell me what to write because it's me doing it, you see. I have got my own head. I use my own brain."

"I know. You seem to think I'm talking down to you."

"No, no," he said, quickly. "You're not talking down to me on this occasion, but you're auto-suggesting me."

"Okay, mate."

"If you're not satisfied with it, I'll be very surprised. But that's entirely up to you."

"How long is the letter?" I asked, dreading him saying he'd kept it brief. To make a decent show in the paper, we needed at least 1,500 words, but I was hoping for more.

Reg called out to another prisoner who said the letter made three A4 pages. I was relieved: with photographs of Reg and Hindley, that should be enough for a spread.

"Okay, now listen," I said. "I've got to put you in the land of reality. No newspaper editor can guarantee using every single word of a letter. Not even the Prime Minister can get that."

"Well, I'll tell you one thing that must be left in, then…"

"Your mate," I cut in.

"Yes, my friend."

"What's his name?"

"It's self-explanatory," Reg said, cuttingly. "Joe Martin."

"How do you spell that?"

"M.A.R.T.I.N," Reg spelled out, sneeringly. "You should know how to spell the word *Martin*."

"Yeah, could be with a Y, Reg," I volleyed back.

"Well, it's with an I."

"Okay," I said, then asked if the letter included what Joe was in prison for.

"I have put it exactly – yes, yes, yes," Reg said.

I told him I would guarantee Joe a mention by making that a condition the paper was getting the letter. But Reg was unimpressed.

"Well, either they do, or they don't," he said. "Because if they don't give it a mention, I don't want the letter published. It's as simple as that."

"Right," I said.

"Okay. Fair enough? Speak to you later."

I should have left it there, but Reg's strong desire to help his mate prompted me to return to Hindley.

"I think you're more of a Christian than she is, Reg."

"Possibly," he said. "I don't know. I'm not talking about myself…" Then, what I'd said seemed to hit home, and he said, angrily: "I don't consider it a gee that you're telling me I'm more Christian than that fucking slut. I should think I am…I don't need you to tell me that, do I? Eh? Pardon?"

"All right."

"I find that a bit insulting really, to even compare me with the dirty fucking slut, eh? I'll phone you tomorrow."

"Okay."

"Right?"

"Okey-doke. Bye."

*

Reg's letter did arrive the next day: three pages of neatly-written longhand; not the 1,500 words I was hoping for, but around 1,000, which, with photographs, was still enough to make a spread. It was well-written and said everything the paper wanted. Indeed, the only thing wrong was that Reg hadn't written it. If I hadn't been corresponding with him for so long, and been privy to how his frenetic mind worked when putting thoughts on paper, I might have been fooled. But the well-constructed, immaculately-punctuated document was clearly the work of someone else – probably his pal, Bradley Allardyce, although I knew nothing of his background to suggest he was capable of such an erudite piece of work. I read the letter a second time, dwelling on emotional, poignant phrases Reg would never have dreamt of, let alone put on paper. Families of Hindley's victims, he said, knew *the scales of sorrow and joy can only weigh down in sorrow for the rest of their lives.* Of the victims themselves, *so many springs and summers and autumns to live through, and at Christmas they would have received their toys with joy, and I know with stark reality that they were deprived of these innocent pleasures and my heart hardens toward the release of Hindley.* Those flowery ramblings were not the creation of someone who, over the past nine years, had shown he could scribble nothing but the briefest of sentences and had the most limited vocabulary.

My initial worry was Tom Petrie; I would not want to embarrass him. He knew me well enough to know I hadn't written the letter myself and sent it to the prison for someone to copy and have Reg sign. But who could blame him if he didn't want to show his Editor something purporting to be from a Kray twin when it clearly wasn't. Then there was Reg himself. I'd listened to the recording of our conversation, heard again how pleased he was with the letter, how keen he was to see it in the paper "in its entirety." How could I possibly tell him: "Nice try, mate, but no way is a newspaper going to run that, much less pay money for it." Apart from when I'd lost my rag, in Parkhurst, at being asked to make that phone call, we'd barely had a cross word, but who knows what would happen if I accused him of trying to con a national newspaper. To be honest, I didn't think I could do that; I would have to get round it some other way; blame the paper perhaps; say that what he'd written was fine, but they couldn't include the Joe Martin references, so they'd decided not to run the letter at all.

In the end I decided not to try to second-guess Tom, just sent him the letter.

Surprisingly, he didn't question its authenticity; just said he liked the letter, and so did Bridget. It was perfect for that week's paper. And, yes, it was probably going to make two pages.

Knowing how quickly a story can be in one minute, and out the next, I didn't let on to Reg that I'd sent the letter to the paper. When he called that afternoon, I just said I'd received the letter and thought it was very good.

"It covers all aspects, don't you think so?"

"Yep."

"That was what I was trying to achieve," he said. "I'm glad you like it, anyway. So would you try and get it in, in its entirety. I know it's a bit difficult, but if it's split up, as you'll appreciate, it will break it up."

"I will make that point to them."

Then, as the letter referred to his friend, I asked him if he wanted Bradley's name in the paper. Reg said he did, but was more concerned with Joe Martin getting a mention. As the letter also referred to Reg meeting Lord Longford, I asked him how many times they'd spoken. "I met him on three or four occasions in Parkhurst," Reg said. "I told him I disagreed with his views. He is quite a nice man. He's a humanitarian and if he had his way he'd let everyone out of prison. But, with Hindley, he is wasting his time and spoiling what could be good efforts on behalf of other people who are more worthy of it."

"Did he try to get *you* out?"

"I suppose in his own way he did voice that kind of sentiment years ago," Reg said. "I don't know, I don't really know. But he would never do anyone any harm."

Keen to beef up the letter, I praised Reg for making nasty comments about Ian Brady, and asked if he felt both killers should have been hanged years ago. Diplomatically, he said he didn't want to get into a debate about capital punishment because innocent people could get hanged. Knowing the paper would want him to compare his case with Hindley, I prepared the way by reminding him how we'd ended our conversation the previous evening. "Sue has told me not to raise my voice to you because I get you going the wrong way."

"No, it's not that," Reg said. "It's not the raising of your voice – I don't mind that at all. But when you compare my case with theirs, it really is a bit insulting, you know. I know you don't mean it that way, but, as far as I'm concerned, I'm like chalk and cheese compared to them people, you know."

"You do realise, I was just thinking, from a newspaper point of view, that it would be good for you to say – Don't compare *my* case with hers."

"No, I would rather stay out of it completely," Reg said. "I'm not writing on my behalf, I'm writing for Joe, and my sentiments against Hindley and Brady. I don't want to bring myself into the picture at all."

"Well, let's talk about Joe, then," I persisted. "If *he* said he'd found God, do you think *he'd* be let out for shopping?"

"I can't speak for Joe…because he's not present and I don't think he would like anything like that."

Fighting to hide my exasperation, I asked: "If you said *you'd* found God, would you be allowed out for shopping trips?"

"I won't get involved in that," Reg countered. "It's a different issue."

"You should have been a politician, mate."

"Pardon?"

"You should have been a politician."

"If you took away her privileges, it would be taking other people's privileges and stuff. I won't get involved in them areas, you know."

"Okay," I said, determined to get Reg to answer at least one point raised in the previous *The People* story: "What do you think about her therapist saying that special facilities have enhanced her feeling of well-being?"

As soon as I heard myself reading the question, I knew that Reg would not have grasped it.

"Pardon," he said.

When I repeated it, Reg said: "Well, it probably has done, but, whether it's justifiable or not is another issue I won't get involved in. I've said what I have to say and now I'm going to leave it at that, please, if you don't mind."

"Okay," I said, feeling strangely defeated. Then I thanked him and said I thought he'd done well.

"I'm very pleased you say so," he said. "So, do you think it will be in this Sunday?"

"I think so," I said.

That should have been the end of it. But, typically, Reg wouldn't be fobbed off.

"Okay," he said. "Shall I phone back and find out some other time?"

I wanted to tell him to wait until Sunday because self-respecting freelances don't like bothering executives with, "Is my story going in?" and "How are you using it?" when they probably won't know themselves until nearer their copy deadlines. But, there was another reason I wanted to forget about the piece until it did - or did not - appear. Earlier that week, I'd told Reg that a dear friend of ours was dying and I was going to be out of reach while we spent time with him. When I reminded Reg, it cut no ice. After a brief "Sorry to hear about that," he demanded to know when I could let him know if the letter was going to be published.

I said I'd find out later that day. I didn't know whether I would, but it would get him off the phone and buy me some time. That wasn't good enough for Reg.

"What time is later today…"

Jesus!

"…then I can phone you."

"Well, I won't be in. But…"

"Would you phone Steph?"

"Yeah, will do…I'm going to be out for a couple of days."

"Yeah, but when will you be phoning Steph?"

"Erm," I stalled "Five o'clock."

"Five o'clock? Well, I'll phone Steph after five."

"Okay." I was sure that would be the end of it. But I was wrong.

"What's the position if they want to break it up?"

"I'm going to say that the condition of using this is that they have got to use Joe Martin."

"Of course," Reg said. "I would like you to try and do me the favour of getting it in its entirety because, as I said, I feel that if you break it up, it won't get home what I've tried to convey. So, can I leave it to you, eh?"

I wanted to scream, 'Yes, you can, you pushy old git,' but, instead, I tried flannelling him. "This is a chance for me to impress you, isn't it?"

"Yes," he replied. "It is really…we've done nothing on the past three occasions… regardless of whose fault it was."

He paused, then, deciding enough was enough, said: "So I'm going to leave you now, Robin."

"Okay, then."

"I wish you luck."

"Well done, mate."

The full text of *The People* story.

Gangland killer Reggie Kray was so incensed that murderer Myra Hindley may be being groomed for release, as The People reported last week, that he has written to us, backing our campaign to keep her behind bars for the rest of her life.

In a dramatic letter from Maidstone Prison, 60-year-old Kray says his eyes filled with tears as he thought about evil Hindley being freed and imagined the stark terror her child victims suffered before their deaths. And he reveals for the first time that he has tried to comfort some of the mothers of the murdered children.

Here, in his own words, is Kray's remarkable letter

"OF RECENT, there has been a lot of speculation as to the possible release of Myra Hindley, which has left me in complete disgust, in that her release should even have reached the point of debate.

Many years ago while at Parkhurst Prison I had the displeasure of being next door in a cell to Ian Brady.

At this particular time I was in the hospital block on the observation ward F2 and I was banged up for 24 hours a day for five years, and though the scum Brady was nearby he was well minded by the hospital staff. I caught only a glimpse of his evil eyes.

My brother Ron had also seen Brady from a distance while at Durham prison and Ron said that Brady was very arrogant! Myra Hindley and Brady perpetrated the most heinous of tortures on little children before cold-bloodedly killing them, and it is my opinion, and the opinion of 95 per cent of the prison population, that the heathen pair should never be released into society. I am not a squeamish person when it comes to blood and violence, but I could never bring myself to read the books written on the barbaric deeds of the evil pair.

And just prior to writing this letter I can honestly say that when speaking to my friend Bradley Allardise (sic) about the possible release of Myra Hindley it brought tears to my eyes, because I could visualise what stark terror the children who were victims went through in ordeal before their deaths.

Stark terror must have reached the very bones of these poor children before they came to the abyss of death, and when I think of the families of these children and how they have suffered it makes me very sad.

I have in the past received letters from the mothers of some of these children to which I have replied and I know that the scales of sorrow and joy, which is part of life, can only weigh down in sorrow for the rest of the families' lives.

I also feel that if Hindley had true remorse she would suffer her imprisonment in remorse and would not wish to be released, and that she would be humble and sorrowful enough to prevent any further suffering of the parents of the children that suffered.

I know that recently, and in the past, Lord Longford has clamoured for the release of Hindley, but I make him wrong on this issue and the same goes for his colleagues who may wish to see Hindley released.

Lord Longford in my opinion is a good man and a humanitarian, but I feel that his concern for the release of Hindley is misplaced and when I met Lord Longford I told him my views on this issue.

Unfortunately, Lord Longford has not done his image any good by clamouring for Hindley's release and my opinion is that he has wasted time on such a person when he could have done so much for others.

In complete contrast to the extreme, I have a friend here at Maidstone prison who has been my friend for 30 years.

His name is Joe Martin, and he is serving a life sentence without, I repeat, without recommendation on length and yet he has already served 28 years in prison.

He has never been outside the gates for even a day's parole and still has no release date, whereas Hindley has had day trips outside. My friend Joe was convicted of the murder of man during a robbery.

He has accepted his punishment like a man, in comparison with the wailings of Hindley, and Joe is recognised as a man of principle throughout the system.

He also has to his merit the fact that he has served his country in the time of war when he fought with the British Army in Korea.

Joe is also a royalist and shows no bitterness to the fact that he has served such a number of years.

Only today, one of the prison screws here at Maidstone said to me, when asked the question of release of Hindley, that he could not understand how she could be considered.

The officer also said that he would welcome Joe for lunch any time at his house to be shared by the officer and his wife.

I would like to add that I am in constant touch with children who I have befriended and in fact I am godfather to some, so I know how sweet and innocent they are and I think of everything that the Brady and Hindley victims have been deprived of.

They had so many birthdays to celebrate. So many springs, summers and autumns to live through and at Christmas they would have received their toys with joy, and I know with stark reality that they were deprived of these innocent pleasures and my heart hardens toward the release of Hindley.

I have always said there is a difference between Mad and Bad and I can feel for those who are maybe Mad.

But in the case of Hindley, she has both symptoms, that of Mad and Bad, and I put my voice beside the families of those who have suffered at the loss of dear children in that Hindley should not be released back into society.

Her punishment of life in prison can never compensate the loss of the lives after torture of the innocent children. God's children.

God Bless.

Reg Kray."

*

On Saturday, Tom Petrie phoned to tell me the letter *had* made a spread. And when I opened the paper the next morning I was delighted: across two pages, beside a photo of Reg, was a white on black headline, *'EVIL HINDLEY ROBBED HER LITTLE VICTIMS OF THEIR BIRTHDAYS, THEIR CHRISTMASSES AND ALL THE JOY OF THEIR LIVES.'* Above it, there was a smaller heading: *'Gangland killer Reggie Kray read last week's People…and then wrote to us.'*

It was a striking layout and as a bonus that would have boosted Reg's ego still further, his letter ran across two columns, below his flamboyant letterhead, which had a head and shoulders photo of him, next to the initials R.K., in bold type. I felt sure Reg would be thrilled, not least, because his letter was run in full - including the Joe Martin mention. But he didn't phone, or write, to say what he thought, much less thank me for arranging such positive exposure. I'd probably impressed him, though, because the next time he rang - a couple of weeks later - he was in a relaxed and chatty mood. I'm so pleased I recorded what turned out to be our friendliest conversation.

"Hello, Robin. You okay?"

"Yeah."

"Been busy, writing, have you?"

"I get up at five o'clock…and write until about half-ten," I said.

"I've been doing that since four o'clock this morning."

"Have you?"

"Yeah, I did that until about 7.30," he said. "I always get up about four o'clock and make lots of notes and discuss them with my friend here - just to start the day. Because I share my thoughts and whatever projects I've got in mind, you know."

"Is this with Bradley?"

"Yes."

"What's he doing time for?"

"He got 12 years for robbery with firearms," Reg said. "He done it out of a sense of adventure really. He went to join the Foreign Legion and had about three months training and got chucked out for different reasons. He was very upset about that and went on robberies, for a sense of adventure rather than boredom. Unfortunately he ended up getting twelve years. But he's doing it well, you know. He is only 26 now. Unless he gets parole, he's got about three or four years left. But he's OK. He's quite happy."

Reg, who knew I was ghosting Chris Lambrianou's autobiography, then referred to a letter I'd written telling him that one of Chris's daughters had been badly injured in a fall.

"Well, the baby is out of intensive care now," I said.

"Very good," Reg said. "You and your wife show a lot of concern for other people, don't you?"

"Very much so."

"Yeah, yeah, yeah. I've noticed this. Your wife, in particular. She's very good. Yeah. It's nice to have time for other people, isn't it, eh?"

"Sue's met Ronnie you know," I said. "Ronnie liked her."

"So I understand," he said. "I can imagine why. By the voice alone, you know. It's very good. Anyway, how are you?"

"Well, I'm struggling with this book, because I need to speak to Chris."

"It is very difficult writing a book, don't you think? Sometimes they flow and sometimes they don't."

I seized the moment to ask what I needed to ask Chris. He'd described a party in a pub and was convinced it was to celebrate Mr and Mrs Kray's wedding anniversary. But the date didn't add up.

"When was your parents' wedding anniversary, Reg?" I asked.

"I don't honestly know," he said. "I honestly don't know. In the East End, peculiar as it may seem, we didn't go on that type of thing. It just wasn't too important."

Thinking Chris may have made a mistake, I said: "Your mum's birthday I meant, actually."

"Fourth of August," Reg replied, immediately.

"I had a feeling it was that because Chris told me something that happened and I just didn't think it was the time."

I asked about the book Reg was working on and he said he was finding it difficult because all there was to say had been said. To me, that was ridiculous. I felt the twins and Fred Dinenage had failed to tell it properly in not one, but two, books. And I thought *Born Fighter* could have been better. "You've got a great story still to be told," I said.

"Fortunately or unfortunately, whatever way you look at it, as each day goes by there is always some more stories cropping up," Reg said. "In the last couple of days, I reached a conclusion on three things, right? It took me sixty years to realise this and I have just told my twenty-six-year-old friend upstairs, so he knows it quicker than I do – or did, I should say. Three things that you should be concerned about and nothing else really: your health, your friends and peace of mind. That is about the most you can ask for out of a lifetime, I would think. I think they are the three most important factors, myself."

"Have you got peace of mind?" I wanted to know.

"To a point," Reg said. "But not entirely. Because every day I get problems. Even though I'm in here, I'm in touch with lots of people, and so I get more problems. If I only had two friends, I would get less problems but the more friends you get, the more problems you get... I mean it works both ways. They can help you or they can hinder you, you know. So, each day unveils another story for me, you know."

"The story of your life in prison would be a possible bestseller, in my view."

"It *would* be a best seller?" Reg questioned.

"Well, possibly."

"Oh, yeah. No doubt about that. Not possibly – it *will* be."

"Well, I always say, possibly," I said. "In life, nothing's guaranteed."

"No. I agree there. Yes. I agree with you there... Who knows what the recipe for a best seller is? No one knows. If we did, we'd all be millionaires, would we, eh?"

"Have you ever heard of a writer called Ken Follett? " I asked.

"No. I can't say I have," Reg said.

"He wrote *Eye Of The Needle*. Heard of that?"

"No, no... was he good?"

"Well, he used to work for me...he's worth 24 million now."

"What kind of writing did he do?"

"He's like a Freddie Forsyth thriller writer," I said, then asked Reg if he'd read *The Key to Rebecca*. It was the book Ken wrote after signing a $3 million three-book deal, on the back of *Eye Of The Needle,* and he'd dedicated it to me as a thank you for publishing his first book, in the seventies, and for introducing him to his American agent Al Zuckerman, who'd helped make him a millionaire.

No, he hadn't read the book, Reg said, adding, without even a hint of irony: "I don't get time for reading."

We spent a few more seconds talking about books, then Reg seemed to realise the cosy chat wouldn't prove profitable. "Anyway it's nice speaking to you, Robin, I'll phone you from time to time."

"We seem quite relaxed now," I said. "We're not having a row."

"Yeah, yeah, yeah. I value you as a friend anyway. Even though we have had our differences, I value you as a friend and I hope you do me, anyway."

"I think you are very straight," I said. And that seemed to press a button in Reg's mercenary mind.

"Thank you. What has happened to that money? Will that be going to them children's mother or what?"

He was referring to his share of *The People* money and I reminded him that I'd be giving it to our mutual friend, Laurie O'Leary.

"Oh, that's okay," Reg said.

I said I'd known Laurie since his days at The Speakeasy, had been to his home, and had had dinner with him at a Chinese restaurant in Stepney. That prompted a rare nostalgic comment.

"Did you ever eat at The Lotus House in Edgware Road?"

I said I had.

"Beautiful there," Reg said. "Smashing food, eh? Anyway, I'll catch you another time, eh?"

"Okay."

"Take care. God Bless. Give your wife my love. Cheerio."

Chapter Fifteen

FOR Reg to say he had "friends" was not only untrue it was pathetic: he was too obnoxious and manipulative to encourage friendship. The only people he could consider friends, inside and outside prison, were those who wanted to use his name and reputation for their own ends, while he wanted to use *them* to keep his reputation alive. To say these people caused him "problems" is also misleading. Whatever trouble Reg encountered was of his own making, either through his craving still to be seen as the powerful, all-controlling crime boss, or ignorance of how the world had moved on since his imprisonment.

At the same time, he was vulnerable to dreamers or con-men with hare-brained ideas, and an easy target for supposed victims wanting to benefit from the fear of the Kray name. Instead of keeping his distance, he positively encouraged violence on the outside, to the point of sanctioning beatings to people he wasn't sure were innocent or guilty. If a pen-pal had come off worst in a row, and had been in contact with Reg, he would feel obliged to help them get even. If someone he'd seen on a visit was owed money, he'd want to help them get it back. For a percentage, of course.

What I didn't realise, until I spoke to John Corbett for this book, is that, the moment he was released from prison, in 1975, Charlie was the person Reg relied on to sort out these "problems." Being the non-violent person he was, Charlie didn't want to get involved, but out of a hard-to-understand loyalty to his brother, he found it impossible to say No. Instead, he'd ask someone else to do what Reg asked, or ignore it altogether, hoping the "problem" would go away. Sometimes it did, but often it didn't and Charlie would then have his brother on the phone, yelling: "Why haven't you done what I asked you? You're fucking hopeless." Hence the verbal batterings I witnessed on visits. On reflection, perhaps, I should have asked Charlie why Reg was always so brutal with him, but, at the time, I honestly thought that whatever problem Reg had with Charlie was a family matter and nothing to do with me.

Fortuitously for Charlie, he was drinking in a Croydon wine bar, in 1982, when he met up with John Corbett. Although just twenty-one, John proved to be not just a valued, trusted friend, but someone able to take the pressure off Charlie. John was already operating successfully on the edge of crime, in the Kent area, with John McCarthy, an ex-policeman turned robber. The two of them were only too happy to travel around the country, threatening people on Reg's behalf, particularly if there was money in it. Unfortunately for them, there wasn't. Not from the people they frightened. Not even expenses from Reg for their time and trouble.

"The whole business was a pathetic shambles," John told me. "All that concerned Reg was being viewed as the guv'nor, who could get things done. People would write to him and if they received a reply – which they invariably did, signed *Your Friend, Reg Kray* – they'd think that Reg *was* their friend and they could ask a favour. All they'd want was his backing – and he'd give it.

"He'd say: 'I'll sort that out for you, don't worry', even though he never knew the full facts. There's always two sides to a story and Reg only listened to one. He'd be on the phone, telling Charlie: 'You'll never guess what these people have done, they need to be given a slap.'

"Charlie wouldn't want to be involved and would beg me and John to deal with it, to get Reg off his back. And we did because I couldn't bear to see the pain in his eyes when Reg was having a go at him. We'd go flying off round the country to sort out who'd upset Reg's new-found friend. At first, thinking everything was as Reg had explained it to Charlie, we'd go crashing into homes and knock people about without asking questions. But we quickly learned that we were hitting a lot of people who'd done nothing wrong. I'm ashamed to admit now we did hurt a lot of innocent people, some badly, just on Reg's say-so. We'd never mention his name, of course, but those on the receiving end knew who was behind it. No doubt whoever thought they were Reg's mate had told them: 'I'm a friend of the Krays – you're in trouble now.' Reg never gave a monkey's. All that concerned him was that he satisfied anyone who'd asked his help, and perpetuated the myth the Krays were still in control."

This, presumably, was why Reg ordered an attack on Peter Sutcliffe, in Parkhurst, two years after Sutcliffe was jailed for life for murdering thirteen prostitutes. Shortly after 6 p.m. on 10 January, 1983, Sutcliffe went into a recess in the hospital wing to fill a plastic bowl with water when a fellow inmate smashed him in the face with a broken coffee jar, inflicting two deep cuts – one from his mouth to his neck, the other from an eye to the ear. Sutcliffe also suffered smaller cuts on an eyelid and below the eye: he needed thirty stitches and an operation to repair superficial muscle damage. The attack was carried out by James Costello, a Glaswegian serving ten years for firearms offences, who was waiting to be transferred to Broadmoor after being diagnosed mentally ill. At Newport Crown Court later that year, when he was accused of maliciously wounding Sutcliffe, the prosecution said his motive was that Sutcliffe was the most unpopular man in the prison. But no mention was made of who initiated the attack

Ronnie, too, abhorred Sutcliffe. When he heard the sex killer was being transferred to Broadmoor, the following year, he immediately asked for a meeting with the Principal and told him he didn't want Sutcliffe in his part of the hospital, "walking down my corridor, past my room, to get food, or I won't be responsible for my actions." He got his way. And if women visiting him inadvertently sat in Sutcliffe's line of vision, he insisted they moved so that they didn't have to look at him.

*

For twelve years, Charlie and Corbett were virtually inseparable. When they weren't seeing their respective partners, they would go on the town, either eating in South London restaurants, or drinking through the night in West End clubs, Charlie revelling in being the centre of attention and introducing his mate to all the well-known personalities – crooked and straight – he always attracted. But one person Charlie did not want John to meet was Reg. For he knew, that once his brother met the guy who was carrying out his 'orders', he'd want to deal with him direct and would make John's life as unbearable as his. For some reason, though, Charlie changed his mind in the summer of 1994 and took John and a dozen or so villains and minor celebrities to visit Reg in Maidstone. If Charlie thought there was safety in numbers, he was wrong: Reg liked John, saw the value in dealing direct, and from then on would phone *him*, not his brother, when he wanted something done. For John, life *did* become, as Charlie feared, a never-ending nightmare, because Reg quickly learned that John's partner in crime, McCarthy, could provide what he craved, and needed, most - drugs. By day, it seems, Reg wanted a clear head to talk business. But, at night, he was happy to be "out of it" on any drugs McCarthy could supply.

"Reg asked for weed, black, slate and Ecstasy tablets, either for himself or others, or simply to trade," John told me. "He obviously liked what we organised because he'd write, saying, 'I feel great tonight, thanks to you.'"

That was the appreciative side of Reg and, if he'd kept it that way, John might have continued to deal with him. But, as with most of his relationships, Reg's intense, demanding nature, as much as wanting something for nothing, tried John's patience too far. "It wasn't just that we were travelling hundreds of miles on wild goose chases, but that Reg didn't want to pay us," John said. "It got to a point when he'd ask me to do something and I'd say 'No, you haven't paid for the last job. When you do, we'll do another one for you. That's the way the world works.' The trouble was that Reg *didn't* know how the world worked. He saw himself as a switched-on wheeler-dealer, but he didn't have a clue about business, especially finance: having no idea about credit checks, he thought he could ask for a loan one day and have the money in his account the next.

"Once, someone from Newmarket suggested Reg bought his big house and converted it into a nursing home. I drove there and, after talking it through with the owner, agreed it was a house worth buying. When I asked Reg about the money, he said we should get a mortgage. It hadn't occurred to him that he might not qualify for one.

"In the end, Reg became a blessed nuisance. He'd ring early in the morning, knowing I'd been out late with Charlie. I'd just be getting into bed and the answer-phone would go, with Reg saying: 'John, John, pick up, pick up. PICK UP.' I'd ignore it and Reg would get Bradley to call. 'John, it's Brad, can we have a quick word?' They wouldn't stop, so eventually, I'd pick up. Reg would say: 'What's the matter with you? Don't you want to speak to me?' I'd say: 'No, can't you go and fucking annoy someone else this time in the morning.'

"'Oh, how lovely for you being out all night,' he'd say.

"'Go and haunt someone else, leave me alone!' I'd yell, then hang up. But Reg would ring back, be aggressive, and try to frighten me. I'd be very calm which would annoy him more. I'd mention his scream–ups to Charlie: 'That bloody brother of yours is driving me mad. Why does he do that?'

"Charlie would say: 'He only has a go at people he's close to. If he didn't shout and scream at you, you'd probably get a knock on the door.'

"'I'm doing the bloody knocking for him!'

"'Yeah, he knows that. He can't afford to lose you.' Then Charlie would grip my arm and giggle: 'Anyway, all the time he's ringing you, he's not ringing me'."

Finally, everything got too much for John and he became more and more unavailable. Reg would ask him to send McCarthy to visit, but the former policeman didn't want to know. He told John that he had friends in the prison and all they kept saying was that Reg kept chasing his boyfriend round the pool table, like a silly schoolboy. "Why do I want to go and see a raving poof," McCarthy said. And he never went.

*

By now, Dave Courtney was visiting Reg every week and starting to do the jobs Corbett and McCarthy wouldn't. Dave was in awe of the Kray twins. In the gangsterish world of debt-collecting and nightclub security in which he lived, he still believed they were the real deal – especially Reg – and he was willing to do almost anything, just to be able to boast, "I work for the Krays." Within months of Reg moving to the Kent jail, the frightening, but witty and likeable South Londoner was a Kray henchman. As he readily admitted to me, he became Reg's "arms and legs," carrying out any task that would keep the Kray image - and Reg's reputation – alive, be it smuggling in alcohol and drugs, hurting someone for a supposed misdemeanour to one of Reg's pen-pals, or silencing anyone threatening to expose a dark side that Reg wanted to keep hidden.

Seeing Reg once a week, Dave soon learned that twenty six years behind bars, had left Reg understanding little of what went on in the outside world. He was trying to maintain some sort of influence outside the prison walls, but had no idea how life had changed since the sixties. "He knew nothing other than the Cortina Mark One," says Dave. "He knew nothing of McDonald's, KFC, or the M25. I told him once that my wife had paid £85 to have her hair done and his mouth fell open. He said: 'That's a month's wages!'"

And Reg was naïve, too. If a fellow prisoner said he was owed a lot of money and Reg would be on half if he got it back, Reg would call Dave, asking him to track down whoever owed the money and threaten them to pay up. Sometimes Dave did, but often he discovered – like Corbett - that what Reg had been told was rubbish and the money was not owed. "Prison breeds paranoia, and Reg suffered from it more than most," Dave said. "Once, he convinced himself that because a guy he'd befriended in prison was living in Spain, he must be a millionaire through contacts Reg had given him. He told me to fly out and threaten him into handing over some money, and to take my expenses and fee from what I squeezed out of the guy. But when I arrived and saw the Rice Krispies box the supposed millionaire was living in, I realised it was another case of Reg's paranoia blinding him to the facts. I couldn't ask the guy for anything, and flew home out of pocket, because, of course, Reg wouldn't pay me a penny."

On another occasion Reg told Dave to visit him as soon as possible, because he had an idea for a TV commercial for Scotch Porridge Oats "that will make a million." Dave arrived to find Reg very excited. "I'm in the gym on the punchbag, being watched by my friend Bradley," he enthused. "I then turn to the camera and say: 'Thirty years of porridge never done me no harm.'" Dave waited for the, er, punchline – but it never came. Dave explained, as delicately and politely as he could, that no advertising agency or TV station would use the Kray name for anything, but Reg didn't get it: he was still in that world where he and Ronnie were famous faces in all the papers. When he learned that Dave ran a security company, employed by London clubs, he quickly – and very seriously – asked him if he would pay for permission to call it "*The Kray Twins' Security Company*," blind to the reality that, like *Krayleigh Enterprises*, the name Kray was a drawback, not a plus.

In keeping with his desire to be seen as the man who could help with anything – even a jail escape – Reg sent Dave to a prison, in Sussex, to wait in a car for a prisoner who was going to climb over the wall. Dave waited for three hours, in constant fear of a "tug" by police, before giving up. He later learned that the prospective escapee had changed his mind but felt it unnecessary to tell the man who'd organised his getaway driver. Of course, Dave was out of pocket again.

*

Whatever passion Reg had felt for the other young men who had shared his prison life, it's clear that no one touched his soul more than Bradley Allardyce. The two met in Maidstone, in 1994, a few weeks after Reg's move from Blundeston. Bradley was in the exercise yard preparing to escape when he saw a patrolling guard. He went back into the prison and ended up in the gym, face to face with Reg, who was working out on the punch ball. Reg was immediately attracted to the tall, dark, good-looking East Londoner, and when Bradley stripped to the waist to work the punch ball himself, Reg was unable to hide his admiration for his stomach muscles. Forgetting all thoughts of escape, Bradley set about conning his way off his current Wing, to be with Reg, in the

Lifers' section. Much to Reg's amazement, he managed it that afternoon by convincing the authorities that he might kill a fellow prisoner he'd been told was responsible for his brother's suicide.

Reg grew to like Bradley so much that, in one moment of soul-baring intimacy, he confided that Ronnie had killed his late wife, Frances – a sensational revelation that Bradley took literally, assuming that Ronnie forced Frances to take the overdose of drugs that killed her, in June 1967. In fact, what Reg meant was that Ronnie's constant bullying drove the poor woman to suicide. That Reg revealed such a personal secret, however, does show how deeply he felt for Bradley.

The two became so close that when Bradley was unofficially offered parole, he turned it down - an astonishing gesture of loyalty that shocked, but impressed, Reg. After that, though, he did become maddeningly possessive – even to the point of demanding to know which of the prison's toilets Bradley had used, who he'd met and what they'd talked about.

*

Early in 2011, I visited Bradley, in Grendon Prison, near Aylesbury, Bucks, and found him desperate to talk about their intimate relationship provided it was off the record. He revealed Reg's biggest regret in life, the one thing he'd missed most since his incarceration, the Mafia nicknames they shared, the real reason Reg had married Roberta, how Reg had danced into his cell in his moccasins, veins bulging, after taking his first Ecstasy tablet. He also confided that he had taken two years to succumb to Reg's sexual advances.

What Bradley claimed *not* to know was that, during his time in Maidstone, a fellow prisoner had threatened to expose Reg to a Sunday tabloid newspaper as a sexual predator, who had drugged and raped him. Which was strange, since I subsequently discovered that Bradley had written a letter for Reg about the expose, which he'd given to a newspaper reporter as a trade-off, on condition that the letter was not published until after Reg's death. The letter, in Bradley's neat handwriting, began: "*I wish for the public to know that I am bisexual. The reason I am coming out into the open is because I have an intense dislike of blackmailers and all they stand for. I prefer not to live a lie and ask the reader to understand my predicament of having been in the prison environment for 26 years in an all male population. It is not sympathy I seek but that the public applaud me for telling the truth…*"

The ginger-haired prisoner, who was in his mid-twenties, had told Ian Edmondson – a *Kent Messenger* reporter who worked as a "stringer" for the national Press – that he wanted £15,000 to tell all about Reg's behind-bars sex life. But the salacious allegations were never printed, thanks to some imaginative and daring "detective" work by Dave Courtney.

A visit was arranged with Reg, and Edmondson outlined the story. Never in his life, I'm sure, had Reg been subjected to such an embarrassing and humiliating experience. For among the prisoner's allegations was one that Reg was so short he'd had to stand on several telephone directories to have sex with him against the cell door – and that Reg had had to have hospital treatment for wood splinters, caused by self-inflicted sexual activity. As if that was not enough, the young man was also prepared to reveal that Reg had been tested for AIDS *nine* times.

Edmondson told Reg he would not be able to write the story unless the man could substantiate what he claimed.

He looked Reg in the eye. "Can he prove what he says?"

Reg nodded. "Yeah, he most probably can," he said

If his accuser had been in Maidstone, no doubt Reg would have found ways to dissuade him from going ahead with his expose. But he'd been transferred to Long Lartin. Later, after Edmondson left the prison, Reg said he *had* to find a way to stop the story – had Dave any ideas? Short of breaking into the Nottingham prison and threatening the prisoner, Dave hadn't. But, a few days later, he came up with a plan to do just that. It was outrageously audacious. It was unlawful. But, he felt, it might just work.

Reg's solicitor, Ralph Haeems, who had represented Dave successfully a number of times, arranged to see the prisoner in Long Lartin, and Dave went along, too, posing as a police detective on a training course. With Haeems having the appropriate paperwork, Dave needed to give only his name, which - to avoid lying - he stated as "DC Ourtney". They were shown into a small room, where they waited until the prisoner was brought in by two officers. As the prison officers left, closing the door behind them, Haeems turned his back.

Recognising Dave from his visits to Maidstone, the prisoner went for the panic button, but Dave was too quick for him and knocked him to the ground. "This wasn't the idea," he admitted. "I wasn't meant to touch him, just give him the little speech Reg had told me to. But he left me no choice. He wasn't knocked out, or in any great pain, but he was on the floor, screaming. I was telling him to forget about doing the story when two screws burst in. Seeing him laying, bleeding, and terrified, they looked at me and went for their batons. "Hold up," I said, "I'm not the prisoner here – start with him." They asked the guy what happened. Wisely, he said he had injured himself by falling over. And when police were called to investigate, he stuck to the same story. After two hours, Dave and Haeems were allowed to leave."

Dave returned from Long Lartin and phoned Reg to say he'd "sorted that thing out." Reg said, "Brilliant," and that should have been the end of the matter. But Reg, not seeming to care that the phone was bugged, then called someone, boasting: "Dave's sorted it out."

For someone who believed he knew it all, that was not Reg's cleverest move.

I kept in touch with Reg by phone over the next few months and early in November, he wrote promising to return a favour. He was his usual positive self, telling me he was busy on various projects, which he was sure would come together in the New Year. Sadly, whatever projects they were would have to wait because, just four months later, Ronnie had a heart attack and died, and the only project that would concern Reg was organising the most spectacular funeral he felt his beloved brother deserved.

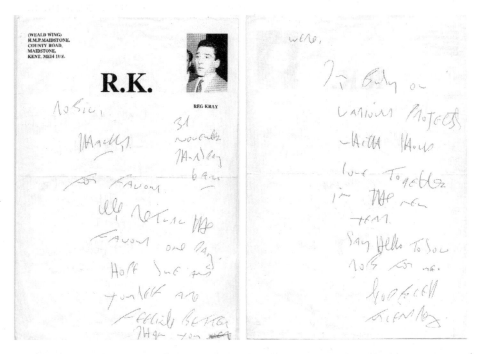

3rd November   Thursday   6 AM   Robin,   Thanks for favour will return the favour one day.   Hope Sue and yourself are feeling better than you were.   Im busy on various projects which should come together in the new year.   Say hello to Sue Rob for me.   God Bless   Friend   Reg

Chapter Sixteen

I KNEW Ronnie was dead even before Charlie heard.

Shortly after 9.30 a.m. on Friday, 17 March, 1995, I was in my study when a reporter from a TV news channel rang, saying someone from Heatherwood Hospital, in Ascot, had told them Ronnie Kray had died from a heart attack that morning. I was shocked; I knew Ronnie was in hospital after collapsing at Broadmoor, but didn't think for a moment he was likely to die. The reporter wanted a quote about Ronnie, but I was more concerned about speaking with Charlie. I felt sure that if a reporter knew Ronnie had died, Charlie would and I wanted to speak with him. But when I rang, Charlie said he'd heard nothing, and he refused to believe it. "It can't be true because I'd have been told," he said. "Or Reg, would have been and he'd have called me."

But it was true. Both Charlie and I phoned Broadmoor and someone confirmed that Ronnie *had* died - at seven minutes after 9 a.m. - and the news had been leaked before anyone at the hospital had had a chance to phone either Charlie, or Maidstone Prison. Charlie was in such a state that I offered to ring and ask someone to break the news to Reg, but he felt it right that he rang himself. A prison officer fetched Reg from his cell and he spoke to Charlie in an office. "Ron's died," Charlie said quietly. But Reg already knew. He said he'd been walking along a corridor past the cells when another prisoner told him he'd just heard it on the radio. Reg was choked, barely able to talk. Later, I would learn that he was angry, too, and not just that the media had heard about the death before the family. The previous morning, Reg had had a feeling something was wrong and had asked to visit Ronnie in Broadmoor, but he was told that Ronnie was not ill enough to warrant a visit. Reg was assured that, if the position changed, he would be told. But he wasn't.

Charlie was concerned that he and Reg weren't being told the whole story. A few days earlier, he was alerted that Ronnie had collapsed in Broadmoor and had been taken to Heatherwood, but nobody could tell him what was wrong. The next morning, as he was about to leave home for the hospital, he got a call that Ronnie was back in Broadmoor. Surely, he thought, the doctors had not had enough time to determine what was wrong with him. Two days later, Ronnie was back in hospital, having taken a turn for the worse. Charlie drove there immediately, with Laurie O'Leary, and they were astounded to find Ronnie in bed, in a tiny room, watched by not one, but three male nurses – as though he was planning a dramatic escape. He looked and sounded all right, but was clearly paranoid: he asked for all the medical bits and pieces to be removed, thinking that the monitor registering his heartbeat was really a tape recorder.

Later, Charlie told me he believed Ronnie's sixth sense told him he was going to die. For as they were heading home after the visit, Laurie said that, while Charlie had gone to buy Ronnie some cold orange juice, Ronnie had asked Laurie to promise to look after Charlie – as though he knew he would not be seeing him again.

Reg was convinced there was more to Ronnie's death than "heart attack", and was all for kicking up a stink until he was told the truth. Charlie calmed him down, saying they were too emotional now; there would be time to demand answers later. What they each had to do first, he said, was have some time on their own, then get together to decide on the best way to handle the funeral arrangements. They agreed to meet in Maidstone Prison the following morning; Charlie would travel down with Laurie and myself. This, of course, put me in a unique position: obviously, I'd have to respect the brothers' grief, but I couldn't ignore the fact that a Sunday newspaper would want the exclusive story of the brothers' emotional meeting. So, later that Friday, I rang Tom Petrie, at *The People* and told him what was happening. "Phone me the moment you get home after the meeting," Tom said. "Bridget will want to play this big, so the sooner we get your copy the better."

At 11 a.m., on Saturday, Charlie, Laurie and I waited in one of the prison's private rooms, and when Reg was brought up from the cells, I watched him and Charlie hugging each other, both crying quietly. Laurie and I looked at each other, not knowing what to do or say. After half a minute or so, we all sat down and, astonishingly, Reg's sombre mood lifted and his positive mental attitude kicked in: he wasn't going to let himself get too depressed over Ronnie's death, he said. He'd felt dreadful not being allowed to see him, as his life ebbed away, but he'd been allowed some rare privileges during the day and night, and was now feeling better. He felt happy, knowing that his troubled twin was at peace at last. "You know, Ron had a premonition of his death," Reg said. "Three weeks ago he told me, 'I'm not long for this world.'"

Then, Reg himself had had a premonition. The previous Wednesday, another prisoner had asked to borrow a suit for a wedding he was being allowed to attend. Reg arranged for him to have a black suit he'd bought off the peg for his mother's funeral in 1982, but, as he handed it over, he had a strange feeling he would be asking for it back before too long. Two days later, Ronnie was dead. Reg started talking about how he was going to organise the funeral from prison. "Ronnie always said he'd like six black horses, so that's what he'll have," Reg said.

"I don't think it'll be possible, Reg," Charlie said, gently. "Chingford Cemetery is six miles from Bethnal Green. It'll take all day. The police won't allow it."

"Ron wanted horses," said Reg. "And he'll have them."

Charlie knew better than to argue. "Okay, Reg," he said. "I'll look into it."

"No," Reg said. "I want to do it."

"Leave it to me, Reg," Charlie said, gently. "Ronnie will have the best. The funeral will be exactly the same as mum's and the old man's."

But Reg would have none of it. "Charlie if it's okay with you, I want to

Gangland killer Reg Kray and his elder brother, Charles, had an emotional meeting in prison yesterday.

They hugged each other and wept in a visiting room that had been made specially available at Maidstone Prison, in Kent.

The meeting was the first time the brothers had spoken since Reg's twin, Ronnie, died from a heart attack on Friday.

Charlie, 67, sat in the room, shaking and smoking nervously, while Reg was brought up from his cell.

As soon as Reg walked in and saw Charlie, he burst into tears and fell into Charlie's arms.

Neither said a word for half a minute, just stood in the middle of the room, embracing each other.

Then Reg said: "What's happening about the funeral? What about the horses? Ronnie wanted his coffin to be drawn by six black horses with plumes."

Charlie shook his head. "Not possible, Reg. The cemetery is in Chingford. It will take all day. The police wouldn't allow it."

"Okay," said Reg. "But what about the cars? I want Ron to have Rolls Royces and Bentleys. I want him to have the best."

"Leave it to me, Reg. He'll have the best. The funeral will be exactly the same as mum's and the old man's."

That pacified Reg. The tears now gone, he want to talk only of positive issues to Charlie and his East End childhood friend, Laurie O'Leary (and writer Robin McGibbon!).

"I was bad yesterday," he said. "Having been refused permission to visit Ron in hospital, I felt I'd been deprived of comforting Ron in his last hours as his life ebbed away.

"But the prison was kind enough to grant me a few privileges last night and I feel in a better frame of mind today.

"I'm still sad at Ron passing away, of course, but I woke this morning feeling at peace. I know Ron is.

"After being locked up for 27 years, he's free at last. He beat the system, didn't he? He didn't die in Broadmoor as everyone expected him to.

"I didn't sleep much last night. But I forced myself not to think back over all the years, because it would have been too hurtful. During my sentence, I've learned to switch off and keep my emotions under control – be dispassionate about thing.

"Yesterday, I wandered around in a trance, my head spinning, and I suppose I'm still in a state of shock at the moment. No doubt I'll have an emotional set back when the realisation of what has happened truly sinks in.

"But, right now, I'm coping with Ron's death well – better than anyone expected, I'm sure – and I intend to throw myself into even more work, such as writing and film projects, because I know that's what Ron would want me to do.

"I feel particularly sad that I was cheated out of seeing Ron in hospital, because a lot of projects I've been nurturing over the past year or so are coming to fruition and I had so much good news to tell him.

"There's so much to remember Ron by, but I suppose what will remain longest is his unique brand of humour. As people close to him knew, he could be funny without even realising it.

"I always think big and when I wrote a book on Cockney slang, I sent it to the then President of the United States, Ronald Reagan.

"I told Ron this on one of our six-monthly visits and he looked at me, deadpan. 'That's nice,' he said. 'What did he think of it?'"

What Reg Kray wants more than anything is to be allowed to visit the Chapel of Rest to say his final farewell to his twin.

And yesterday he and brother Charles revealed they would be making an appeal to the Maidstone Governor to make this possible.

> After the hour and a half hour visit, Charlie said: "Reg hadn't seen Ron for nine months and it would be terrible for him if he wasn't allowed to say goodbye for the last time. They were twins after all.
>
> "I can see no reason why he should not be allowed to go. I'm keeping the location of the Chapel of Rest secret, so Reg could easily be taken one day, or night, without anyone knowing.
>
> "The authorities will surely know, after all these years, that there is absolutely no security risk. Reg has never once thought of escape and never will.
>
> "Even if someone said, 'we've got a plane waiting for you', Reg would simply say: 'I'm going to see my brother, then I'm going back to jail.' Apart from anything else, he would do that out of respect for Ron.
>
> "After the insensitivity of what happened to Reg last week, I hope the authorities feel they would like to make amends and allow Reg to see Ron's body. It would be a humane gesture, and one that Reg would be forever grateful for."

deal with the arrangements, I've got all the time in the world to think about what to do for the best."

As bad as Charlie felt about Ronnie, he knew it was worse for Reg, so he agreed, comforting himself that organising the funeral might help his brother cope with his grief.

"I'll make sure Ronnie has the best send-off possible," Reg said. "I want 20 Rolls Royces and Bentleys for all our friends. And we *will* have six black horses. And they *will* take Ron all the way to the cemetery."

While trying to remember all this intimate detail for the next day's *People*, I could not help thinking: as gangster funerals go, Ronnie's promised to be the biggest and most spectacular. Who was going to pay for it?

By Monday, Reg was even more suspicious over Ronnie's death after hearing that East Berkshire Coroner Robert Wilson had held the inquest at his home, over the weekend, without informing the public, a decision several lawyers had called unlawful. In a "hearing" lasting just three minutes, Mr Wilson read statements aloud to himself, then recorded "death by natural causes," by fax to the coroner's office, at Slough. Reg was furious and, predictably, Charlie was in the firing line. First thing on Monday morning, Reg phoned him, angrily accusing him of not asking enough questions. "We could be fobbed off with any old rubbish," he fumed. That night, still angry, Reg phoned a local TV station, saying he was delaying the funeral until he'd been given some satisfactory answers and he was instructing a solicitor to get them.

One worry playing on Reg's mind was that Ronnie's heart attack – if he'd had one – had been brought on by a struggle. Ideally, Reg would have liked to have seen for himself if Ronnie had any bruises, but he was hardly likely to be released to see the body in the coroner's mortuary. Even if he gave permission for Ronnie to be moved to English's, the East End undertakers handling the funeral, there was no guarantee he would be driven there from Maidstone; in fact, as one of the country's highest profile prisoners, Reg was doubtful he would. In the end, Ronnie *was* taken to English's, and thanks, in no small part, to Chris Rogers, security chief at Maidstone Prison, and Debbie, his prison officer wife, Reg was allowed to go there and see him. Unknown even to Charlie, they drove Reg to English's on Wednesday afternoon, took the handcuffs off, and allowed him to spend fifteen minutes with his brother in the Chapel of Rest. No one knows what Reg said, or did, but one thing is certain: being allowed to pay his respects made a positive impact on him, and he certainly let Chris and Debbie know how much he appreciated their compassion.

Although there was no bruising on Ronnie's body, Reg still had misgivings, but confirmed the funeral could go ahead the following week, and asked Charlie to make sure all those who would be involved were at the prison to discuss arrangements with him the next day. I had to be there because Reg wanted me to handle the Press and TV, but Charlie asked Sue to go, too, because he wanted her to read a poem and say a few words about Ronnie on his behalf.

Apart from the three of us, there were six other people there – Chris and Debbie Rogers, Dave Courtney, who was to handle the security, English's Funeral Director, Paul Keyes, and manager, Alan Jackson, Frank Fraser, who Reg wanted as a pallbearer, a woman who was a florist, and a younger woman, who Reg stroked and cuddled, then held both her hands. He did not introduce her and, as far as I could tell, she was not going to play any part in the funeral.

As Chris Rogers sat in a corner, smoking a pipe, Reg made it clear he was orchestrating proceedings and, with unconcealed pride, told us he'd written a brief eulogy for Ronnie. As he wouldn't be allowed out of handcuffs on the day, he had recorded his words, and wanted us to hear them. All of us knew Reg's voice wasn't attractive at the best of times, so I'm sure I wasn't the only one who feared the worst. But nothing could have prepared us for the awfulness of what Reg played us, on a cheap, crackly, old-fashioned tape recorder. What he had written was okay, if brief and wholly inadequate, in my view, but it was his weak, nasal voice, as much as the dreadful quality of the machine, that made the recording inappropriate. When it finished, we all sat in silence. We knew we had to say something. But what? Who had the bottle to be honest? Who was going to tell Reg Kray that what he'd clearly devoted a lot of thought to would embarrass him?

I wasn't, for a start. Nor was Sue. Frank Fraser was motionless and silent beside me. And Charlie, the English representatives, the florist and the young woman were looking down, not having a clue what to say. It was left to the irrepressible Dave Courtney, sitting opposite Reg, to relieve the tension.

"No, no, mate," he boomed. "That won't work in a church. You should ask Sue to read it." To his credit, Reg took it on the chin; who knows, perhaps deep down, behind all that cocky arrogance, he knew his strengths and weaknesses; knew that the ludicrous recording would do nothing for his credibility; might even make him a laughing stock.

"Yeah, you could be right there, Dave," he said. "I wasn't sure whether a recording would work." Confident now, both Charlie and Frank quickly said that Dave was right, and there was a quiet mumble of agreement from the rest of us, lest Reg was not convinced. But he was, and looked at Sue.

"Would you be happy to read it for me, Sue?"

Sue, who was experiencing her first visit to a prison, nodded: "Of course, I would, Reg."

"I've written out what I've just played," he said. "I'll give it to you before you leave, with another poem I'd like you to read."

Reg, then went round, speaking to everyone – except Charlie and Frank – about their jobs. Mine would be arranging a national newspaper photographer to take exclusive behind-the-scenes photos, and to sell exclusive TV rights to the highest bidder. Even in his grief, Reg had not lost sight of the commercial value of what he clearly wanted to be a State occasion.

For me, choosing the photographer was relatively easy. The funeral, and the razzmatazz likely to surround it, promised to resemble a showbiz event, and I needed someone used to working in that mad, frenetic scene. There were only a handful of snappers I'd consider, and I plumped for *The Sun's* Dave Hogan, a gentle giant of a man, who was one of the most accomplished showbiz photographers – and likeable and trustworthy, too.

Selling exclusive TV rights was less straightforward. Neither the BBC, nor ITV, was prepared to pay anything, which was hardly a surprise. Sky News offered £2,000, provided it went to charity, which, on this occasion, was not what Reg had in mind. In the end, I reached an agreement with *London Tonight* that was so attractive I was shocked the news editor, Simon Harris, offered it. And it had nothing to do with money.

I was discussing the deal with him and reporters Phil Bayles and Geoff Hills, over tea and biscuits at London News Network's HQ, in Waterloo, when I mentioned that Reg wanted to produce his own commercial video of the funeral. Simon thought about it for a moment, then said he was prepared to provide Reg with footage from all five cameras that would be covering the event – including pooled film from a helicopter the TV companies were sharing. It was a surprisingly generous offer, but what did he want in return?

"Total exclusivity in the church," Simon said. "Before, during and after the service. We plan to broadcast about eight minutes that evening."

I wish I could replay that scene, in LNN's restaurant, because I'd love to see my expression: I'm sure I did my best to look cool and unimpressed, and I'm equally sure I failed. For Simon's offer was one I'd never have dreamt of suggesting: it was simple, so straight forward; an agreement that gave both parties what they wanted. I'm sure I felt like a poker player trying to conceal he had an unbeatable hand. And then someone came to our table, saying there was a phone call for me.

Sue was on the line, saying she'd had a call from Reg, telling me not to go ahead with *London Tonight*.

"Why?" I wanted to know.

"He's got his own video man," she said.

"*His own video man?*"

"Yes," Sue said. "Bill Curbishley's arranged it." The Who's manager was a close friend, to whom Reg felt indebted.

"What? Just one guy? One camera?"

"Apparently so," Sue said.

"Okay," I said, feeling that what I now had to do was anything but okay.

What Simon had offered was too good to turn down. No matter who Reg's "video man" was, he couldn't compete with five professional cameramen – one in the church, four at vantage points along the route to the cemetery – and *eight-minutes* coverage on the day.

I walked back to the restaurant, not sure what to do. His own "video man"! What did Reg think the funeral would be like – a genteel village fete? Part of me felt I should explain the phone call to Simon and walk away from the deal. Another part cried out to ignore it and grab what was clearly a heaven-sent opportunity. By the time I reached the table, I'd made a decision.

"That was Reg," I said, with a warm, wide smile. "You've got a deal."

As we shook hands, all I could think was that Reg and I were going to have one almighty battle. But it was one I was determined to win. We did have a row: a long, loud one. I did my best to convince him that he'd be stupid not to accept the deal, but, pig-headed, as usual, he told me *he* was organising the funeral, not me, and Curbishley's man would have exclusivity. I couldn't accept that, however, and, that night, I typed a letter which I would deliver personally to the prison early the next morning.

In it, I impressed on Reg that *London Tonight's* cameramen would provide TWENTY video tapes, covering every significant moment of his brother's last journey – four hours' footage from five professionals, just for allowing one camera in St Matthew's Church. Crucially, I told him that all this would be in addition to what he was planning on his own – not instead of. And I stressed

Saturday a.m.

Dear Reg,
    I've driven down to Maidstone to deliver this letter
because it is vitally important you have not
misinterpreted what I have been saying in the last 24
hours. I fear that you are making a massive mistake that
you will regret for the rest of your life, and I can't sit
back and let that happen – not without a battle anyway.
    When you asked me to approach TV stations concerning
rights to film the funeral service, I did so, and, because
I have got to know the top people well over the years, I
was given a lot of time to talk the matter through fully
and frankly.
    ITN, London Tonight and Sky News were all interested,
naturally. ITN would give the funeral 1 min. 30 secs
(quite a lot of time by TV news standards), but would not
pay for the right to film inside the church. Sky News, as
you know, were prepared to pay £2,000 to be inside the
church, provided the money was paid to a charity.
    London Tonight have very, very little money to spend.
In fact, when I squeezed £1,000 out of them for an
exclusive interview with Ronnie Knight.s wife, Sue, in
Spain, I was told it was the first time ever they had paid
for anything!!
    But, yesterday, they agreed to a proposal I put to
them which left me tingling with excitement. It is
staggering. Unbelievable almost.
    For the privilege of filming in the church, they
agreed, not only to lead their Wednesday programme with an
EIGHT-minute (!!!) coverage of the entire funeral, but
said they would hand over every single piece of footage
filmed by FOUR cameras – one in the church and three at
vantage points along the route and at the cemetery.
    This would be around TWENTY video tapes, covering
every single significant moment of dear Ron's last
journey. TWENTY tapes for you to do what you want with.
TWENTY tapes for you and Charlie to watch on your own, if
you like.
    The programme would show eight minutes. But you would
get ALL the footage from their four cameras…FOUR HOURS!
    And for what? Simply for allowing a camera into the
church!! As I said, it is almost unbelievable. (And I take
full credit for pulling it off!!)
    Reg, my dear friend, what you have on offer is not a
substitute for anything you are planning to do on your
own. It is an ADDITION.
    Over the years, you have poured a lot of energy into
projects. Some have come off and earned you a nice few

quid; others, no doubt, have turned out disappointingly.

I doubt that you will have an opportunity like this one in your life again. At the very worst, you could sell the tapes for very serious money.

But, you know, it is not only the financial aspect that concerns me. It is what you and Charlie and all your friends - like Sue and me - would be missing out on. Think about it for a moment, Reg: your beloved twin brother being given something resembling a State funeral and you have the chance to have FOUR HOURS of film of it for nothing.

Have your mate do his video. Use Bill Curbishley's expertise. You'd be a fool not to.

But, in my humble opinion, you would also be a fool - and a very poor businessman - not to see a once-in-a-lifetime opportunity when it is staring you in the face.

I feel very strongly about this, Reg. That's why I've driven to Maidstone to deliver this letter when I should be playing with our new puppy or trying to write my novel.

that, in my opinion, he was making a massive mistake he would regret for the rest of his life. Meanwhile, I told *London Tonight* nothing, just prayed my letter would change Reg's mind. Thankfully, it did. He didn't call that weekend, which caused Sue and I some anxiety, but he did, on Monday morning, congratulating me – almost in passing – on writing a "good letter," then telling me to go ahead with *London Tonight*. He also said something that gave me a clue why he'd had a change of heart. Bill Curbishley, it appeared, wasn't laying on a "video man" for free, as Reg thought. The cost was £15,000! What, I wondered, would Reg have done about *London Tonight's* fabulous offer if he hadn't had to pay for a "video man"?

Most people expected a big turnout, but the crowds that morning of March 29 surprised everyone. In a radio interview, Frank Fraser likened the funeral to the State occasion given to Sir Winston Churchill, and he was spot on. No one was counting, but from the massive football crowds I'd been in, I'd say there were 200,000 or more in Bethnal Green, and along the six miles to Chingford. And while I do think Reg lapped up being hailed as a celebrity by the masses chanting his name, it would be churlish not to credit him for the way he conducted himself throughout a stressful experience. With such intense emotional pressure heightened by all the accompanying ballyhoo, he could have been forgiven for cracking under the strain. But, throughout, he maintained a dignity that was impossible not to admire. He sat looking at the coffin, as Sue read the poem, Invictus, that he had chosen, but stared ahead when he knew the poignant moment had come when Sue would read the words he'd hoped to speak himself.

"*My brother, Ron, is now free and at peace,*" Sue read. "*Ron had great humour, a vicious temper, was kind and generous. He did it all his way, but, above all, he was a man. That's how I will always remember my twin brother. God Bless. Affection. Reg.*"

Apart from tensing slightly as Sue emphasised "vicious", Reg listened impassively throughout the brief reading, gave a nod of approval, and mouthed "Thank you" as Sue stepped down from the lectern. The reading was crucially important and that Reg was satisfied with it was evident: as Sue finished, the anxiety that had been etched on his face had gone and colour was back to his cheeks. I could see him visibly relax.

As I have no siblings, it is impossible for me to empathise with someone who has lost a brother or sister, let alone a twin. But, at that moment I did feel a certain warmth towards Reg, forgave him his cocky arrogance, and even liked him a little. The feeling didn't last, of course. The next day, Reg phoned, angry that I hadn't arranged a photograph of Ronnie's body, and I wondered yet again, why I didn't tell him to get out of my life. For reasons, I had yet to find out, Dave Hogan had not gone into the Chapel of Rest to take a picture, but Charlie had told Reg that I'd stopped him. Quite honestly, I did not feel it was my place to suggest what some would consider a macabre intrusion of privacy. That decision would have to come from the Kray family. Certainly Dave Hogan would not have presumed he had permission.

My conversation with Reg, which I recorded, was brief – just a few seconds – and left me in no doubt that Reg was unimpressed with me:

"It wasn't done, was it, eh?" he snapped.

"The photographer was there, Reg," I said. "The fact that Charlie said what he said to you is nothing to do with me."

"You're both over twenty one," Reg fumed. "It's no good passing the buck, is it? It seems to me, me and you just can't get on. So, I'm going to speak to Charlie. Is that okay?"

"Yes," I said. "Please do."

"Okay, cheerio," he said.

That should have been that. But, a few days later, we had a blazing row over *London Tonight's* footage, and Reg's insistence to do something himself when it was clearly better done by someone else.

The *London Tonight* contract was with my company, because the programme would not deal with a convicted criminal. But Reg and I always understood that the tapes would be used to make a commercial video to benefit us both. Call me naïve, if you like, but I felt that I and Laurie O'Leary - who had produced and distributed a number of videos, as manager of the medium, Doris Stokes – had the wherewithal and contacts to produce, package and promote that video, so I was shocked when Reg demanded I send the tapes to him because he was going to do it himself. Naturally, I refused: not only was it madness for Reg to contemplate such a complex operation from behind bars, but I didn't want to be kicked into touch, after pulling off the deal.

So, we had words again. Loud, foul ones. And then, a few days later, I received a letter from Reg's solicitor, Stephen Gold, demanding I sent the tapes to Reg because they were his copyright. Legally, this wasn't the case, but in the end, Sue and I didn't want the aggravation, so I agreed to send the tapes, on condition I was paid for the part I'd played in giving him the opportunity to capitalise on his brother's death. Unused to being on the wrong end of a bargaining session, Reg wasn't happy, but arranged for someone to pay me what I asked, and I sent the tapes.

If Laurie and I had been left alone to edit that fascinating footage, we'd have produced and marketed a good-quality product, highlighting the significant moments of Ron's remarkable farewell, and made sure it was on sale in all the established retail outlets soon after the funeral. As it was, the video Reg produced was dreadful quality, amateurishly edited, and with no voice-over describing the astonishing scenes and identifying the personalities present. And it wasn't marketed and promoted well, or soon enough, to make an impact. A great shame, in my opinion, because *London Tonight* had access to many intimate, behind-the-scenes moments that would have formed the basis of a unique historical document of an occasion that fascinated thousands who were there and millions who saw it only on TV, not only in the U.K., but throughout the U.S. on CNN.

For Dave Courtney, the funeral was a poisoned chalice. Within the security business, he was acclaimed for organising such a massive operation, and his high-profile performance unquestionably opened doors for him. At the same time, the powers-that-be in Whitehall and Scotland Yard were shocked that one man could produce such a formidable show of force and, before the flowers had died on Ronnie's grave, moves were being made to close those doors and put Dave out of business.

Reg's careless phone call after Dave's visit to Long Lartin only made things worse. The Roger Cook TV programme was already looking into Dave's activities when they were given a tape recording of Reg's phone call. Suddenly Dave was no longer merely the man in the Darth Vader coat at the centre of Ronnie's funeral spectacular, but a Kray henchman, silencing one of Reg's gay lovers. Unfortunately for Dave, that phone call helped the Cook Report produce an investigation so damaging that his business never recovered.

No doubt Reg lost as much sleep over that as he did about the £14,000 security bill he promised to pay, but never did.

*

That eventful 1995 drew to a close with the two remaining Kray brothers facing a dreadful emotional experience that would leave Charlie, in particular, with little will to live – a trauma that would, eventually, lead to his demise.

Chapter Seventeen

IT began on Christmas Day. Judy's children were with their father, so Charlie took her and Gary to the Croydon Park Hotel for lunch. They had a lovely time, but on the way home, Gary didn't feel well, and looked weaker, and more frail, than usual. He perked up enough to see in the New Year with a family friend, in West Norwood, but, two days later, his back was so painful he went to a doctor, who immediately ordered an X-ray. When Gary went back for the results the next day he could barely walk, and was taken by ambulance to King's College Hospital, in Camberwell, where he had various tests. On 19 January, a doctor there called Charlie into his office. "Mr Kray," he said, gently. "I'm sorry to have to tell you, your son has cancer."

All Charlie could think to say was: "How bad is it? Can you operate?"

"I'm afraid not," the doctor said. "It's gone too far."

"How long are we talking about?" Charlie asked, thinking, hoping, for at least a year, perhaps two.

The doctor shook his head, sadly. "I'm afraid eight weeks. At the most."

When Charlie told Sue and I, he said all he kept thinking was: why can't it be me? I'm coming up to seventy. Why does it have to be Gary? He's only forty-four. He's in the summer of his life.

He decided not to tell Gary and I do feel he was right: his poor son would not have been able to handle it. At sixteen, he'd been told to leave the family home after Charlie and the twins were arrested, and had never recovered. He wasn't the brightest of kids, but being abandoned by his mother, amid the shame of his dad being labelled a gangster, shattered his confidence, and he was a lost soul, profoundly introverted, to the point where most people thought he was handicapped. Gary's condition was something Charlie never discussed, not even with close friends, and no one ever mentioned it. We all knew, though, that Charlie adored Gary and would do everything to protect him. So, he kept the terrible truth from his son, pretending he didn't have anything serious and would be going home when he was better.

The twins, of course, had to be told the truth and when Gary left hospital, both Ronnie and Reg asked to see him. With Gary now in a wheelchair and so weak that even the shortest journey was painful, the 160-mile round trip to Broadmoor was out of the question. But Charlie knew Reg desperately wanted to see his nephew, so, in the first week of February, Laurie O'Leary drove them to Maidstone, Gary stretched out in the back of the white Mercedes, his head in his dad's lap. Charlie told me later that, funerals apart, taking Gary to see his uncle for the last time was the saddest journey he'd ever made.

Charlie had told the prison about Gary's condition and was allocated a special visiting time so they could all be alone. They spent just half an hour there before the strain of the drive took its toll on Gary, and all the time they chatted, Reg sat stroking his hair and rubbing his shoulders. When Charlie wheeled Gary to the exit door and looked back, Reg was standing there, tears streaming down his cheeks.

*

With emotional turmoil facing him over the coming weeks, Charlie didn't need any further stress, but he got it when, in the first week of March, he saw this big headline in the *News of the World*: THE GREAT BRAIN ROBBERY, with a smaller heading below: *Docs have pickled Ronnie Kray's bonce in a bottle – now his wife has half a mind to sue.*

At first, Charlie thought it was a sick joke, but it was true: Broadmoor's top medical staff had secretly ordered Ronnie's brain to be removed before his funeral and examined by scientists who believed criminal behaviour might be brought about by chemical imbalances in our little grey cells. The story had come to light after someone from the hospital had tipped off Kate, who told the newspaper. Outraged to learn that part of Ronnie was in a jar with a little paper label, she accused Broadmoor of theft and was now threatening legal action. Charlie was outraged, too. And so was Reg when told that no one had sought their permission for the bizarre operation. Reg ordered his solicitor to ask Broadmoor why they had not been approached, but got nowhere. A Tory MP brought up the matter in the Commons, describing the operation as "gruesome," but he didn't get anywhere either.

What bothered Charlie was the memory of those quiet moments in the Chapel of Rest when he'd watched Reg stroking Ronnie's face and shoulders, saying, over and over: "You're at peace now, Ron, you're at peace now." He felt sick – and, no doubt, Reg did, too – knowing that Ronnie was *not* at peace, and that they had been deceived in a callous, cynical manner. A couple of weeks before the story appeared, one of the staff at English's had collected Ronnie's brain from a laboratory, in Oxford, and buried it in a casket beside his coffin. But no one had thought to tell Ronnie's brothers, or his ex-wife.

*

Sue and I visited Gary in hospital, but weren't with him when he passed away, in St. Christopher's Hospice, in Crystal Palace, on 7 March. Charlie rang to tell us Gary had gone, and urged us to join him and some close friends there. When we arrived, Charlie was uncharacteristically hyper and stumbling over his words, as though he was nervous. He immediately buttonholed Sue and was – strangely – insistent that she went with him to say a final goodbye to Gary. Sue wasn't sure she wanted to, but Charlie took her arm and led her down some stairs to the Chapel of Rest. She gently kissed Gary's forehead, said some appropriate words, then, after a few minutes, made to leave. But Charlie, on the other side of the bed, didn't want to: he kept stroking Gary's hair and adjusting his jacket and tie, and bed covers, softly saying, over and over again: "My poor Gary, my poor Gary."

Sue comforted him and did her best to coax him to leave, but still Charlie didn't want to. She got the impression he'd already spent a lot of time with Gary and was using her as an excuse to spend more. Eventually, Sue did encourage him to rejoin the others, but Charlie clearly didn't want to leave his son and, as they went out, she saw him look back over his shoulder at Gary's frail, childlike body, as if he couldn't bear leaving him on his own.

A few days later, Charlie admitted to me that he was dreading organising the funeral. The thought of gathering at the same funeral parlour, carrying the coffin into the same church as they'd carried Ronnie just a year ago, then burying Gary in the same plot in the same cemetery, was emotionally crippling, and he admitted that it was a blessed relief when Reg offered to make the arrangements. I'd like to think Reg made that offer because he felt Charlie's pain and wanted to spare him further suffering, but I don't. I believe he was motivated by selfishness and a craving for attention. Having wallowed in the adulation at Ronnie's funeral, he wanted more of it at Gary's – even though he wouldn't be there. Why else would he arrange for a recording of himself, reading a poem by his favourite writer, Kahlil Gibran, to be played to the packed congregation? Why else would he arrange for an empty limousine to travel directly behind the hearse, in a symbolic gesture that he was there in spirit, if not in person. As his former Parkhurst pal, Steve Tully, had told me, Reg never made a magnanimous or charitable gesture without something being in it for him.

*

For all those terrible weeks since Gary went into hospital, Charlie was convinced his son had no idea he didn't have long to live. But Gary did. Once, when he was alone and being comforted by Diana, he suddenly said: "Is dad going to be all right?" Unable to bring herself to ask Gary what he actually meant, Diana just assured him that, Yes, of course, his dad would be all right.

Well, after we'd buried Gary in the rain that afternoon, Charlie was far from all right. All he could think was that he'd never see his gentle-natured son again – and the hurt didn't go away. For the next two months, he suffered the most stressful panic attacks, either in bed in the middle of the night, sitting on his own with a cup of coffee, or driving the car. Suddenly, the finality of death would swamp him and he would break out in a sweat. He told me that the very idea of never seeing his beloved son again was too horrible to contemplate, and he'd stay where he was until the panic passed, trying to convince himself that he would see Gary again.

With Charlie's sadness came depression, deepened by his lack of confidence and self-esteem, and, two months later he was still vulnerable, and easy prey for the undercover police who sucked him in and, tragically for Charlie, changed the course of the last years of his life.

*

On the day of Gary's funeral, Patsy Manning, one of Charlie's friends from Birmingham, introduced him to a friend, nicknamed "Indian Joe" Sunner. He, in turn, introduced a man who'd driven them from the Midlands – a short, stocky guy in his mid-thirties, who said his name was George.

Two months later, on 9 May, Manning invited Charlie to a party at the Elbow Room, a Birmingham club, owned by one of Charlie's friends. When Charlie said he had nowhere to stay, Manning told him a friend owned a hotel in Moseley and Charlie could stay there free for two nights. At the hotel, Manning greeted Charlie, accompanied by two men, "George" and "Deano." Charlie had never seen Deano before, but recognised George as "Indian Joe's" driver.

The group were joined by another gentleman, who George introduced as Jack from Newcastle. Jack was staying at the hotel, and, before going on to the Elbow Room, told the barman to charge all the drinks to his room. In the toilet, Charlie let slip to Deano that he was short of money and Deano gave him fifty pounds. At midnight, Charlie rang Judy, enthusing about his wealthy friends.

The following week, Jack and a friend, named Ken, travelled down to Kent for a charity night at John Corbett's pub, and brought a football supposedly signed by the Newcastle United team, which they auctioned. A week later Jack and Ken travelled south for another charity evening, in aid of St Christopher's Hospice, and Charlie introduced them to many of his friends – including Ronnie Field and Bobby Gould. Two weeks later, Jack invited Charlie and Field to Newcastle for a business meeting and sent two airline tickets. Charlie and Field were introduced to a third man, Brian, and plied with drinks at a five-star hotel. On 11 July, Jack loaned Charlie £500, so that he and Judy could travel to Birmingham to a party for Charlie's seventieth birthday at the Elbow Room.

Charlie and Judy stayed at the same Moseley hotel - again free of charge – and, shortly before leaving for the party, Jack gave Charlie a gold-plated cigarette lighter, as a birthday present from him and Brian. On 20 July, Jack rang Charlie, asking to be booked into the Selsdon Park Hotel, near Judy's home, then persuaded Charlie to join him and Field and Gould for a drink.

Charlie spent nearly five hours of the afternoon of Wednesday 2 August at my home with me, working on the updates to his autobiography. He left to go to Judy's house and he and Judy had just had dinner when there was a knock on the front door. Six policemen – four detectives and two uniformed – searched the house for two hours, then arrested Charlie and took him to Ilford police station, where he was charged with conspiring to supply two kilos of cocaine worth £63,000 and 1000 Ecstasy tablets worth £20,000. He was kept in a cell overnight. The next evening, I drove Judy to the police station and, in the few minutes they were allowed to talk, he told her that the lovely, wealthy, generous guys he thought were his friends were undercover police, who had twenty tape recordings of him promising to supply drugs over a two-year period.

The next morning, I sat in Redbridge Magistrates' Court, in Ilford, surrounded by newspaper and TV reporters, covering the hearing on the back of the morning's headlines *"Kray brother in £78m sting."*

£78 MILLION! It was ridiculous: the man who'd sat in my lounge had no money in his pockets, and no idea how to put together even the most modest business deal – let alone a multimillion pound drug operation. Apart from that, in the twenty years I'd known Charlie, I'd never heard him talk of drugs, much less deal in them. I was convinced there was some mistake: that someone had set Charlie up; that, when the truth came out, he'd walk away, a free man. Sadly, there was no mistake. He had been set up, but, far from proving his innocence, the truth would prove his guilt and send him to prison for twelve years.

Reg had no sympathy for someone he and Ronnie scorned. The only way he could have helped was to pay a firm of private investigators that John Corbett wanted to use to find evidence that might back up Charlie's defence of entrapment. But Reg was against supporting Charlie in any way – even though Reg had been given a huge gift by Karl Crompton, a convicted criminal from Blackpool, who, that May, had won £10.9 million on the National Lottery.

Crompton had written to Reg in Parkhurst and, as with all correspondence he felt might prove useful, Reg had kept his letter. Reading about Crompton's win, Reg had written to him, suggesting he visited him in Maidstone. Crompton did and, as a result, decided to give his favourite gangster £100,000. Even a small part of this would have paid the investigators' bill, but instead Reg chose to give Bradley Allardyce £50,000 for a deposit on a house, and the rest to other friends, leaving Corbett to settle the bill by remortgaging his house. That Reg gave his older brother the cold shoulder came as no surprise to those close to the family. Throughout their lives, Reg never had time for Charlie and, even if he'd been given a million, his brother wouldn't have got a penny.

*

Even today, I find it hard to believe that Charlie was so foolishly naïve and trusting that summer. Yes, he was devastated by Gary's death, and grateful for any sympathetic shoulder to cry on. Yes, he'd squandered the film money, and, with little confidence and self-esteem, was vulnerable to any generous stranger with a friendly smile, and fat wallet, who told him he was great. And, yes, deep down he was still emotionally troubled by his cowardly betrayal of Diana, the only woman he had genuinely cared for. But, surely, a warning bell should have rung when people he barely knew gave him a birthday present, fifty quid for nothing, and flew him 300 miles to stay at a five-star hotel – with all the food and drink he wanted – at their expense. Most people would have questioned their benefactor's motives, but Charlie basked in the adulation, believing the generosity of his new-found friends was because they liked him. After all, had he not been feted in bars and clubs across the land by strangers captivated by his charm, as much as the allure of the Kray name?

With John Corbett and Judy, I was cleared to visit Charlie in Belmarsh Prison, in South London, where he was kept on remand – with Field and Gould - until the trial at Woolwich Crown Court the following Spring. I went to the prison every week for eight months and, throughout that time, Charlie maintained that he'd believed that Jack and his pals were genuine businessmen; and that drugs were never mentioned.

However, the prosecution's case was that, believing Jack was a drugs dealer, Charlie told him that he had a mate who could supply five kilos of cocaine every two weeks for two years. The first exchange, arranged to be made at the Selsdon Park Hotel, was aborted, but took place at The Swallow Hotel, at Waltham Cross, in Essex, where Field and Gould gave Jack two kilos of cocaine, in return for £63,000. The police case was that Charlie had set up the deal and within hours of the trial beginning, it was clear from what Charlie said on the police tapes that he knew what was going on; that even if he was not involved directly in the supply of the drugs, he was going to profit from it.

Faced with that damning evidence, Charlie had only one defence: that George was an undercover policeman who had infiltrated Gary's funeral to be introduced to Charlie, so that he could be entrapped into committing a crime. Believing Jack and his pals were wealthy, Charlie played along to squeeze some money out of them: that he never had any intention of supplying drugs, and was bluffing, to get money out of people he believed were drug dealers. The jury should disregard everything they heard Charlie say, his barrister, Jonathan Goldberg, said, because it was all invention, designed to impress; Charlie would have promised Scud missiles or gold bars if he thought it would help. Goldberg painted an unflattering picture of Charlie as a charming, but gullible, old man who lived like a pauper and didn't know his limitations. That was certainly the Charlie I knew, but it was not the point: he could be heard on tape, promising to supply cocaine – not as a one-off transaction, but regularly over two years.

Some of Charlie's friends, who popped into court and sat near me in the public gallery, would listen to a couple of hours then tell me: "Charlie's going to walk, you know. He's been stitched up." But, again, that missed the point. Of course, he was stitched up. Undercover police asked him if he could get drugs and they arrested and charged him when he said he could – and did. End of story. The big question was: *Why* was Charlie set up? *Why* was he targeted as a drug dealer when all those who'd met him knew he hadn't the wherewithal to be one. As Dave Courtney, the court jester, said: "Charlie couldn't deal a pack of cards, let alone drugs."

After speaking to key people, I believe the authorities wanted Charlie, even at seventy, off the streets, but, in June 1997, after he was found guilty, all who knew him were mystified. It seemed incomprehensible, and wholly unfair, that he would probably end his life behind bars.

Charlie was sentenced to twelve years for conspiracy to supply drugs. He appealed, hoping to have it reduced, but was philosophical when it wasn't. And in the three years he was incarcerated, he never once whinged, or blamed anyone but himself. Early in his sentence, he asked John Corbett to take Judy to see him in Long Lartin prison, and urged her to start a new life without him. Reluctantly, she agreed to stop visiting and, eventually, moved to Australia with her three children. As with his previous sentence, Charlie was a model prisoner – so much so that a prison officer was moved to write in an official report, that Charlie was *"very polite...adhered to regimes and expectations... was approachable to staff...caused no problems and was cheerful and polite and never disrespectful to staff."*

In the autumn of 1999, Charlie was transferred to Parkhurst, but the wear and tear of the years, coupled with the trauma of Gary's death, wrecked his health and, early in 2000, he was taken to St Mary's Hospital suffering from serious heart problems. Confined to a wheelchair, he was thrilled to see many old friends – none more so than Diana, who made the long trip despite working at the Ideal Home Exhibition, in London.

Knowing he would not recover, Charlie told Wilf Pine that he didn't want a funeral like Ronnie's. He'd never been a gangster and didn't want to be remembered as one. Despite his numerous affairs, he had been so happy with Diana, and he wanted his body taken to her home, then, after a quiet service, buried, with no fuss, beside Gary, at Chingford. When Reg was taken to the hospital, Charlie was unconscious and Reg was asked by the doctor if he wanted him resuscitated. After a brief discussion, Reg said he didn't. Asked if he wanted a priest present when Charlie passed away, he said: "No priests, no vicars. Nothing religious."

Later, when Wilf told him what Charlie had said about his funeral, Reg said: "If that's what he wants, that's what he'll have." But, from what happened later, it was clear he was determined to treat Charlie in death the way he'd treated him in life – contemptuously, without a hint of respect.

*

As Sue had spoken on Charlie's behalf at the funerals of Ronnie and Gary, it was no surprise that Diana wanted her to speak for her at Charlie's. Of course,

Sue agreed and they spent most of the day discussing what Sue would say and read. Everything was going smoothly, but, the next day Diana phoned her, beside herself with fury. "That bastard, Reg, has told me Charlie can't be buried at Chingford," she said. "There are only two spaces left in the family plot and he wants them for himself and Bradley Allardyce. Can you believe it?"

Unfortunately, Sue could: after what we'd experienced and heard, nothing surprised us where Reg was concerned.

For Diana, the prospect of Charlie being denied his dying wish was unthinkable and she started considering having Gary's body exhumed and reburied with Charlie – at the Upper Norwood Church where he gave Diana's daughter, Claudine, away on her wedding day. Thankfully, Reg didn't put her through that: for some reason we never discovered, he had a change of heart and gave Charlie priority over his young lover. But he insisted on handling the funeral arrangements, and although she feared the worst, Diana felt it best for all concerned to leave him to it. If Reg had had his way, I'm sure he would not have allowed Sue to read Diana's eulogy, but Diana knew how much Charlie – like Ronnie – admired Sue's voice. So that was one battle Reg didn't win.

Everyone who knew Charlie felt he would have been horrified by the show that Reg laid on, that sunny Wednesday, 19 April. It wasn't as ostentatious as the funeral he staged for Ronnie, but the eighteen limousines and patrolling minders outside English's and St Matthew's Church, did smack of a gangster's farewell. However, Charlie would have been delighted with the warmth of affection generated by 300 mourners crammed into the church. That he was, by far, the most popular of the three brothers was evident when Freddie Foreman's son, Jamie, read messages from Charlie's friends and acquaintances. Being an accomplished actor, Jamie was used to delivering written lines under pressure, but his voice frequently cracked with emotion, and loud sniffing among the congregation showed that he was not alone in being touched by such a huge demonstration of affection. Then, tears flowing, Jamie spoke about the Charlie he knew – a tribute so nakedly honest and loving it made even the supposed hard men weep.

Few people, if any, would have expected to hear Shakespeare recited at a Kray funeral, but that's how Sue began her personal tribute. She read those beautiful words from Romeo and Juliet: "And when he shall die, take him, and cut him out in tiny stars, and he shall make the heavens so bright, that all the world will be in love with night." Sue then went on to say: "My friend Charlie's bright smile lit up any room…Charlie was a delight to work with… he was always smart and clean and smelling sweet…I can still hear his wonderful laughter when recalling some of the great times he'd enjoyed with friends…but he was more than a friend to Diana and their memories span more than thirty years…"

However, it was Diana's own tribute that best summed up Charlie. I noticed that Reg made a point of not looking at Diana as Sue read: "Charlie and I were a partnership and, like all partnerships, it had its highs and lows. We shared a wonderful life that spun us in all directions. We had a superb time, which we enjoyed to the full. There was lots of laughter and joy and the occasional sadness. There were many good times shared with friends from all walks of life…I know he takes with him a small piece of everyone of you here. We have all lost someone special…I will especially miss Charlie's wonderful, blue, blue eyes. A picture of that enchanting smile will remain forever in my heart until the day when I also walk into the light and am reunited with Charlie." And then, in a poignant reference to an in-joke they'd shared twenty-five years before when they were broke, Sue smiled at Diana and read: "Charlie, I just want to tell you how much I love you. I love you twenty-two quid."

Reg did not look at Sue either. By now, he was married to Roberta and he was more interested in holding her hands and whispering in her ear than listening to Diana's praise for his brother. Sue went on to read Stop The Clocks by W.H. Auden, then some beautiful words about fatherhood, for Diana's son, Dean, and Claudine. She finished her tribute with the poem by an anonymous writer, Weep Not For Me. The service was simple but dignified, befitting the man it was for, and Reg should have left it there. But he evidently thought his voice would add to the proceedings because a recording of him reading the poem, Do Not Stand At My Grave And Weep, – the poem Sue read for Charlie at Ronnie's funeral – was played to the hushed church.

It was a mistake, as it had been for him to play his tape at Gary's funeral: his feeble voice simply did not have the gravitas to be anything but embarrassing. It was a shame Reg didn't have anyone around him with the guts to give him the advice Dave Courtney had given him. But that was Reg, especially in his later years. He believed he always knew best.

He was supremely hypocritical with Charlie's funeral. He'd despised Charlie for supposedly living off their name, but he broke his promise to Wilf and gave his brother a spectacular gangster-style farewell he knew Charlie didn't want. Reg did it for his own ends, no question about it. Watching him waving regally to the hordes from the graveside, responding enthusiastically to Frank Fraser's call for "Three Cheers for Reggie," told me all I needed to know about what he wanted that day.

*

I never saw Reg again. We'd had no contact since our row over the video footage of Ronnie's funeral and, after his sickening betrayal of Charlie, I had no desire to see him. What was there to say to a man who disliked his brother so much that he denied him his final request in such a self-serving manner? For Reg, the feeling was mutual, I'm sure. I have a tape-recording of him saying he valued me as a friend, but there's no evidence he did. On the contrary I feel he viewed me more as Charlie's friend; someone with good contacts, to be used when it suited him. Yes, I think he had a grudging respect for me because I wasn't a Yes man; that I wasn't fazed by his reputation, and shouted and screamed as loudly as him when he was trying to bully me. But we were never going to be best buddies. I don't think he ever forgave me for demanding money for the *London Tonight* deal. He was the one who always demanded, nipped a few quid, as he would say, and he must have hated me scoring a point over him.

When Reg died from cancer, six months after Charlie, Sue and I were spared the dilemma of whether to attend his funeral. Having ghost-written Barbara Windsor's autobiography, we were relaxing in Cyprus and only read about the poor turn-out after the funeral. I wasn't surprised that Reg's send-off bore no resemblance to the affectionate farewells of his brothers. From what I saw and experienced, he was truly an unloved individual.

Ronnie, on the other hand, was someone I liked and, if he were alive, would still be visiting. He had a welcoming warmth that made you feel he was pleased you'd made the effort to go, and, even today, sixteen years after his death, I still remember, with great affection, giggling with him over the silliest things. With Reg, I always left whichever prison he was in, wondering whether either of us had got anything out of the visit. But with Ronnie, I always left on a high – although, most times, sad too, reflecting that, had his paranoid schizophrenia been treated when it was first diagnosed – in the fifties! – everything might have been different, for him and the family. One has only to read his distressing letters to me to have some idea of the torment Ronnie's condition brought on when he was emotionally stressed.

With the appropriate medication, Ronnie inspired nothing but affection. That's why he had so many visitors. And that's why Charlie encouraged Sue to visit *him*, not Reg. "You'll like Ronnie," he said. "But Reg's an animal."

Charlie, of course, we miss dearly. He had his irritating foibles and was cowardly in that he allowed innocent people to be hurt on Reg's instructions. But I forgave him a lot, because of the bad hand he'd been dealt in life. As Dave Courtney so succinctly puts it: "Imagine being seven and your mum gives birth to those two!"

A Final Word

One evening, a couple of years after *Me and My Brothers* was published, in 1988, Charlie and I were having a bite to eat in Crystal Palace and I asked him if he trusted me. I told him to think carefully because I wanted to put a proposition to him and it depended on his answer. Charlie said he didn't need to think – the answer was Yes, a hundred per cent.

"In that case," I said, "here's my proposal. I'm not daft. I know that you didn't tell me the whole truth for the book. But what if you did now, and we locked it away, to be published after your death, for Gary's benefit? It would be a sensational story and Gary would get the lion's share of the money it earned."

Charlie thought it a great idea; in fact, he said he'd been thinking along the same lines himself. At the time, I believed him, because it *was* a great idea and would, unquestionably, have earned Gary a nice few quid, as his dad would have said. But Charlie and I never did pursue it. And, having heard what John Corbett told me for this book, I now know why. Apart from anything he might want to keep secret about the twins, Charlie would most certainly not have wanted me to know that he wasn't the whiter-than-white character he'd portrayed himself to be; that while not actually carrying out Reg's orders himself, he'd arranged - albeit reluctantly - for people to be hurt or intimidated on his behalf. Sue and I were shocked to hear of Charlie's involvement. And disappointed, too, for we had bought into the charming image he had presented. We did genuinely believe him when he said he had never had anything to do with his brothers' violence.

We'll probably never know whether it was this help in maintaining Reg's status as a top gangster that lay behind the police drugs sting that effectively cut short Charlie's life. For, even fifteen years after his arrest, the reason he was targeted remains a mystery. Like all his close friends, I'm still puzzled why someone somewhere decided that, at the age of seventy, with little money and no power, Charlie should be coerced into committing a crime, and then spend his last few years locked up with murderers, terrorists and sex fiends.

At one time, the Krays did have information – and photographs – that would have damaged the reputations of people in high places, particularly a high-profile peer, who, Ronnie had discovered, was regularly having sex with under-age boys. But this material, which might possibly have changed the Establishment's approach to the Krays' prosecution, had been lost. Charlie had left it with a member of his family for safe keeping, in case of an emergency, but when that "emergency" came, the material could not be found.

So, in 1996, when he was targeted, Charlie was in no position to blow the whistle on the sexual shenanigans, or whatever, in the corridors of power. Indeed, with the movie windfall long gone, he was back, living hand to mouth, scrounging around for cash, scrounging drinks off supposed admirers, still dreaming of that big-money deal his wide range of contacts might - with John Corbett's expertise - help him put together.

What wouldn't have helped Charlie that summer, was that the cheering and chanting of Reg's name by the hero-worshipping masses at Ronnie's funeral, the previous year, would have done nothing to lessen the fears within the Government and police that the Kray name still wielded power in the East End. Worried by that massive support, the men in suits in Whitehall would, Charlie believed, have been thinking of ways to keep his brother inside when - in 1998 - he completed the 30-year sentence recommended by trial judge Melford Stevenson. Throughout his time in jail, Reg had kept his nose clean, had finally expressed remorse over the McVitie murder, and was about to marry a respectable woman. Now, with far more dangerous killers being given lesser sentences than the twins, the Press – especially *The Sun* - would be bound to say: Enough is enough, and campaign for his release. What better way to counteract that, and make Reg ineligible for release, than to discredit the only Kray brother still free? Make him out to be a conniving drug baron with the money and contacts to flood Britain's streets with drugs. That would quieten the Press, wouldn't it? How could they demand Reg Kray's release when his brother was such an evil criminal?

This was Charlie's thinking as he languished in Belmarsh Prison awaiting his trial. And if he was right, it is sadly ironic that Reg's inflated ego would have played a big part in the reasoning behind the sting. For by insisting on such over-the-top security for Ronnie's funeral, Reg scored a spectacular own goal, and played into the hands of authority. The police were more than capable of handling the crowds, but Reg, desperate for a lavish "State-occasion" send-off, demanded a huge security presence befitting his brother's legendary status. As a result, Dave Courtney laid on 150 of his biggest, toughest nightclub doormen to ensure that no one spoiled Reg's big day. What message did that awesome show of strength send out to the thousands in Bethnal Green and millions watching on television? That, if necessary, the Krays could still marshall a small army? That it would be wise to get the one remaining Kray off the streets and into prison as well?

What wouldn't have helped Charlie in the months to come is Dave's attitude to the Commissioner of Police, Sir Paul Condon. A few days before the funeral, the two met - with Charlie - to discuss security arrangements. Sir Paul wanted the police to handle the security, but Dave, then a brash, know-it-all, thrilled to be working for the Krays, told him that his men would be more of a deterrent to trouble-makers than Sir Paul's young PCs, more used to controlling pop fans. To compound the gauche, offensive insult, Dave told the police chief to "just get your lot in the streets and do the holding hands bit and leave everything else to me." It was an arrogant and insulting remark and Dave – now older and much wiser – bitterly regrets making it. Charlie told him that being associated so prominently with the Kray name would come back to haunt him. And so it proved, not only with The Cook Report, but with other police-motivated actions that blighted not only Dave's security business but his personal life, too. Was it merely coincidence that, at the very time Dave was having doors slammed in his face, the plan to entrap Charlie was taking shape. I don't think so.

There are those who think that Charlie was targeted simply because he was in the wrong place at the wrong time, unwittingly mingling with known drug dealers being watched by the police. But I don't believe that, because Charlie and his co-defendants - neither known drug dealers - were the only ones arrested. Another theory, put to me by one of the barristers in Charlie's case, is that, having run up huge expenses in a surveillance operation that had produced no results, Jack and his team went for Charlie - through a likeable and trusted, but woefully naïve friend – to get them off the hook.

One thing is certain: even now, fifteen years later, John Corbett and Steve Wraith still think of what might have been, had they been available when Charlie asked them to meet his new friends. He was in awe of guys who, in his own words, were "tall, good-looking with bundles of money" and the fun-loving Geordies fitted the bill: thinking he'd fallen on his feet for once, he urged John and Steve to meet them. Each wanted to, but, at the time, it was inconvenient. Which is unfortunate, because both feel they would have tumbled that Jack and his mates were not what they seemed, particularly Steve, who was well-connected at Newcastle United and would have detected that a football that Jack claimed had been signed by the team for a charity auction was a forgery.

Anyone who doubts that Charlie was a marked man should know that, after setting up the first meeting in Birmingham, it was Jack who kept calling him – not the other way round. In fact, having squeezed £500 out of Jack to travel to Birmingham, for his birthday party, Charlie borrowed the same amount from John to repay Jack, to get him off his back. It didn't work, and, being trusting, gullible - and broke - Charlie was a pathetically easy victim of the undercover team's carefully-spun web.

As one might expect, Reg had no sympathy for Charlie, saying he'd been stupid to put himself on offer the way he had. And in suggesting that his brother would not have been caught out had he not been living the life of a playboy on the Kray name, Reg missed the point that it was indeed the name that had made Charlie a target.

No matter how badly I feel about Charlie's duplicity and irritating wishy-washiness, I still feel, even now, a deep sadness that his life ended so miserably – and intense anger that his brothers' stupidity and selfishness destroyed his life.

While researching this book, I learned that the twins were given a chance to take responsibility for the Cornell and McVitie murders and allow Charlie and the so-called "firm" to walk free. While on remand, their solicitor, Ralph

Haeems, told them that he'd seen all the police evidence, and it was impossible for them to be found not guilty. If they changed their pleas to guilty, all charges against everyone else would be dropped. Reg thought for a moment, then said: "I don't think we can do the bird without our boys." Ronnie looked at him. "We won't have to," he said. "We're still going not guilty."

That selfish decision meant that Charlie would be convicted of a crime he did not commit and sentenced to ten years. What makes me even angrier, however, is that, for some reason, the twins summoned Charlie in the middle of the night to tell him they had murdered McVitie.

By telling him, they made him an accessory after the fact of murder. And that, tragically, transformed what should have been a happy, carefree life into one beset by problems, worry and everlasting shame.